DOWN AND OUT

DOWN AND OUT

Daniel Lavelle

WILDFIRE

First published in 2022 by
WILDFIRE
an imprint of HEADLINE PUBLISHING GROUP

1

Cataloguing in Publication Data is available from the British Library

Hardback ISBN 978 1 4722 7909 5

Typeset in Minion by CC Book Production

Printed and bound in Great Britain by Clays Ltd, Elcograf S.p.A.

Headline's policy is to use papers that are natural, renewable and recyclable
products and made from wood grown in well-managed forests and other
controlled sources. The logging and manufacturing processes are expected
to conform to the environmental regulations of the country of origin.

HEADLINE PUBLISHING GROUP
An Hachette UK Company
Carmelite House
50 Victoria Embankment
London EC4Y 0DZ

www.headline.co.uk
www.hachette.co.uk

For Grandma

Contents

Author's Note

I have disguised some of the identities of case studies that appear in this book. I decided to provide pseudonyms to protect the privacy of some interviewees and other people who feature within its pages. Some interviewees requested to have their names changed, and some names used are composites of several people. I have provided pseudonyms for former teachers, care workers, school peers, care peers, Emmaus Companions and front-line charity workers. I have altered the names of buildings and locations, including schools, care homes and foster placements.

I have only used real names when interviewees gave consent for me to do so, or if the information they provided is already in the public domain. Where published research, books, newspaper articles and videos are quoted, their work has been cited and is available in the Notes section (pages 279–293).

Introduction

When I zipped up my tent on that first night sleeping rough, I felt no despair. I had picked a grassy patch near a local bridle path. I listened to the wind rustling through the trees, and the pitter-patter of raindrops as they bounced off my nylon roof. I had always assumed something like this was going to happen to me. The reasons why I ended up in a tent that night are multiple and complex, yet few people would have been surprised. I was just another care-leaver who had lost control of their life. What made me think I was so unique that I could avoid the inevitable breakdown?

I'd spent three years living in a ground-floor flat in Mossley, a small town on the foothills of the Pennines in Greater Manchester, before I found myself in that tent. I was about to finish university; five years of hard work had been leading to this moment. I should have been happy and excited for what the future held.

I wasn't.

As you step back from a painting, its shapes begin to merge and become blurry. My memory of the week or so I spent in my tent, which occurred during a catatonic drunken stupor eight years ago, are difficult to recall in detail. I do know that I could have surfed on friends' sofas or even stayed with my parents, with whom I was finally on good terms, but I couldn't bring myself to tell anyone about my predicament. I had just graduated with a 2:2, and landing on my arse was one disappointment I wanted to keep to myself.

Since the coalition government took over from Labour in 2010, austerity has eviscerated the nation's social infrastructure. Cuts to welfare, the health service and social care, along with stagnating wages, insecure jobs and a failure to build enough affordable homes, have contributed to a mounting homelessness crisis. This crisis has reached every corner of the UK: not just the capital and major cities, but also idyllic villages, market towns and seaside resorts. In these places, rough sleeping has become visible in almost every doorway, bus shelter and underpass. The increasing number of people at the sharp end of this crisis is impossible to ignore, but rough sleeping represents only a tiny part of a colossal problem. Homelessness, a term which includes anyone lacking suitable, stable and/or long-term housing, is almost impossible to quantify accurately due to the number of people living in temporary accommodation or sofa-surfing, and because many homeless people have transient lifestyles. The number of people reported homeless between 2016 and 2021 varies between 250,000 and 320,000. At the time of writing, a Crisis study found that approximately '305,000 single people, couples and families registered homelessness applications with local authorities in 2019/20. Of these, 289,000 (95%) were judged as homeless or threatened with homelessness.'[1]

The circumstances that precipitated my journey to the streets seem entirely of my own making when viewed in isolation. I racked up considerable rent arrears, was drinking heavily, and moved out of my flat without being evicted. Surely it was my fault? However, when digging deeper, some might be surprised that I'm writing this at all. I attended special-education schools from the age of nine, was expelled at fourteen, and completed my secondary education with no qualifications. I lived in the care system from the age of twelve. In my early twenties I worked a full-time job, took night classes and completed an Access to Higher Education course to get accepted at Manchester Metropolitan University in 2010. But by the end of my third year, I was firmly in the grip of self-loathing and depression. Over the course of those three years, my grandparents had passed away, one of my best friends had died suddenly, and my mother was in hospital, having suffered multiple organ failure. My immediate family members struggled with substance abuse and were in trouble with the police, and one was placed in a psychiatric ward. All of this caused me to withdraw into myself. Aftercare support from social workers had concluded a long time before, and weeks would pass without me speaking to anyone, especially in the summer months, when I wasn't compelled out of my hovel to attend university. I left my flat to buy junk food, white cider and other cheap booze. As a result, my health deteriorated, and my weight ballooned, exacerbating my self-loathing; trapping me in the same self-destructive cycle that befalls most of the people you see on the streets. I barely registered my mum's illness, in truth, and only visited her once in hospital. She was emaciated and delirious, yet, sitting at her bedside, I felt nothing.

Looking back, I'm hit with the horror that I should have felt at the time – but if you don't care about yourself, how are you supposed to care about anyone else?

Towards the end of my tenancy, my flat resembled a bomb site. Piles of unwashed clothes, empty beer bottles and food containers were strewn around every room. I was in thousands of pounds of arrears, and had become paranoid about debt collectors visiting me. I wasn't worried about them taking my things; I just didn't want anyone seeing the state of the place. I wasn't evicted. I wasn't even threatened with eviction; I just handed in my notice and left. I wish I could say I was forced into homelessness by an unscrupulous landlord, an addiction to hard drugs or something more dramatic – but it was sloth, shame, and overwhelming paranoia that saw me land on the streets. Many of the mistakes I made were my own, and I deserve a substantial amount of blame, but in hindsight, I can't help feeling that if I had had more support when leaving care, I could have avoided my deterioration.

Avoiding this same deleterious path to the streets has become increasingly difficult over the last decade, especially for the poorest and most vulnerable in society. My fellow care-leavers are estimated to comprise 25 per cent of the homeless population in the UK.[2] Families break down for a multitude of reasons, and it's not always because of mistreatment. I don't blame my parents. When I was diagnosed with Attention Deficit Hyperactivity Disorder (ADHD) at the age of six, my psychiatrist told my parents that he'd never treated a more severe case than mine.

I was tempestuous, extraordinarily hyperactive, aggressive,

and I didn't sleep. My parents, who had problems of their own and were offered little support from social services, were not equipped to cope. When I turned seventeen, social services moved me from my semi-independent unit into a place of my own, a two-up, two-down terrace in Oldham. My case was referred to a private care management provider. They assigned me a key worker, who would visit me a few days every week. I'd lived in the care system since I was twelve, and even though the foster placements and children's homes could be fraught and chaotic, the presence of others was comforting, especially at night. I wasn't ready to be alone. A good semi-independent unit can prepare care-leavers for life outside the system. They can teach budgeting, cooking and cleaning – but it does not prepare people for loneliness. Before this, I had moved homes eleven times in five years. This deprived me of a strong support network. Among care-leavers, I'm not alone in struggling to cope with independence. According to the Centre for Social Justice, 57 per cent of care-leavers find it difficult to manage money and avoid debt.[3]

I only spent a few weeks in that tent – occasionally packing up and moving to different sites along the bridle path, or to spend a night on a campsite, or, on some days, to kip on my brother's sofa in Oldham – but I spent almost two years homeless. Perversely, I was fortunate in that the only thing keeping me on the streets was my paranoia; most rough sleepers aren't so lucky. According to Crisis, 'Two-thirds of homeless people cite drug and alcohol use as a reason for first becoming homeless.'[4] It was warm in May, those first weeks I spent by the side of the canal, but in the depths of winter, homeless peoples' dependencies only get stronger as the need to fight the cold, numb the pain and stave off boredom intensifies. Being dependent on drugs and alcohol also reduces one's chances of getting accepted into temporary accommodation, such as hostels and shelters, which often impose strict rules of abstinence. My hypochondria prevented me from even contemplating using hard drugs, and my weak constitution curtailed any risk of severe alcoholism – even though I often drank to oblivion. Yet, despite this, getting off the streets was still an ordeal.

After the first few days of inertia and morose self-pity, I decided to look into my options, which turned out to be scant. I visited a local housing advice service for assistance, where a rather officious-looking advisor wasn't particularly helpful. She told me I wasn't in 'priority need' to receive help, as I did not present any vulnerabilities that would exceed those of my homeless counterparts. 'I have to establish that you would be worse off than me if I were homeless,' the advisor explained.

I was homeless, but not homeless enough. It may interest people to learn that local authorities are so depleted of resources that they operate a misery contest for housing, a sort of *X Factor* for the destitute. Maybe my audition would have gone better if I'd rocked up with a few missing teeth and pissed myself while singing 'Oom-Pah-Pah'. Typically, things like pregnancy, disability, fleeing domestic violence or having spent time in prison would make one eligible for priority housing. But the paranoia that had plagued me for much of the past three years had won out again, and I had given a fake name, the wrong age and false housing history. This meant I couldn't tell them I had learning difficulties and was in receipt of Disability Living Allowance at the time, because I'd have had to verify it with a confirmation letter. That letter would have had my real name on it, and the jig would have been up. I don't understand why I did that. I don't understand a lot of my decisions back then.

Austerity has made getting on the housing register more difficult, but the roots of the housing crisis can be traced back to Margaret Thatcher's government. Thatcher's Right to Buy scheme was wonderful for a generation of social renters who were enabled to buy their council homes, and for Tories who benefited at subsequent elections; but they were terrible for millions of families who now languish on long social-housing waiting lists.[5]

In 2009, David Cameron pledged to strengthen families and fight poverty. Cameron said that Labour had failed Britain's poorest citizens, and 'it falls to us, the modern Conservative Party, to fight for the poorest who you [Labour] have let down'.[6] A decade later, thousands of families found themselves homeless and raising their children in converted shipping containers. In August 2019, the Children's Commissioner for England found that 210,000 young people were homeless, either living in hostels and temporary accommodation or sofa-surfing.[7] According to a Local Government Association report, between 2016 and 2018 one in ten new homes in England and Wales were created in office blocks,[8] such as Terminus House in Harlow, known locally as a 'human warehouse' and described as a form of 'social cleansing' by local Tory MP Robert Halfon.[9] Placements in temporary accommodation are often cramped, overcrowded, miles away from family and friends, and in areas rife with crime. If families struggle to find affordable homes and are being packed like sardines into overcrowded office blocks and shipping containers, what chance do entrenched rough sleepers have?

There are some hopeful signs, but much more needs to be done. According to a BBC report, local authorities in England are building council homes 'on a scale not seen in decades',[10] but the numbers are still a long way off meeting people's needs. The lack of affordable housing stock, coupled with stagnating wages, has led to the so-called 'Generation Rent': young adults unable to buy their own homes and forced to depend on the private rental market. A Centre for Housing Policy review into the private rented sector found that living conditions have improved, but 1.35 million privately rented properties still do not meet the Decent Homes Standard, which New Labour introduced to tackle poor quality and disrepair.[11]

Research conducted by Shelter and YouGov found that around 2 million adults renting in the private rented sector have become physically ill because of housing problems such as unaffordable rents, poor conditions and the threat of eviction. The research also found that '45% of private renters (or 3.8 million adults) have suffered mental health issues as a result of their housing problems, with nearly one in three (2.8 million adults) saying this has kept them awake at night.'[12] The Building Research Establishment found that poor housing costs the NHS £1.4 billion a year,[13] a financial burden comparable to smoking and alcohol. Such anxiety and stress can start people on the road to homelessness by exacerbating mental health conditions and increasing the probability of depression and substance abuse.

There are ways out of this crisis, but it will take a political will that has hitherto been absent, and is likely to remain so for the foreseeable future. The Conservative Party is obsessed with shrinking the state, free markets and home ownership, but they already subsidise people's housing costs through the welfare system. Wouldn't it be more efficient to spend that money on long-term and affordable social housing rather than enriching private landlords who have no interest in meeting the needs of the poorest renters?

Many factors contribute to the record levels of homelessness in the UK. While the government's pitiful record on house building is key, austerity has undoubtedly made things worse. Cuts to drug and alcohol dependency services mean that people don't benefit from early intervention and struggle to get the appropriate support when addiction has overcome their lives. Stagnating wages, insecure employment and changes to the welfare system have all contributed to people losing their livelihoods. From education to the health service, policing and social care, the coalition scaled down every inch of public life with their austerity programme. The results have been catastrophic for the poorest and most vulnerable in UK society. Thirty-one per cent of UK children live in poverty,[14] while more elderly citizens experience severe poverty in the UK than anywhere else in western Europe.[15] Since 2010, more than 20,000 police officers have been cut.[16] Over the same period, violent crime has risen to record levels.[17] A lot of the suffering caused by austerity is hidden away from view. Most people don't come across the poor kids having to skip their lunches or patients dying in hospital corridors, but it's become impossible to avoid the homeless. The tent cities, sleeping bags in doorways and desperate men and women with their hands out at cash machines are things we all pass by every day. Homelessness is now part of all our lives.

As the state has shrunk over the last decade, homeless provision has become the domain of the third sector. Unlike the government, charities can't guarantee their funding, and predominantly rely on donations and subsidies to survive. This limits the quality of service they can offer. More crucially, charity absolves the government of responsibility and engenders a sense of tolerance for desperate issues, such as rough sleeping, when there should be outrage. In December 2017, the charity Action Hunger installed 'homeless vending machines' in Nottingham, which provided food, clothing and other essential items to homeless people on a twenty-four-hour basis.[18] Even though the people who devised this scheme probably had the best intentions, the message it sends to the general public is that rough sleeping is now an acceptable part of society. Toby Neal, a Nottingham City Councillor, agreed: 'This is a well-meaning but misguided and ill-informed attempt to address complex problems faced by people with accommodation and health issues. There is no evidence that it helps, and [it] may distract people from finding long-term solutions.'[19] The scheme ultimately failed.

The third sector has an interesting relationship with accountability. Charities like Emmaus and the YMCA that provide accommodation to service users usually offer support rather than 'personal care'.[20] The legal distinction here is important; offering 'support' means that these charities are seldom monitored by the Care Quality Commission nor Ofsted. This lack of oversight allows the third sector to devise whatever schemes they like, with their own rules and regulations, making their quality of service pot luck (this would certainly turn out to be my experience). Moreover, charities are not obliged to comply with Freedom of Information requests (FOIs),[21] which frees them from scrutiny and keeps the fourth estate – and you – in the dark. This is something I have discovered repeatedly throughout my investigations.

A more conspiratorially minded person would argue that this was all part of the Tories' plan to keep the working classes down. This idea gives the incompetent politicians who've been running things for the last decade far too much credit. The Big Society was supposed to step in. With our entrepreneurial and philanthropic spirit, you and I were supposed to march along and pick up the slack. Like the Victorians before us, the Tories believed charity would provide the nation with a safety net. That hasn't happened – and it's not for want of trying. The number of charities listed on the Charity Commission's register reached an all-time high in 2018, with over 160,000 new charities joining, and their collective income exceeded £75 billion for the first time.[22] Despite the best intentions of those who work in third-sector organisations, they've been unable to compensate for the cuts to public services.

For so many homeless people, it's not statutory aid but a stroke of luck, the kindness of a stranger or their strength of will that finally gets them off the street. So it was for me. During my brief stint sleeping rough, I was bedding down along the bridle paths in Saddleworth, a collection of quaint villages that lie along the old West Riding of Yorkshire and are connected by the River Tame, which meanders through the countryside. Each village is filled with grey stone cottages, Range Rovers and, in the summer, village fayres. During the day, I would wander aimlessly along the banks of the River Tame or booze at friends' houses around Mossley.

As Frosty Jack and other cheap booze became my close companions, I was drawn into the social circles of people who had been comforted by these drinks for years. That's how I met Walter, who was fifty-five at the time, a year before I took to the bridle paths. On my jaunts along the Tame, I would often meet up with him in an area known locally as Mossley Beach. (It isn't really a beach, more of a riverbank, but I suppose you could call it one if you're a bit sloppy about details.) A former welder from Oldham, Walter wore a woolly hat in all weathers and had a long white beard. He sat on a camping chair and hurled stones into the river for Rover, his scruffy little Yorkshire terrier, to fetch.

'Danny, Danny, Danny!' he would say when greeting me. 'Fuckin' 'ell, man, you alreet?'

Walter swore constantly. Every sentence began with 'fuckin'', and every other word in it was bridged by 'fuckin'', and each finished: 'do you know what I fuckin' mean?' Cross a drunk Jack Duckworth from *Coronation Street* with ZZ Top's Billy Gibbons, and you've got Walter.

'Where've you been, man?' he asked me.

I told him I'd left my flat and that I was looking for a place to live.

'Get the fuck out of it, man.' He made some more sympathetic grunts and asked if I'd tried Emmaus, the local homeless charity that offered full-time work in exchange for bed and board. Walter's advice would prove to be the first step towards me leaving that bridle path.

Not long after, in May 2013, I folded up my tent for the last time and began the process of entering Emmaus. But this was merely the beginning of my journey out of homelessness. Over the next two years, I would experience all the bureaucracy, austerity, precarity, anxiety and charity mentioned above, and gain a deeper understanding of what it means to be homeless today – and why so many people cannot make it off the street.

Chapter One

Is Charity Broken?

'Charity is a cold, grey, loveless thing. If a rich man wants to help the poor, he should pay his taxes gladly, not dole out money at whim'

– Clement Attlee (per Francis Beckett)[1]

'If you are suffering, whoever you are, come in, eat, sleep, and regain hope. Here you are loved.' Abbé Pierre's words are at the heart of what Emmaus claims to offer Britain's homeless. Pierre, a Catholic priest and former member of the French Resistance, founded Emmaus in Paris in 1949 to help the rising number of people made homeless by the Second World War. The people he rescued from Paris's streets recycled old rags to earn their keep. Emmaus in the UK operates in much the same way as Pierre's original community, except they're secular and receive their income from the benefits system and second-hand furniture.

Emmaus communities in the UK accept people who have experienced homelessness and social exclusion. Those who live and work in the communities are known as Companions.

Companions can expect three meals a day, a bed every night and a paltry weekly allowance if they commit to working forty hours per week in Emmaus' social enterprise and agree to observe a strict regime of rules. Drink and drugs are off-limits, and Companions are expected to remain sober inside the community's walls. They must give up any benefits, except housing benefit, which is pocketed by the community. Companions are not protected by conventional housing or employment rights; legislation has specifically excluded them from receiving the minimum wage,[2] and they are not allowed to receive any additional income. I didn't know any of this then.

Walter told me to return later one evening to meet some of the Companions living at the Mossley community, who used the 'Beach' as their evening drinking haunt. I got to the Beach at around 6pm and waited half an hour for the Companions to materialise, but no one did. On my way back to the tent, walking through the estate, I saw Walter and Rover.

'They weren't there,' I told Walter.

'Oh, fuckin' hell, man. Well, if they're not at the fuckin' Beach, they'll probably be at the fuckin' Tyre or summat . . . you know what I fuckin' mean?'

For once, that question was valid, because I didn't have a clue what he meant. It turned out that the 'Tyre' was an area of wasteland, a few hundred yards from the Beach near a derelict factory. The Companions used a worn rubber tyre, which must have come from an excavator or digger, as a seat while they blotted out the memories of their day's toil with black lager and white cider. They were all middle-aged men and well into their session when I arrived a little after dusk. Some of them were perched on the eponymous tyre, while others sat on camping chairs or the ground. The Tyre and the Beach functioned almost like local sanctums for the socially excluded. People would visit the Companions – who were village elders of a sort – for counsel, booze, roll-ups and occasional drunken scraps.

Walter introduced me. 'This is Danny. He's on his arse.'

Sebastian, a portly Companion from Stoke who looked like a ten-year-old boy trapped in a fifty-year-old man's body, began to extol the virtues of the charity while slurping a can of Kestrel Super. 'It's great,' he said enthusiastically. 'You get food and your own room and bathroom. You only get a thirty-five quid allowance, but everything else is paid for.'

It sounded wonderful to my weary ears. All I would have to do was drag myself out of bed every day, carry a few sofas and reap the rewards. I didn't care that I would be going from completing higher education to the bottom rung of the social ladder. Any grand ambitions I had once had for my future had been replaced by an overwhelming need to check out, to not care, to yield to a tide that was out of my control and let it wash me up where it wanted. Emmaus provided that opportunity.

To get accepted by Emmaus, one must be referred to the community by an agency, local authority or another Companion. That evening I returned to Walter's house, accompanied by Tom, one of the Companions I had met at the Tyre. Tom and I were the same age, and we seemed to get on well enough. I told him I was interested in living at Emmaus, and he suggested I come and visit the next day, promising to vouch for me to the community manager. I arrived the next morning, a hot, cloudless day, during his fag break. He stood puffing on a roll-up in front of the converted textile mill in which the Emmaus community was based.

'All right, Danny,' he said. 'I haven't had the chance to speak to the manager yet, pal. He's in later, though.'

Tom was about twenty-seven, but his dress sense, attitude and cadence were of a bygone era. He didn't care for 'modern music', didn't 'do' films, preferring to spend his downtime with a spliff and a few episodes of *The Real Housewives of Orange County*. He laughed at his own jokes, which were usually at someone else's expense – often mine – and would prefix every sentence with 'basically' or 'technically'. Whenever asked for his opinion, he'd rev up his response with a machine-gun rap of pronouns: 'Well, me, myself, personally, I think it's a good idea, me.'

Later that afternoon, Tom introduced me to Kevin, the community manager. A squat and spritely man, Kevin had been a prison officer at Strangeways. The Companions complained about Kevin in one way or another, but most had a lot of respect for him. He was frank and officious, but I always found him fair, and he was usually willing to turn the other cheek on minor discretions.

Aside from general questions about my background, eligibility for housing benefit and willingness to work, Kevin was primarily concerned about whether I was a self-harmer or a drinker. The community had just banned a male Companion known as 'Slasher', a nickname he earned after prowling the community's hallways one evening with a bread knife, which he'd used to cut himself. I assured Kevin I was neither, and after briefly deliberating with George, a 'core' Companion who had lived in various Emmaus communities for the past twenty years, they accepted me into the community. I was given an en-suite room with a fifteen-foot-high ceiling and everything I needed to live in comfort – except a telly. TVs were prized commodities in Emmaus, and how quickly you got your hands on one depended on who you knew and where you worked within the community.

My room was next to one of the most interesting men I've ever met. Michael Leadbetter – or 'Mick', as everyone knew him – was from Hull, and although he was only in his early fifties, his dehydrated complexion produced deep wrinkles that made him resemble an eighty-year-old. His dress sense boasted as many layers as his personality: a couple of T-shirts – a bright purple one on top – worn underneath a blue denim jacket, covered by a scraggly leather jacket that matched his scraggly beard. Mick was eccentric, funny, provocative and clever, but a hopeless drunk, pointlessly anarchic and self-destructive. He was from a generation of working-class hippies who – hypnotised by Pink Floyd and sixties psychedelia – dropped out and never quite managed to drop back in. Mick had gone to grammar school, was well-read and articulate. I managed to give him the impression that I had those qualities too, and we bonded over sixties rock and games of chess in which he would prevail even after six cans of the black stuff. Mick was also very fond of taunting me. He would blast out Bonzo Dog Band's 'Slush' each morning, knowing that the maniacal laughter that loops throughout the track freaked me out. He also enjoyed preying on my lack of work experience by asking me to fetch such things as tartan paint or a left-handed screwdriver.

We lived above the shop at Emmaus, so there weren't many excuses for being late. Even if your alarm didn't go off, there'd be a knock on your door to rouse you out of your pit. Nevertheless, I turned up for my first morning meeting, held among the higgledy-piggledy assortment of dining furniture and sofas on the old mill's first floor, fifteen minutes early. I wanted to impress upon Kevin what I'd assured him of at our interview: that I wasn't a drinker and was up to graft. A few minutes later, I was joined by Sebastian, Tom, Mick and a dozen others, before Rabbit, the community cook, who looked like a waxwork model of D'Artagnan that had melted slightly, entered the room. He was called Rabbit because he loved the sound of his own voice.

'Alreet, you shower of cunts!' he announced to the room, who issued a collective murmur in acknowledgement. 'Alreet, lad,' Rabbit said to me while pulling up a stool next to the café bar. 'Sleep well?' he asked, winking in Tom's direction.

'Err . . . yeah,' I said, confused by the smirk broadening across his face.

'Deep sleeper, is it?' Rabbit asked, as he sprinkled tobacco into an empty Rizla paper.

'You were lucky then, pal,' Tom said before I could reply.

'Why?' I asked.

'Well, you got the short straw in that room,' Rabbit said.

Behind me, I could hear Mick laughing into his mug of black coffee.

'Because,' Rabbit continued, gesturing towards Mick, 'that mad fucker is usually screamin' his 'ed off till early doors. 'Ere, at least you'll learn alt' lyrics off *Dark Side of the Moon*, soon.'

'And *Slim Shady*,' added Tom.

I quickly learned that on most evenings, Mick, after quenching his thirst at the Tyre or the Beach, would unleash the complaints he'd been harbouring all day in a series of drunken rants. These episodes were like a daily broadcast of events through 'channel Mick'. If he was pissed off about something you'd done, these tirades were the only way you'd find out: 'And you, Danny, stop leaving the pallet truck in the middle of the road. You don't listen. You always know best. Well, you don't. Time-wasting bastard!'

Like George, Mick was one of the 'core' Companions. There were seven of them living in Mossley when I arrived. The core Companions reminded me of Brooks from *The Shawshank Redemption*: institutionalised long-timers unlikely to leave, and even more unlikely to cope if they did so.

On my first day, I was assigned to the warehouse to work under Mick. The happy-go-lucky hippy from the Tyre transformed into a cantankerous grump during the day. It took him until the early afternoon to shake off his hangover and delirium tremens (DTs) from the night before, which produced a temperament that wasn't fit for customer service. In the afternoon, he would become giddy as he anticipated the black lager awaiting him on the Beach. A pink tutu had been donated to the community one day, and Mick decided to wear it for the rest of the afternoon, striking the odd ballet pose as he went to and fro from the warehouse to the shop floor. It was also in the afternoon that Mick would pepper you with jokes that would have made Bob Monkhouse wince.

'Danny, sorry about giving you stick earlier,' he said as he passed me in the yard one afternoon.

'No worries, I'm used to you by now, you miserable twat.'

'Yeah, well, the thing is, I didn't get much sleep last night.'

'That makes two of us – but that's all your fault, to be honest. Why not try less shouting?'

Mick laughed and continued: 'No, no, listen, I was up all night wondering where the sun had gone.' He paused for a second. 'And then it dawned on me.'

He walked off, leaving me rooted to the spot, wondering what on earth he was talking about . . . and then it dawned on me.

Mick wasn't earning as much as the other Companions in the community, as he was confined to the warehouse where the only opportunity to make some side money was by slashing the bottom of sofas in the hope of procuring loose change. His sole instruction that first morning was 'find gaps; fill 'em in.'

The gaps he was referring to were spaces on the shop floor that needed restocking with furniture. I began finding and filling, but after an hour of this, I was at a loose end.

'I don't care if you've got nowt to do,' said Mick after he noticed me contemplating the ground. 'But you need to do something. The last thing you want to be known as is a lazy bastard. 'Cause it will stick.'

After I'd spent a few months in the community, Mick and I would set up a chessboard in the warehouse and make our moves between delivery trips. Walking inside Mick's warehouse was like going on a safari into his mind. The chaotic hodgepodge of furniture, scrap wood, and anything from kayaks to parachutes strewn inside the storage bays made for a post-Blitz ambience which was peculiarly pretty but completely impractical. After a few days, I made the colossal mistake of attempting to organise all of it. Mick expressed no objections to this during the day, but everyone heard about it on 'channel Mick' that night:

'Danny, you don't know what you're doing! That's my fuckin' warehouse. I have my system; you have no respect!'

I was moved on to the van crew the next day. The van was the only place (aside from the positions controlled by the 'core', who weren't fit enough for the van job) where one could pursue a side hustle. The single drawback was that it was also the most taxing job at Emmaus. It involved driving across Tameside and Greater Manchester, collecting and delivering furniture. I started with two men, Bob and Fred. Bob was our driver and, according to Tom, a pervert:

'He's not right, him,' Tom said one night while giving me a breakdown of everyone in the community.

'Why?' I asked.

'I went into his room once, and, I swear down, he had pictures of fanny all over his walls.'

A single man deprived of female attention keeping visual stimuli for when nature called didn't strike me as all that unusual. 'What, pictures of naked women?' I asked, unmoved.

'No – fanny!' Tom reiterated, sniggering. 'Fuckin' giant pictures of fanny. No faces or owt – just fanny!'

But even if Bob was a record-breaking wanker behind closed doors, at work, he was quiet, harmless and got on with things. Fred was also quiet, but slightly more on the ball.

'Right, listen, mate,' he said that afternoon. 'You seem like a good lad. If we get a tip, you don't say fuck all, 'cause we're supposed to hand them in. Right?'

'Right,' I affirmed.

Down and Out

Tips on the vans were scant and, in my experience, always offered by those who could least afford it, which made one reluctant to accept them. The wealthier customers were too concerned about us scratching their posh decor to even consider a gratuity. The real opportunities to make cash came from collecting valuable pieces of furniture and selling them on to another dealer or a customer whom you knew was interested in buying what you'd collected. Stained mattresses presented an opportunity to make some side cash, too. We weren't supposed to pick them up because they were impossible to sell. Who wants to buy a stained second-hand mattress? We told people that we couldn't accept the mattress as a donation, but we could take it to the tip for them for £20. We were paid a £35 weekly allowance and had £10 put into our savings each week. If you ever wanted to get out of Emmaus, your savings would only help you achieve this after several years of service. Is it any wonder that Companions tried to make a little extra?

Even though I worked hard, I was hopeless on the vans. On one windswept and wet afternoon, I was attempting to load a bedside cabinet on to a toe sack truck so that I could cart it on to the van. I must have been wrestling with this thing for five minutes. Trying to load it back-facing, front-facing, on its side and upside down, not realising that what was impeding me was my failure to place the cabinet's legs between the bars on the truck's shovel. When I finally figured it out, I looked up and discovered almost everyone in the community wearing mixed looks of confusion and amusement.

'Clueless,' said Mick, to roars of laughter.

Fred, who was less amused, marched over and picked up the

cabinet, strode to the back of the delivery van and launched it inside. 'Simple!' he shouted. 'Are you taking the piss?' he said.

Fred had me replaced. I had only been living and working in the community for about two months at this point, and had already been excluded from the warehouse and the van crew.

After a few months, I felt relieved that some structure and stability was being reintroduced into my life. I even got used to Mick's evening routine of drunkenly shouting over Pink Floyd albums. Mick might not have known it, but he restored some of my self-confidence. The conversations we had about literature, film and particularly music helped me feel more human, and that my life wasn't geared solely around survival. Despite his own madness, he helped re-establish my perspective on life, constantly reminding me that Emmaus was no place for someone as young as I was, who had just graduated from university. The first few months I spent in the community had restored some normality to my life. I was grateful for the respite, but as time wore on, my feelings changed.

Apparently, side hustles were not exclusive to the vans, and the staff had started to investigate stealing from the community.

Tom warned me that people thought I was a grass: 'They've been bang at it for years, pal. You come along, and now we're being investigated.'

I was already suffering from cabin fever from living and working with the same people; people who were damaged, dysfunctional and temperamental. The atmosphere of suspicion made me feel like the walls of the cabin were collapsing in. When I first entered the community, my critical faculties had been blunted by a desperate need for sanctuary, but living there for six months had sharpened them. The true nature of the place came into focus. Many of the Companions had lived there for decades; they frequently lamented their lot in Emmaus, but for them, it was either the community or the street. They were trapped. I also realised that I was doing full-time manual labour for no pay, with no basic rights protecting me from being returned to the streets.

It struck me that the relationship the Companions had with Emmaus was similar to the one that Victorian paupers had with their workhouse masters. This observation is shared by Professor Bill Jordan, who, in his book *Social Work and the Third Way*, compares Emmaus to the workhouse: 'At one level an Emmaus community in the UK could be seen as a privatised form of indoor poor relief – a workhouse, operated according to strict rules, with informal systems of surveillance amounting almost to a blood and guts panopticon.'[3]

On a sunny spring day in May 2017, four years after I had first entered the community, I travelled to Birmingham to interview Simon Grainge, chief executive of Emmaus UK, in his offices at the city's refurbished Custard Factory. Grainge didn't recognise these similarities: 'I think that kind of thing very often comes around where people's perception of Emmaus is not complete, shall we say, and I think that's where people dip into it and they don't fully understand it.' He added that Emmaus provides people with a sense of purpose and belonging: 'It's about people regaining their self-esteem by being able to work and support themselves, rather than being in receipt of charity.' One can appreciate why the word 'workhouse' would trouble Grainge. It conjures up images of Oliver Twist and meagre slops of gruel.

Companions have to adhere to a strict regime, but clean water, central heating, flat-screen tellies – if you can get your hands on one – and the Human Rights Act set Companions apart from their Victorian counterparts. I was not expected to break boulders or pick oakum to earn my keep, and there was more on the menu than watery porridge, but the fundamental relationship that other Companions and I had with the charity was much the same.

Emmaus was established in the UK forty years after Pierre opened the first community in Paris.[4] Today, Emmaus UK has grown to become the largest wing of the charity outside France, with twenty-nine communities catering to over 800 Companions across the country. Camilla, Duchess of Cornwall, is a patron and the president is Terry Waite, a former aide to an Archbishop of Canterbury. The organisation's goals are perfectly aligned with Conservative notions of community and volunteerism. A House of Commons select committee report, issued shortly after the Conservative-led coalition government took power in 2010, stated: 'We regard the challenge to government presented by charities such as Emmaus as a litmus test of the government's Big Society project.'[5] Nobody talks about the 'Big Society' any more, but at its heart is the Tories' *raison d'être*: the desire to whisk us back to Victorian Britain, where small government and laissez-faire capitalism was all the rage. In 2011, the then-prime minister David Cameron pledged to dismantle big government and build the Big Society in its place.[6] One can see why Emmaus would be a poster child for the Big Society; the charity practises precisely the kind of philanthrocapitalism that the concept preaches.

The do-it-yourself-'cause-you're-on-your-own-mate philoso-phy of the Big Society has led to the fragmentation of many social services. A homeless person might approach a hostel and receive accommodation with a support plan. Let's say they have a substance dependency and mental health issues. They will be referred to an alcohol and drug support service and, separ-ately, a mental health support service. All these organisations will be non-profit groups, charities or private companies, and are likely to be independent of one another. Due to the Data Protection Act, these services will be unable to share informa-tion about their clients with each other unless the client agrees first, so things like missed appointments and other issues can go unreported. These services must be returned to the public sector so those who need help with things like homelessness, dependency, health and employment can have them addressed concurrently, and different branches can communicate with each other without being impeded by red tape.

In 2018, St Mungo's – a hostel and outreach charity – was caught up in a scandal when a *Guardian* investigation[7] found that some of their staff were handing over their client's infor-mation to the Home Office to assist their Hostile Environment Policy. The brainchild of Theresa let's-stop-being-the-nasty-party May, the Hostile Environment was designed to make life as miserable as possible for migrants without leave to stay in the UK. It has fostered a severe lack of trust among rough-sleeping communities for the outreach teams that purport to have their best interests at heart. Even homeless people who aren't vul-nerable to repatriation are reluctant to share their information with charities because they're worried that it could be used against them in some way. This is a sorry state of affairs, especially considering that one of the significant problems homeless organisations face is keeping track of their service users and sharing vital information about their background, health and other issues with other providers.

The irony here is that while the government celebrates charities like Emmaus, who are increasingly running the nation's social infrastructure, it is still footing the bill. A significant proportion of Emmaus' revenue is comprised of housing benefit. When I later went on to live in Emmaus' St Albans community, the amount someone living in shared accommodation could claim in housing benefit was £78.50 per week. But this cap did not apply to claimants in supported accommodation, and before I finally left Emmaus in 2016, I was receiving £182.15 per week in housing benefit. Emmaus St Albans reported that their housing benefit receipts rose to £300,564 for the year leading up to 30 June 2016.[8]

This financial burden was evaluated in 2008 by the Cambridge Centre for Housing and Planning Research. Their report, which used the Village Carlton Emmaus community as a case study, claimed that by housing twenty-seven Companions in Emmaus, rather than in alternative accommodation, the hypothetical annual saving to the taxpayer is £557,362. Emmaus often cite these findings in their promotional material. However, the findings are based on interviews with just eleven Companions, carried out during one week of the year. Moreover, the study seems to ignore the fact that Companions are working full-time. If they're capable of working in Emmaus, they're capable of working outside of Emmaus. And if they were in full-time work, they would be paying tax.[9]

Down and Out

I moved on from Emmaus Mossley in late 2013 and returned to the housing advice centre. By this time, my severe paranoia had subsided, and I disclosed my personal details, including my disability. Despite ticking a crucial box on the misery checklist, I was given the same spiel as before: I would have to be especially destitute to get help. My parents were away, so that night, I tried desperately to find a sofa to stay on, but none was forthcoming. I spent a bitterly cold and wet November night wandering Oldham, making my way around the shopping centre until it closed, followed by circuits of Tommyfield Market. My sobriety and renewed mental clarity allowed me to view my terrible choices and severe misfortune with clear eyes. While I should have been in tears, I was laughing maniacally at what a parody my life had become. The ground was too wet to sit on, so I spent most of the night huddled underneath a bridge at the Civic Centre. The housing advice centre called me the next day and offered me a place in supported accommodation in Openshaw, Manchester. I don't know if they'd initially missed something on my application or if I just got lucky, as I can't recall them explaining their offer. I was just grateful to get it.

I spent around five months in Openshaw. I can't remember my support workers' names, but they were some of the best I've come across. And after five months, they helped me find a council flat back in Mossley.

I took pride in this place; I got fit, started blogging and, with renewed self-confidence, applied to the University of Melbourne to study for a master's degree in journalism. I was accepted, and after five months in my flat, I gave it up and moved to Australia. I was born in Melbourne and moved in with my biological father's side of the family. They hadn't seen me since I was an infant, and they paid for me to go out there, allowing me to live rent-free in the beginning.

I was uncomfortable as soon as I got off the plane in Melbourne. Australia is a beautiful country; the trunks of the luscious eucalyptus trees look like they're made of suede; gorgeous white shores look on to crystal-blue horizons, and the whole place looks polished, clean. But it is hot. Bloody hot. It's also so bright that I found myself reaching for sunglasses on a cloudy day. Plus, the country boasts the largest variety of ways to be killed since Spain circa 1492. In Britain, our animals are quaint, fluffy things that star in children's books; in Oz, they're the stuff of nightmares. Twenty-one of the world's twenty-five most venomous snakes live there, along with crocs, white sharks, giant bounding rats (kangaroos) and monstrous arachnids. A tiny spider can murder you in your garden out there; the creepiest thing one might come across in a British garden is Alan Titchmarsh.

The bigger problem for me out there was getting a job. I arrived in Melbourne in mid-September 2014, but I couldn't begin my master's degree until February 2015. In the meantime, I had to look for work if I wanted to continue staying with my uncle in the suburbs, but getting on the employment ladder was an even more arduous task out there. Just like the UK, 'essential' skills and health-and-safety training rackets have cosied up to Centrepoint (their version of the Job Centre) in Australia, and even menial jobs require one to have their 'tickets' in order.

I returned to my parents' house for Christmas 2014 with the intention of going back to Melbourne afterwards to start my masters. But while I was at my parents', my uncle phoned to tell me that I could no longer stay with him. He'd thought that I would only be shacking up with him temporarily until I found my own digs, but I'd been there just under three months, and my uncle wanted his own space again. I had no job and little money, and because I couldn't afford the rents out there, I didn't use my return ticket.

Back to square one. This was my fault. The decision to go out there was impulsive, and I should have done more research into what to expect, but I took a risk to try and improve my life, and my failure resulted in me hitting rock bottom again. This is something I've witnessed time and again throughout my experience in hostels and while reporting on homelessness. Clearly, the safety net isn't good enough.

I moved in with my parents for a while, but as much as I love them, we've never been able to live with each other over long periods. I was having no luck finding a job and I grew desperate. I expected that things would soon break down at home, and, as I didn't want to be at the mercy of Greater Manchester's housing service again, I looked to escape the north entirely. Time heals all wounds, and I thought things at Emmaus could be different. I knew what to expect, what to say, what not to say, so I applied to live at the Emmaus St Albans community.

The community support manager was full of smiles and niceties when she collected me from the train station. She drove me to the community and guided me to a box room, which was fully furnished – and even included a TV! I was given a handbook detailing the community's rules, which, like those at Mossley, were centred on abstaining from alcohol and drugs.

The handbook also included the system of reprimands used for various infractions, which were illustrated in a table of ascending severity. Alcohol and violence earned one an immediate 'ban' – the length of which depended on the offence – while things like tardiness and verbal abuse would earn you a verbal warning, followed by a written warning, a final warning, and eventually a ban. The manager left and told me to relax before tea at 5pm.

The community was inside a large red-brick building in what must have been a hospice or nursing home. While Emmaus Mossley did all their business under one roof, Emmaus St Albans had many shops across Hertfordshire. It was a hot and humid day, and the stress of moving had welded my shirt to my back. I changed and went outside for some fresh air. The community was warmly decorated and had a spacious and manicured garden where chickens roamed free; there was even a friendly house cat roaming the corridors. Mossley, by contrast, felt cold and austere, the comparison with a workhouse made more evident by the Victorian mill we had lived in. When the Companions returned from work, I expected to be repelling banter, but each of them, with a few exceptions, introduced themselves cordially, invited me to eat at their table and bombarded me with questions.

There's no other word for it. It was nice. They were *nice*. The atmosphere in Mossley had a working-class gruffness to it, whereas in St Albans, the ambience was gentle, fluffy, very middle England and middle class – it was soft. Maybe this perception was conditioned by my background (saying 'actually' in Manchester is enough to be considered a snobby bastard). Perhaps they were just normal and 'it's grim up north'.

I fitted in easily at St Albans. There wasn't the same hustling culture, and everyone got the opportunity to work across the enterprise in a variety of roles. I enjoyed selling to people, booking deliveries and arranging collections. In some of the shops, the operation was run entirely by Companions. This responsibility nurtured a sense of purpose; I felt like I was valued and contributing in some way. Mossley was populated by your bog-standard northern miserabilist, while St Albans was a cornucopia of eccentricity. Every type of personality lived there, from laddish boors and rule sticklers to artsy hippies and fantasists. I'd had no friends to speak of in Mossley, but I made several in St Albans, some of whom I'm still close with today. In the room next to mine was Dominic Smith, an aspiring magician from nearby Hatfield, who, to my relief, wasn't prone to evening screaming matches with himself. Dom and I exchanged scarcely a passing glance in the first few months. The first time I spoke to him, he was fixing his leather jacket and attending to his wispy goatee in front of a mirror in the hallway.

'Hey, Danny!' he shouted. 'Boom! How do I look?' He pointed his two index fingers at me like they were guns.

'Err . . . like a fifties greaser,' I offered.

'Exactly, exactly, the ladies love it, mate.'

'Good luck!'

I headed to the garden to puff on a few roll-ups, where I was met by Conor, a diminutive Irishman in his late fifties. Conor had the appearance and voice of a mysterious sage, the kind who appears to protagonists in fantasy novels offering riddled guidance. Every time I spoke to him, I half expected to find myself fighting a dragon moments later.

'How goes it, Dan?' he asked from his corner of the garden. The late-evening sun only illuminated half of his face; the rest was shaded by the tree that loomed over his table, reinforcing the eerie quality of his character.

'Good, ta,' I replied.

'Why stand when you can sit?' Conor said, pulling out a garden chair for me. I accepted his offer and parked it next to him. He continued: 'A wise old man told me, "Why stand when you can sit, why sit when you can lie down, and if you're lying down, why not have a little sleep?"'

I couldn't think of what to say, so I said nothing. To break the unbearable silence, I told him about Dom going out on the pull.

Conor pondered this for a moment, then answered: 'There's nothing like a bit of warm arse.'

I wished I'd said nothing.

One Companion with his head firmly in the clouds was Wilfred, a warm and kindly looking man in his early sixties. When Wilfred wasn't talking about his struggles with diabetes, he was regaling us with his military escapades. Wilfred claimed he was in the parachute regiment and had served as a sniper in Lebanon.

'I score quite highly on the psychopath metric,' he blurted out randomly to Dom and me at breakfast one morning.

'The what?' I replied.

'Well, you have to be a psycho to be a sniper,' Wilfred said.

'Ah, right,' I said, not knowing what he was talking about and hoping this would be the end of it.

'I had to shoot who they told me to shoot; you can't ask questions in that situation,' Wilfred insisted.

'What, even women?' asked Dom.

'Yeah, one time there was this woman walking towards a roadblock. She had a burka on and a kid with her. She was ordered to go back, but she kept on coming. I had to shoot her because we didn't know if she had a bomb underneath her clothes,' Wilfred explained.

'Did she?' I asked.

'Nope,' Wilfred said.

'Jesus, that's dark,' said Dom. 'Did it affect your confidence?'

'No,' Wilfred said. 'I told you I score high on the psycho test.'

A few days later, Dom and I watched *American Sniper* in the lounge. There's a scene in the film where Chris Kyle, a real sniper played by Bradley Cooper, has to gun down a woman in Iraq in identical circumstances to those Wilfred had described. After this Dom and I would ask Wilfred about his military exploits and see if we could match them to other films or TV shows.

As I spent more time in the community, the sweetness shown by staff struck me as insidious. Some of this was subtle, some less so. Emmaus, like a lot of homeless charities, thinks that sleepouts, which usually entail a coterie of charity bods huddling together inside sleeping bags for the night, are a fantastic way of raising homeless awareness among the general public. Presumably because passing by real rough sleepers in their sleeping bags during the morning commute is too obvious. Sleepouts are a terrible idea – and an appalling one when you're asking formerly homeless people to take part. It would be like asking women at a refuge if they wouldn't mind being beaten up to raise awareness for domestic violence.

Like Mossley, St Albans was content to allow Companions

to become as paralytic as they liked in the neighbouring park, but prohibited such behaviour on the premises. The policy was taken a lot more seriously here, and Companions had to pass a breathalyser test every morning before they were allowed to work. Emmaus' policies around abstinence are indicative of why charity is not capable of meeting the growing challenge of homelessness. A significant proportion of homeless people have issues with substance dependency. No one with serious substance dependency issues could survive in Emmaus, as they wouldn't be fit enough to complete the work, which is full-time and labour intensive. This would be fine if the charity had the resources to screen those who are referred to them properly, but they don't. New recruits are often referred to Emmaus communities by outside agencies. In my experience, these recruits would – understandably – lie about the severity of their dependency issues so they could get off the streets or leave the bleak hostels they lived in. The staff would rumble these Companions when their addictions inevitably got the better of them, and back to the streets or the hostel system they would go.

Dom explained that a Companion who was kicked out for drinking in his room took to living in the local park, just beyond the threshold of the community's back garden. Dom took pity on this Companion and brought him food in the evening.

'They asked me why I was giving him food. I was given a verbal warning for doing that,' he told me. 'They didn't explain what rule I had broken.'

In response to Dominic's claims, Emmaus said: 'It is not unusual for Companions to provide food for people living outside of the community, and it is not something they would be reprimanded for. There is no record of any kind of warning being given to Dominic for passing on food.'

Homeless people often have complex needs, and when rules are enforced as strictly as they are in Emmaus, many will be forced to return to sleeping rough. But there is another, perhaps more fundamental way, in which charity is broken. In my experience, I cannot honestly say that it is in the interest of third-sector providers and charities to end homelessness. Emmaus managers often boasted about new communities opening around the country. What should give charities pause, however, is that their expansion is also being celebrated by our politicians, but for entirely different reasons. In 2017, the current leader of the House of Commons, Jacob Rees-Mogg, rejoiced at the news that the number of food parcels handed out by leading food bank charity the Trussell Trust had reached almost 1.2 million. Rees-Mogg said:

> To have charitable support given by people voluntarily to support their fellow citizens I think is rather uplifting and shows what a good, compassionate country we are. Inevitably, the state can't do everything, so I think that there is good within food banks. The real reason for the rise in numbers is that people know that they are there, and Labour deliberately didn't tell them.[10]

'The state can't do everything.' Look how ready the government is to use charitable growth to absolve itself of responsibility when the real reason that charities are expanding is that politicians aren't doing their jobs. Indeed, the state is not omnipotent, but even relatively poor countries have homelessness levels that are a fraction of the UK's, so we must be doing something wrong.

If charities like Emmaus are genuinely committed to 'ending homelessness', then their ultimate aim must be to cease to exist – yet they celebrate expansion in a way that would make venture capitalists feel uneasy. If we truly want to end homelessness, we must take a holistic approach to housing and social care, and not condemn people to the streets or turn them out again for the same reason that saw them there in the first place. The fact is, charities like Emmaus are compromised from the start, as ending homelessness would be bad for business. No homelessness: no homeless charities. People have pointed out to me that one could make the same argument about hospitals and sick people, but this point only works if you believe that homelessness is just as inescapable as illness. If our goal is to end social ills like homelessness, then we must conclude that philanthrocapitalism, which depends on social problems enduring, is, at the very least, counterproductive to that aim.

I learned the true extent of St Albans' obsession with abstinence when I received my first verbal warning. When winter came along, flu had invaded the community, and everyone was bedridden at some point. A member of staff visited a Companion who had struggled with heroin addiction in his past. The staff member knew that the flu was causing absences, but rather than realise that this Companion was the latest flu victim, they assumed he was withdrawing from heroin and accused him of using again. This accusation tipped me over the edge, and I decided to confront my support worker, Will.

I told Will that this Companion, whom I knew well, was not using heroin. Not content with leaving it there, I started to pick on other things that were bothering me in the community. When I'd been battling the flu myself a week earlier, I'd asked Will for some painkillers. He'd looked through the medicine cabinet and found some Strepsils. He read the back of the pack and shook his head: 'I can't give you these,' he said. 'There's alcohol in them.'

I'd tiptoed around the eggshells at the time, but now I decided to stamp all over them. 'Was I gonna get pissed from some *Strepsils*, Will? That was fucking ridiculous.'

'No, it wasn't! There are people here with drinking problems, and we want to reduce any potential triggers.'

'So, I suppose you're gonna throw out the deodorant 'n' all then?'

'Yes, if it's got alcohol in,' Will replied unequivocally and without hesitation.

'Why?' I shouted.

'Well, the odour could encourage people to go out and drink.'

'Will, alcohol is odourless. Are we gonna ban television as well? Because God forbid that someone should see a beer advert. Fuck me; everyone's on the piss every night in the park.'

As good as it felt to put him right, it was pig-headed. I received a verbal warning, and my head was veering ever closer towards the chopping block. My spiralling behaviour had potentially life-threatening consequences for me one evening when Dom, Noel – a Companion from Cumbria – and I were in the lounge. Dom was sitting at a computer on one side of the room, while Noel and I were vegging in front of the telly on the other.

Callum, a moody Companion, came into the room to work on the computer next to Dom when I shouted 'Shut up!' in Dom's direction. Dom hadn't said anything, but that was the joke. It wasn't particularly original or funny, but it passed the time.

'What did you say?' Callum shouted back.

'I wasn't talkin' to you!' We squared up and exchanged some harsh words. I saw Callum was balling his fist up, so I pushed him backwards. When he found his feet, he reached into one of the pockets in his shorts and retrieved a knife, and was about to advance at me with it when Dom and Noel got between us. Callum offered to fight me outside.

'What? When you've got a knife?'

He slammed the knife on the pool table and stormed out of the room, calling for me to follow. Noel and Dom tried to calm him down and ushered him upstairs.

'You don't want me out there – it won't be much of a fight,' I called.

'Maybe, but I'll be the second-best you've ever had,' he shouted back as he headed for his room.

Him being 'the second-best I'd ever had' didn't really make sense, and I almost told him as much, but I let it go, though.

The next day, I had a difficult time convincing the staff to act appropriately in this situation. The fact that Will was on duty didn't help things. I told him that I wasn't prepared to live with someone who threatened people with knives. The ensuing argument took such a farcical turn that Will ended up disputing what kind of knife it was, and insisted the only reason Callum had had it was because he was still in his work clothes (he wasn't), and that he'd only produced it because he was backed into a corner (also nonsense). Firstly, who cares why he had the knife? Secondly, pen knife, carving knife, Stanley knife, or samurai sword, I don't think it would have made a difference if the blade had penetrated my heart. Imagine that level of logic on the Accident and Emergency ward:

'What's wrong with the patient?' a busy doctor asks a paramedic (I imagine that's how it works).

'He's been stabbed in the heart,' the paramedic replies.

'Oh no! What sort of knife?' the doctor asks for absolutely no reason at all.

'P . . . P . . . Pen knife,' the paramedic says apologetically.

'You bother me with this?! Throw him to the curb. He'll be fine!' the doctor rages as he turns on his heels.

They finally kicked Callum out, but a month later, he returned. With regards to the knife incident, an Emmaus spokeswoman said:

In this particular situation, which was witnessed by a number of people, a Companion had been backed into a corner when he pulled a pen knife, [which] he had been carrying for work that day, from his pocket. When the altercation was broken up, he admitted he shouldn't have reached for the knife, and left the community.

When, at a later date, [this Companion] applied to return to the community, Danny was consulted to see how he would feel about him living there again. While he did raise some concerns, Danny did agree that this individual should have a second chance and be allowed to return to the community.

In fact, I was never happy about him coming back, but I was worried that my own position in the community would be jeopardised if I remained obstinate. It didn't matter. Shortly after Callum's return, I was evicted from the community. Every move you make in Emmaus is being observed and scrutinised by someone. I was on bad terms with the staff and several Companions. On my last day working in the community, I was delivering furniture with a Companion who derived most of his jollies from winding people up. As we drove through the city streets, we got into an argument that ended with me demanding that he pull the van over so I could walk home. Before I got out, I punched a hole in the windscreen. The day after, the support manager handed me a twenty-eight-day ban and I was given seven days to move out. I was lucky that Goldsmiths had accepted me on a journalism course by then; the university's halls saved me from returning to the hostel system.

I spent over a year in Emmaus communities in total, but I never felt the 'love' Pierre spoke of; instead I felt exploited, demoralised, and angry. Even though Companions satisfy the basic legal tests that define employment, they have no employment rights protecting them from things like unfair dismissal. Being sacked from an Emmaus community means not only losing your job, but your home, too. In my experience, the precariousness of this arrangement fostered feelings of suspicion among Companions, both of the staff and of each other – creating the 'blood and guts panopticon' Bill Jordan speaks of. It's common for workers, especially in low-paying and labour-intensive jobs, to look sideways at the work ethic of their colleagues. In Emmaus, this preoccupation was heightened. We worked hard, lugging heavy items of furniture around for minuscule rewards, and anyone perceived not to be pulling their weight earned a reputation for laziness that was almost impossible to shift. This, coupled with living among the people you work with, created feelings of confinement and paranoia.

People I've spoken to over the years will invariably defend the charity by arguing that Companions volunteered for the scheme, which, of course, is true, but only in the sense that everyone who works chooses to. The fact is the work is obligatory, and if they don't do it, the alternative could be a doorway. There's a strong argument that Emmaus Companions should be considered employees and be protected by employment rights. Workers are usually considered employees if their employer controls where they work, and if there's a mutuality of obligation – they exchange their labour for some kind of remuneration.

Paul Johnson, a solicitor, formally of the Oldham Law Centre, who has practised employment law for more than thirty years, said: 'It appears to me that Emmaus have total control over when, where and how the Companions work.' And there is also a mutuality of obligation – Companions are compelled to work forty hours a week, and Emmaus must provide subsistence in return. There's no guarantee that an employment tribunal would accept this argument, and it has yet to be tested in court.

Companions could also be entitled to fundamental housing rights. All Companions sign a Right to Occupy agreement when they enter Emmaus. This can be terminated with reasonable notice and does not confer the protections against eviction provided under the Housing Acts (formerly the Rent

Acts). Johnson said that just because an agreement *says* it's a licence, that doesn't mean it *is* one: 'In the leading case on this subject (Street vs Mountford), the Right to Occupy agreement said that it was a licence, but the House of Lords decided that it was a tenancy and that the Rent Acts did apply.' Johnson explained that, based on the House of Lord's decision,[11] one could argue that 'Companions have exclusive possession of their rooms, even though Emmaus has reserved a right to enter.' Companions would be considered tenants if this argument was accepted; nevertheless, it too has yet to be tested in court.

Simon Grainge rejected the idea that Companions are more vulnerable to unfair treatment due to their lack of legal protections, and he doesn't think the charity could survive if they had them. Grainge also rejected the comparison with a typical worker, because 'huge allowances' are made for Companions. 'I've seen that with many Companions who have actually moved on from communities and gone to work for an employer, and it hasn't worked for them. What kind of employer do you think would accept twenty to thirty fag breaks during the day, and the ability to say, "I'm not functioning today; I need to go to my room"? All that sort of stuff goes on, on a regular basis, in communities.'

I think this is nonsense. The work involved lugging heavy furniture around, sometimes up and down tower blocks. It was one of the most labour-intensive jobs I've ever done, and I've worked in construction, warehousing and landscaping. When I put this to Grainge, he said: 'It is exactly the kind of labour that many other people are expected to do on the minimum wage,' and then reiterated that the 'huge allowances' Companions enjoy means they are not ordinary employees.

Of the many Companions I've spoken to throughout the years, all of them, without exception, agreed that the work is hard. Dom, who has worked in busy kitchens, pubs and butcher's shops since leaving St Albans, said: 'Everyone took their work very seriously; if you didn't work, you were asked to leave. Every job I've had after Emmaus was easier; it was the hardest job I've had.'

One of the critical reasons that charities like Emmaus have continued to avoid scrutiny is the lack of accountability in the third sector. The Freedom of Information Act 2000 provided a public right of access to information held by public authorities. The hope was that public institutions would become more accountable and have fewer places to hide from scrutiny. Private organisations, charities and other third-sector organisations do not have to comply with FOIs. So much of the homeless provision in the UK is provided by these organisations, and yet they are not held accountable. When they make mistakes, you're unlikely to find out about them, and if you do, there's often no regulator interested in making improvements, which might explain why Emmaus thinks nothing of making people work for no pay, with no rights protecting them from being returned to the streets for as little as having an empty beer bottle in their room.

In May 2019, I found myself sitting with Joules Humm on Brighton beach. It had been nine months since his son, Jake Humm, had hanged himself in his semi-independent bedsit at the YMCA. Joules had his entire life wrapped up in Jake; he'd even dedicated his left arm to him. Every tattoo on it is a reference to his son. Joules was adamant that local services in Brighton had done all they could to help Jake, and that his son had been determined to take his own life, but as I listened to him tell Jake's life story, I began to have doubts. Jake died when he was twenty-two. He had been bouncing around Brighton's broken housing system since he was sixteen. By all accounts, Jake was generous, gregarious and had loads of heart, but he was also a self-destructive depressive who'd struggled with alcoholism since his teens. At the beginning of August 2018, Jake was living in semi-independent accommodation with the YMCA Downslink Group. He had been sober for nine months, but relapsed when a close friend died by suicide. Jake's mental health deteriorated dramatically, and he went on a three-week-long drinking binge before taking his own life. It took two days for his body to be found. Anybody who was paying attention to Jake's social media accounts in the weeks leading up to his death would have realised he was in crisis. They read like a diary, with Jake documenting his bingeing and frequently expressing suicidal thoughts. In one post, he explicitly stated that he hoped the alcohol 'puts me in my grave in the next few days.'

The YMCA describes itself as 'the largest provider of safe, supported accommodation for young people in England and Wales. We offer more than 8,800 beds, which includes everything from emergency accommodation through to supported longer-term housing and youth hostels.'[12] Although the YMCA is regulated by the Charity Commission and the Regulator of Social Housing, much of the support offered in its accommodation is unregulated. The semi-independent home where Jake died is self-regulating because it provides support rather than 'personal care'. As I explained on page 10, this means that its support is neither monitored by the Care Quality Commission nor Ofsted, even though residents may be as young as sixteen. Having investigated his case, I had a multitude of questions. Had staff attempted to have Jake sectioned? Had they considered moving him into accommodation with more intensive support? How many times had they contacted him in the weeks before his death? And what were their thoughts on staff taking two days to discover his body when he was known to be suicidal? The YMCA didn't answer those questions, but it did say:

> Our review concluded that there were no errors or omissions in the service we provided, despite the sad outcome. However, we did identify some changes we could make, such as, for example, introducing a ligature risk assessment whereby potential ligature points could be identified and promptly removed if a resident was deemed to be at risk of suicide or self-harm.[13]

I don't know who decided that organisations providing 'support' rather than 'personal care' get to avoid regulation and are able to write their own reviews, but it seems ludicrous. Imagine if a suspect died in police custody and the chief constable announced: 'We've had a long look at ourselves and concluded that we'd done absolutely nothing wrong.' I can't claim that Jake would still be alive today if services had intervened in his life in a more meaningful way, but I think he would've had more of a chance if the quality of support was better.

Aside from their lack of accountability, charities also provide services according to their own philosophies. The number of charities registered in England and Wales is currently around 185,000. The Charity Commission is tasked with enforcing rules and offering guidance, but regulating such a large group of organisations with so few resources, in an area where the law is often obscure, is a difficult task. This makes the quality of support a postcode lottery – and sometimes a lottery within the same postcode. This lottery can even apply to the service provider. Take the difference between Emmaus Mossley's policy on alcohol and the policy in the St Albans community. In Mossley, a preponderance of Companions drank themselves into a stupor after work. The staff knew it – you'd have to be blind and noseless to miss it – but the Companions functioned the following day, so it was tolerated, even when they were trembling with DTs and their health was visibly deteriorating. In St Albans, breathalysers and officious managers would have seen Companions in Mossley thrown out on their first day. Neither scenario is ideal. A better approach would be for homeless provision to be returned to local authorities' social and housing services, where health experts, officials in central government and local authorities can debate and agree upon a clear plan to tackle this crisis. As that's unlikely to happen while the Victorian tribute government is in office, provision for an adequately resourced regulator would at least keep these charities on their toes.

A year after I left Emmaus St Albans, Emmaus Mossley tweeted that Mick had gone missing. A couple of weeks later, an article in the *Manchester Evening News* reported that a man, believed to be

Mick, had drowned in the River Tame.[14] I read this while sitting in front of a swanky Mac computer on Goldsmith's campus. I looked around at my classmates, as my guts tied themselves in knots, and considered the perverse contrast between the relatively petty anxieties over our assignments and grades, and the worries I used to have. I left the room in a way that wouldn't draw concern. I wasn't distraught. Mick's death was deeply upsetting, but it didn't surprise me. I don't know how he ended up in the Tame, but I'd routinely found him passed out at the Tyre, in bushes and on staircases. Once, I witnessed him fall into the canal, and I can recall people telling him that he'd be in deep shit if there were no one to fish him out. Emmaus was far from ideal, but Mick was better off inside its walls than on the street. At the charity, he had shelter, food, running water and other home comforts. He had a regular job that he could go to every day, and, despite his angry protestations, he seemed to enjoy being the warehouse master. Mick said he was very proud of the work he did there and felt like he was contributing to the wider community. He told me he intended to spend the rest of his life with the charity – and in the end, he did.

I missed his funeral, but returned to the Beach to find out what had happened to him. The Companions had pinned a print-out picture of Mick to one of the trees on the riverbank. Tom, Sebastian and Rabbit, as well as Walter and Rover, were perched on camp chairs around a fire. The atmosphere was sombre, and not much was said. Nobody really wanted to talk about it. Neither did I. What could we say? I kissed my fingers, touched Mick's photo and drew a cross on my chest. I'm not religious, but it felt like a respectful thing to do. Walter looked up at me without saying anything, but gave a slight nod of approval.

Emmaus solved two of Mick's problems: lack of shelter and unemployment. What they didn't address was the reason he'd found himself homeless in the first place. Mick was an alcoholic. There wasn't an evening that I spent at the charity when he wasn't three sheets to the wind, falling over and shouting himself to sleep in his room – if he made it there at all. While Companions are banned for drinking on-site, they can drink themselves to death off the premises. Most homeless people have substance dependency issues, and these issues are often the reason why they became homeless in the first place. Returning them to the streets for the same reason they were there originally achieves nothing but keeping those people trapped in a miserable cycle. As much as the Tory government and its Big Society scheme has relied on charity to do the heavy-lifting, charity does not hold the answer. We must find another way for people like Mick.

Chapter Two

Trauma

In 1997, my key worker entered the classroom and presented me with a green paper parcel, which she unfurled, revealing a thick white powder. I leaned forward and gathered as much of it as I could with my tongue, making sure not to miss a speck. I was told the bitter taste in my mouth was going to make me better, make me good.

The classroom was in a special-education school – let's call it Dippydale – for children with learning, emotional and behavioural difficulties, which is government-speak for angry brats. I was there because, as soon as I could form memories, I was told there was something wrong with me – and they had a point. The psychiatrist who diagnosed me with ADHD when I was seven didn't need to strain his diagnostic skills too much. During our first session, I was doing my best Spider-Man impression on his bookshelves when I was supposed to be arranging a series of simple pictures into logical sequences.

I was born in Melbourne, Australia, but I only have vague memories of the city, as my parents moved to the UK when I was three. My mum was born in Leicester and grew up in Norton, a bucolic and boring hamlet on the English–Welsh border. She met my Australian father in her early twenties when he was visiting his relatives in the area. She followed him Down Under, had me, then followed him back when he got accepted into the University of Manchester. Mum wanted to be closer to my grandma, so we moved into a small two-up, two-down terrace in Greenfield, one of Saddleworth's collection of sleepy old textile villages. The area is populated by a mix of tradies, city commuters and the nouveau riche, who look down their noses at visitors from the places they've left. It's also home to eeh-bah-gum Yorkshire men and women who defiantly troop the white rose at any given opportunity, even though the area has been governed by a red-rosed Lancastrian council since 1974.[1] My earliest memories are in that house. They are coloured by fear and violence. For legal reasons, I can't discuss the trauma that my family and I suffered during my infancy, but it left an indelible mark on our lives.

While it's nearly impossible to identify a single cause behind one's route to homelessness, when looking into the lives of homeless adults, one will find that many started on their route to destitution in childhood. More often than not, homeless people will report having suffered from trauma in their early years that went untreated and contributed to worsening mental health. According to a survey conducted by Evolve Housing, a London-based homeless charity, 79 per cent of the 156 partici-pants reported at least one childhood trauma. While Evolve stops short at claiming there's a causal link between childhood trauma and homelessness, they do say there's 'a disproportion-ally high level of those experiencing homelessness following traumatic childhood experiences'. Evolve added that 'separation and loss in childhood is a highly traumatic experience that affects the direction of those who experience homelessness.'[2]

When the dark clouds of this period cleared, I enjoyed the most blissful time of my life. It was just me, Mum and my brother Ollie against the world. Mum couldn't work and look after us all day, so we didn't have much. The clothes my brother and I wore were hand-me-downs, and our older and better-off cousins donated toys they'd grown out of. We didn't have money for holidays or leisure outings, so we had to make our own entertainment, which mostly took place on the trippy purple heather-strewn moorland at the back of our terrace. We would scour this terrain looking for 'clues', which, looking back, was Mum's ingenious way of encouraging us to pick up litter. The rest of our time was spent painting rocks, fiddling with Lego or bashing away on my cousin's old Nintendo NES. When our giant Ferguson video player wasn't jammed up (usually due to our failure to understand the importance of pressing the eject button before we introduced a new video), we'd watch *Ghostbusters* and *Milo and Otis* (the only videos we had) on a loop. The real treat was when Mum would play 'Riders on the Storm' by the Doors on her record player. She'd close the curtains, turn off the lights and gradually increase the volume as the Lizard King's ominous tones overlaid the rolling thunder, and we'd sway in the dark.

Mum made the place look nice enough, but our furniture was old, broken and dangerous. My first major scar came from one of our rickety armchairs. The cushion on the right armrest had come off, exposing a rusty nail, which jutted out menacingly from the hardwood. On one dry summer afternoon, during an

ADHD-fuelled tizz, I managed to impale my right arm on the giant nail as I hurled myself on to the seat. Curiously, I didn't feel a scintilla of pain when the nail bore into my soft infant flesh. I only registered the injury when Mum alerted me to the streaks of scarlet trickling down my arm and on to the cool ceramic tiles on our kitchen floor. It was only when I caught sight of my wound that the tears and panic kicked in. Mum rushed me to hospital for twenty stitches. I was so reckless when I was small that I was *the* reason the local playground got safety pads placed underneath the swings. Mum petitioned the council when wild swinging caused me to fall and crack the back of my head open – for the umpteenth time.

One good thing to come from this is that I got interesting scars for my troubles. I used to feel that the way I got the scar on my arm was lame, so I invented what I imagined to be cool alternatives. My most creative tale was that the wound was a result of shielding my face from a savage knife attack in Moss Side, a notoriously rough area in Manchester. I kept this habit up well into my twenties, until I realised that accidents could be just as impressive to strangers as shark attacks.

It was hard for Mum. She didn't work, and had to play the role of both parents. In my infant mind, she was two people. I thought she was an angel at night. I recall her in her nightie, golden hair resting elegantly on her shoulders, telling us bedtime stories she'd made up. During the day, though, I felt like an angry imposter had borrowed my mum's face in order to give us a hard time. The flowing hair was tied up in a tight bun to match her brusque, I-mean-business attitude; the only stories we were told were 'Get off the Nintendo and go to your room,' and 'There's no afters if you don't eat those sprouts.' Mum insists she hated doing this, but felt that in the absence of patriarchal discipline, she had to exert some control over us – especially me, as I was already well on my way to becoming a little bastard.

One of the typical traits in ADHD folks is a challenging combination of hypersensitivity to criticism and overactive emotions. Things that would inspire a hint of irritability in most people would produce a wellspring of stress in me that could overwhelm my whole body. I still struggle with this today. Only now I have a coping strategy. Well, it's not so much a strategy, more of a dysfunctional habit, which involves taking the back of my left hand and biting down on it as hard as I can until the wellspring is depleted. When I was a kid, books, ornaments and any other inanimate objects I could get my hands on bore the brunt of my anger.

I would march upstairs, screaming blue murder after Mum had said something unreasonable like: 'Don't dance on the coffee table, Danny! You'll hurt yourself.' I'd empty any shelves or drawers, and the contents would make their way to the bottom of our wooden hill with almighty thuds. I would scream every name under the sun at her. Sometimes I'd do this for hours, before collapsing in an exhausted heap. Then came the guilt, the tears and the apologies. Mum would always forgive me.

When she needed respite, my brother and I were sent half a mile down the road to my grandma's house. Grandma was a remarkable woman. She was born in Liverpool in 1933 to a working-class family and lived through the Blitz. My brother and I would be on the edge of our seats as she told us about fussy wardens, rations, the gas mask she had to begrudgingly wear in her Anderson shelter, and the way the sky turned red over Merseyside after an intense night of Luftwaffe bombardment. Grandma was sporty. She excelled at netball and hockey, and was even selected to bowl swing for Lancashire Ladies cricket team before she suffered a severe knee injury. She told me that her surgeon removed cartilage from the wrong knee, leaving her with a steadily worsening limp for the rest of her life. Luckily, she was a proper clever clogs. She won a scholarship to university to study geography and became a secondary school teacher – a remarkable achievement for a working-class woman at that time.

You wouldn't know her roots if you met her, as she concealed them underneath a polite, bourgeoise veneer – unless she was under stress, which was most of the time when I was around. These conflicting identities would make for eloquent yet terse bollockings: 'You utterly puerile . . . shyster!' she would bellow in broad Scouse after I'd done something unspeakably naughty, like climbing into the boot from the backseat when she was driving. Then the phone would ring, and Hyacinth 'Bouquet' would answer. She was also a well of unique and eccentric phrases. A clever turn would be met with 'The brains of you and the price of fish' (I still don't know what that means), while a bad mood received 'What's bitten your tail?' And her *pièce de résistance*: 'Such is life in all its phases. When you're dead, you go to blazes.' That one is inscribed on her headstone.

She could be spectacularly stubborn and unapologetic, refusing to give way in any argument, even if it meant forgoing sleep. But she was also kind and empathetic. I've always been a worrier, especially during the uncertainty of night. Grandma would nurse me to sleep. First, with improvised stories. The most memorable ones were about Hat, Skat, Minto and Bongo, four dinosaurs that the fictional versions of my brother and I would visit through a mystical portal in our backyard. Grandma would begin the tale, and we would fill in the blanks as she went along until our eyelids grew heavy. She'd then lift our infant heads, punch our pillows and tell us she'd created a magic hole in which our worried minds could rest.

Even though I was challenging, Mum just about managed to cope with me during my early years. This changed when my education began to deteriorate. The erratic, impulsive hyperactivity was tolerated at home. Mum was in her mid-twenties and had plenty of energy and free time to keep up with me. At school, it was a different story. ADHD was scarcely part of the lexicon back in the early nineties, and even those who were aware of the condition dismissed it as a medicalised way of describing naughty boys. The teachers at St Mary's, the dainty Church of England primary at the bottom of my road, had far less patience than my mum and grandparents when I decided to leap up inexplicably in the middle of lessons to manically pirouette and cartwheel around the room like a pissed-up gymnast. They had even less patience for my Olympic-level tantrums.

Like many primaries, St Mary's had their pupils ring a bell to announce the end of breaks. This was a coveted task. When it was finally my turn, I raced up to the top floor as fast as my six-year-old legs could propel me, retrieved the bell and raced back down, barely able to contain my excitement. I was gonna ring the fuck out of that bell, ring it as it had never been rung before. Everyone would know break time was over when I was finished, and they were going to line up for me. When I burst through the front doors, though, I couldn't believe my eyes. All the kids had already lined up. It turned out that in my excitement, I had forgotten to grasp the bell's clapper, so on every step back down to the playground, the bell had been ringing, alerting everybody that break time was finito. The wellspring was rising. I threw the bell to the ground and ran away.

These outbursts began to add up. I was finally excluded from St Mary's at age seven and went to Ferney Field, a special-education school in Chadderton, Oldham. I don't recall much from my time there, save for a rainy trip to Chester Zoo, smiley-faced potatoes and gloopy semolina at lunchtime, and, of course, bad behaviour. This was the schooling equivalent of a naughty step, which I stayed on until the education authority found another mainstream school that would have me. That lucky school was St Chads, another C of E in Saddleworth, this time in Uppermill, Saddleworth's unofficial capital.

I only lasted a year at St Chad's. This time, a tonne of bricks rather than a final straw broke the camel's back. As well as being bullied for my off-the-wall behaviour, I began to get a verbal kicking for my unfortunate facial features. My two front teeth had decided to outgrow the rest of my face, leaving me looking like a were-rabbit, and the kids at school chose to remind me of this at every passing opportunity. 'Hey, Divelle' – that's what they'd taken to calling me, on account of me being a bit of a div – 'pick up your teeth, they're filing the floor away!' Or: 'Oi, mong boy, what's Elmer Fudd like in real life?'

I was too young to know about self-deprecation back then, and didn't have the emotional capacity to take it in my stride.

On the day that I'd finally had enough, I ran across the classroom to lamp a lad who had been mocking me by sticking his two front teeth out; I threw a pencil case at another kid who was laughing, and pushed a table over in the direction of the teacher. This incident became a legend in Saddleworth over the years, becoming increasingly dramatic as it was told back to me. 'Are you the Danny who threw a table and chair at the teacher?' one kid might ask. 'Didn't you knock out your teacher?' another would enquire as the story got recycled a few years later. It wasn't as bad as all that, but I still got expelled.

Before I ended up at Dippydale, I spent nine months at Grange House, a special ed boarding school for dyslexics near Leominster. Grange was like a hippy holiday camp. It was by far the best school I went to. They seemed to understand that sitting an ADHD kid in a classroom and expecting them to remain still, silent and attentive when every cell in their body wants them to bounce off the walls was not a good idea. Grange was education in motion. Geography was taught on hills and in the woods, biology was explained to us at the side of ponds as we examined newts at the bottom of our little blue fishing nets, and the school dedicated whole days to PE.

Grange charged high fees to match the public-school vibe they were going for, although the education authority picked up my bill. The school was inside ornate Tudor manor houses on sprawling farmland. We had house teams – Croft, Wigmore and Ambry – homework was called 'prep', and we wore smart uniforms. Unfortunately, the headmistress – and owner – was not using her lofty funds judiciously. The Independent Schools

Tribunal shut the school down for being 'incompetent, inefficient, and exploitative of staff'.[3] I later learned that the headteacher at Grange, Ellen Hamer, was jailed for six months for fraud. According to *Worcester News*, she pretended that a trust ran the school and created false documents supporting that claim. Her barrister said that while she was very good at teaching, her business sense 'was lax in the extreme'.[4]

No mainstream schools would take me, so at the age of eleven, I ended up at Dippydale. Dippydale believed discipline was the way. The smart blazer and elegant pastel blue shirt that I'd been so proud to wear at Grange was replaced by a plain white shirt with a garish blue-and-white striped tie, tucked inside a loud blue jumper. The uniform let everyone know we were 'special'.

I only travelled to and from school on Monday mornings and Friday afternoons, as I was a resident during the week. The school was situated in the middle of nowhere on the foreboding West Pennine Moors under the shadow of Peel Tower, a monument to Robert Peel, a former prime minister and founder of the modern police force, which added to the punitive atmosphere of the place. Dippydale was co-educational, but was attended mainly by naughty boys – and the boarding house was exclusively for naughty boys. We were taught in small portacabins until a bigger building made from bricks and mortar sprung up a few years later.

Like much of the social care and support services in Britain, the education at Dippydale wasn't tailored to people's individual needs, or even the needs of an identifiable group. I had ADHD, but I was academically competent. Before I got expelled from St Chad's, I'd been in the top sets in English and maths – I wasn't completely daft. However, at Dippydale, I shared classrooms with kids with severe learning difficulties. Inevitably, the education we received was very different from a mainstream school. Emotional outbursts, fights and restraints routinely disrupted teaching. The soundtrack on Dippydale's corridors was 'Get the fuck off me, now!'

The favoured restraint at Dippydale was known as the B52. It involved lining up three chairs next to each other and plonking an unfortunate child on the middle chair, while two members of staff sat on either side of them, locking the child's arms out straight across their laps with one hand, and pushing the child's head into his or her own lap with the other. It earned its witless name from a bomber used in the Second World War. I guess this was because when staff contorted children on the middle chair of three, they resembled the shape of a plane. Going through the B52 was almost a rite of passage at the school, and I'd soon have my turn.

In the all-boys boarding house, every move we made was heavily regimented. We had to line up before entering the main house, then progress, one by one, to remove our shoes, replace them with slippers, and line up again to go upstairs to get changed and iron our uniforms for the next day. Afterwards, we'd line up for the evening meal. We'd eat, and then it was time for chores, which consisted of setting and clearing the dinner table and pot-washing. One of the benefits of being in the boarding house was that one got to do things that most people never get to do. We'd do activities ranging from banal pursuits like board games to more exotic hobbies like dry skiing, rock climbing, abseiling, kayaking and sailing. At 9pm it was bedtime.

I had enuresis (I pissed the bed). There were four boys to a room, so it was impossible to hide this embarrassing problem from my roommates and, unlike Las Vegas, what happened in the boarding house always left the boarding house. I'd be in the middle of lessons, and one kid – let's call him Crater Face – would rest his head on his desk, pretend to be asleep and mimic snoring, only he'd replace the classic whistling sound after the snort with a hissing one, which was supposed to be the sound of piss, I guess. Other times they'd just hum R.E.M.'s 'Nightswimming' in my general direction. For a set of 'special' kids, they were brilliant at taking the piss, especially when it was about piss. Crater Face was less covert when staff were absent:

'Hey, Goof Troop! Did you piss the bed last night?!' he'd shout over to me during break time.

'Yeah,' I'd reply in resignation.

'Good man,' he'd say, as everyone in the playground sniggered.

My key worker at the time, let's call him Mr Lanky, a gangly, po-faced, condescending prick, thought he could remedy this by waltzing into my bedroom every morning before my roommates had awoken and asking me if I was dry – only he would spell it out, as if that would keep it secret. 'Are you D-R-Y?' he would ask me. We might have been div kids, but we could still spell . . . and smell.

I didn't need excuses to distract myself from schoolwork and behave badly, but the bullying gave me more of them. The first time staff turned me into a B52 was over something spectacularly trivial. On one morning break, I scored six goals on the football pitch, but they were all assisted by a flash new boy called Billy, who dribbled past all the opposing players before generously passing to me for a tap-in. Billy was so good that he probably would have become a professional if it wasn't for the disadvantages of being at Dippydale and the other challenges he must have faced. I was livid about this. Before Billy arrived, I thought I was the best footballer among the juniors. Not any more. The wellspring exploded out of my head when break time ended. I refused to go back inside, and instead fled across the fields in a spectacularly pathetic tantrum. The staff chased me down and dragged me back into school and into the music room, where they placed me on the middle chair of three. I knew all the lyrics to the school's soundtrack by this point, and belted them out with furious gusto: 'Get the fuck off me now, you fucking bastard cunts. Fucking get off me!' I was so upset and helpless as I sat there, immobilised, that I spat on the floor in frustration. A third teacher, who was standing over me, took a tissue, gathered up my spittle and wiped it over my face.

After these incidents wound down, once I had no more energy to shout, scream, and struggle, the school's headmaster would arrive for the post-restraint warm down. The head-master – let's go with Mr Cue Ball, on account of his perfectly round, shiny, baldy head – got so close that I could feel his oniony breath warming my face as he tried his best to make me cry. 'Master Lavelle, you've been doing so well, and now you've let yourself down. We know what happened in your past; we know it's a lot of baggage. Let it go, son,' he would say gently. He'd then trot out more emotionally manipulative lines until I was in floods of tears, followed closely by a sense of guilt and desperate apologies. I sometimes wish I could transport my adult mind into my eleven-year-old body and tell Baldilocks that my aggression came from the reformatory atmosphere that pervaded his school's corridors, and my tears from physical pain and exhaustion.

In mid-December 2020, Oldham Council handed me fourteen bulky folders in two bulging carrier bags, containing my social services records, logbooks and educational reports. There it all was: my personal baggage, embodied. I selected a folder at random, and as I flicked through its contents, the blood ran cold in my extremities and it felt like a million alarm bells were going off all at once in my chest. I don't know what I was expecting. But what I read in the thick bundles of photocopies was a one-sided character assassination; a comprehensive collection of my worst moments, presented uncontextualised and without nuance. Some of it was pure fiction. Lies. I came across like a nightmare child. On almost every page, I found the same adjectives: immature, bizarre, silly, abusive, aggressive, violent. During a read-through of a collection of log entries from my time in children's homes, I discovered misrepresented accounts of – what I'd thought to be – private conversations with members of staff whom I'd trusted. The experience induced a panic attack. One of the worst ones I've ever had, and the first one in years. The consequence was 150mg of Sertraline, weeks of respite and a subscription to Sam Harris's mindfulness app.

When the drugs and mantras had helped me pull myself together, I began reading my logs from Dippydale. I couldn't find any reference to the restraint in the music room, nor did I find any detailed descriptions of their techniques. Reference to restraints are euphemistic: 'held', 'escorted', and so on.

The school seemed oblivious as to why I wanted my records. In fact, when they discovered I was now a journalist with bylines in the *Guardian*, they asked if I would come and give a talk to their students. *The fucking nerve*, I thought. Still, because they didn't seem to sense trouble, I decided to ring the school and ask them directly. A chirpy administrator asked me how they could help.

'Does the school accept that they used to restrain kids on three chairs that were placed next to each other, with the child in the middle and two members of staff sitting beside them?' I asked.

'Are you meaning where you were sort of bent forwards?' the admin replied.

'Yes,' I said.

'I think that was called a B52. We're no longer practising that at all – Team Teach took that out.'

My heart leapt into my mouth. I couldn't believe it. I'd been positive that the amiable facade would crumble away as soon as I broached the subject of restraints; I certainly hadn't expected them to 'fess up. When I asked why the school stopped using the restraint, the admin told me that they 'presumed' it was unsafe, and that Team Teach had removed it from the training the school received.

After a bit of digging, I contacted a former principal tutor at Team Teach, an organisation that provides behaviour management training to schools. The tutor, let's call him Larry, began working for Team Teach in 1997, and said the restraint I described sounds like a technique used in prisons. 'We used to warn people about tipping people forward because of asphyxia,' Larry said. I told Larry about the incident in the music room, and he said he knew of incidents involving teachers wiping spit back on children. He said that at one training session, someone had asked him if doing that was OK. He said that he told them that it wasn't. 'Daniel, I believe you,' Larry said. 'I'm aware of some of the practices in those days – they weren't good; they weren't acceptable.'

I didn't think much of the restraints at the time, as it wasn't the worst thing to have happened to me during my short life, and they were a frequent occurrence at the school. As time passes, I've become detached from such incidents; I almost perceive them as injustices that happened to someone else, a little boy I knew a long time ago. Now, when I think of what happened to that little boy, it keeps me up at night, brings me to tears at the most random of moments, and routinely causes me to disappear into disturbing fantasies where I track down the school's staff.

As my behaviour deteriorated, the brain-sucking ratcheted up a notch. I'd visited shrinks when I was an infant, but they seemed to be more interested in observing me as I messed around with Lego and scaled the walls. As an older boy, they demanded seated introspection, and I was never good at sitting still. The first time I went for a bit of one-to-one shrinkage, I was with Grandma. I was still shorter than her back then, and I remember clinging to her white coat like a timid lamb hiding behind its mother as we shuffled into the psychiatrist's office one blustery autumn morning.

'Can my grandma stay?' I asked the psychiatrist, a diminutive young woman sporting thick-rimmed spectacles and an even thicker woollen cardigan.

'No, I really need to talk to you alone,' Dr Cardy said behind her notepad.

I felt my heart sink all the way down to my shoes. I knew why I was here. Something was wrong with me. Only I didn't know what and I didn't want to know, either. Grandma shot me a tight-lipped smile as she left the room. I looked anywhere but at Cardy as I bashed two conkers together.

'So, how are you, Daniel?' she asked.

I said nothing, and carried on conker bashing.

'Are they fighting?' she asked.

I don't know why this question made me so uncomfortable, but my insides crawled. I leapt out of the chair and fled. A security guard eventually found me, and the therapy session that I should've had with Cardy took place on the pavement with the guard as we waited for Grandma to collect me.

I had more of these sessions while at Dippydale, which I didn't run away from. The verdict: I still had ADHD and needed meds, which I took. They did the trick. There was a marked difference in my behaviour and attentiveness, my schoolwork improved, and when I was twelve, I returned home and became a day pupil.

Then, I decided that I didn't need the medication. I was already reluctant to accept that I had a problem; as far as I was concerned it was everyone else's problem. During a meeting with Dr Cardy, I regurgitated the routine, ill-thought-out criticisms typically levelled at my condition: it is arbitrary labelling of personality traits; an overly diagnosed, overly medicated condition invented solely to line the pockets of the pharmaceutical industry. 'All I need is willpower and some coping strategies, and I'll be fine,' I told Cardy.

Psychiatry has always seemed like the medical equivalent of rummaging around in the dark, and I still think ADHD is too broadly defined, thus overly diagnosed – but the meds were working. Cardy didn't offer any resistance to my medical expertise, though, so off the meds I went.

As with trauma, it would be impossible to draw a causal link between ADHD and homelessness. However, ADHD traits, such as inattentiveness, dramatic mood swings and a propensity to blurt out and do whatever just happens to flash through one's mind, can produce negative outcomes in later life. A diagnosis of ADHD in childhood can be a strong predictor of criminality and substance dependency in adulthood – well known pathways to the streets.

There is not enough research into how ADHD predicts homelessness. However, a unique peer-reviewed clinical study funded by the National Institute of Health in the US found that ADHD substantially increased the risk of homelessness. The study, published in 2017, tracked 134 Caucasian boys aged between six and twelve years old diagnosed with ADHD in the 1970s. When the researchers caught up with the boys three decades later, they found that '24 per cent of probands reported having been homeless. This lifetime prevalence is substantially higher than the 11 per cent estimated rate in the adult white population.'[5]

If the traumas I suffered in early childhood set me on the road to destitution, a relatively new and misunderstood neurological condition saw me careering towards that destination. Then I was separated from my family and placed in the care system, which removed many exits to safer ground. If I was going to avoid homelessness, the odds weren't stacked in my favour.

Chapter Three

Care, Criminalisation & Displacement

I never thought I would go into care. It seemed like a horror story, something that only happened to fictional characters or people in the news. But by the time I reached the front door of my new foster home, the whole thing felt inevitable; my life had spiralled from one catastrophe to the next. This was just the latest one.

As well as my disruptive education and bad behaviour, my mum's budding relationship with my new stepdad was adding to tensions at home. My stepdad and I now get on. He's my dad, I love him, and that's that, but our relationship has been fraught over the years, especially around the time I was at Dippydale. He was the new entity in the household, swallowing all my mum's attention, and someone else who was telling me what to do. Dad's a solicitor, and his approach to parenting was not too dissimilar to the manner in which a lawyer badgers witnesses on the stand. During one bath time, I failed to convince Dad that I'd used the soap.

'Yeah, I've used it!' I shouted after he'd asked me for the fifth time.

'You're lying!' he shouted back. 'Why is the soap in precisely the same position as it was when I ran the bath? And why is the water still clear?!'

'Fuck off!' I said.

Then the lecture began.

Dad was an entertaining chastiser. He had a series of greatest hits that he could've filled a double-sided compilation album with: *Now That's What I Call a Bollocking*. My all-time favourite was when he told me off for relentlessly teasing Ollie on one fraught afternoon at Grandma's house: 'Now listen, boy, and listen well!' he growled. 'You're nine years old, now; you're halfway to being eighteen!' He was halfway to being sixty at the time, so by his logic we should've been preparing for his retirement.

I can't recall the precise timeline of events before I entered the care system. The memories I have of that period are like smudges that blend into a painful, emotional blur. I remember that things reached breaking point at home after the millennium, when my teenage hormones began to rage. Home broke down for a variety of reasons. The details of this aren't important, and going into them here would only bore you and upset my folks. Suffice to say that my behaviour was difficult to manage, social services offered little support and my parents had their own crosses to bear.

I returned to sleep at Dippydale's boarding house the night before I went into care in 2000, aged twelve. Social services reasoned that it would be easier to get me to cooperate if the school's 'care' staff surrounded me before I was taken to my new foster home, but I was never going to resist; I didn't want to be at home either. I was sharing my room with Crater Face that night, and he was more upset than me.

'Why are you crying, you soft bastard?' I said.

'Shut up. I'm just worried. I hope you're going to be OK!' he said.

I ended up having to comfort *him*.

The next day, Mum arrived at the school to collect me with my social worker, and we travelled down to my new home late that morning. Mum was in floods of tears when it was time for her to leave. I felt nothing. I hugged her, but I didn't like her at that moment; I didn't like her for a long time.

The foster home was in Longsight, Manchester. My foster mother, 'Auntie' Brenda, was a plump, tattooed and foul-mouthed middle-aged white Mancunian; my foster father, Jim, was a reclusive and quiet elderly Jamaican man.

When Mum and the social worker left, it was just me and Brenda in the living room. She quizzed me a bit about school, before giving her appraisal of my appearance.

'The first thing we need to sort is that on your 'ed,' Brenda said.

'What's on me 'ed?' I asked, while groping my crown.

'That fuckin' mop!' she replied through a wheezy cackle as she sucked down her thirtieth B&H of the day.

Brenda had three kids from a previous marriage. A short time later, Lisa, Brenda's youngest daughter, burst into the house with her small army of three kids in tow. Lisa had given all of her children obscure Latin names. Lucia, Ciro and Luca were full of beans, cheeky and fun in small doses, though I'd soon find myself leaving the house when they were around just to get some peace. After brief introductions, Lisa shared Brenda's view that I needed a haircut.

'Mam,' Lisa said in the Mancest of Manc whines. 'We'll take him to the Arndale tomorrow. Get him a pattern!'

'You see Ciro?' she asked me. Ciro had a streak of wavy lines and stars shaved into his afro. I nodded.

'Like that. Get you some swagger.'

The next day, on a crisp and bracing autumn afternoon, Brenda, Lisa, the kids and I headed into town to get my wig chopped. As well as adolescence and resentment, the feeling of adventure explained why I wasn't as upset as I could've been. I'd gone from living in parochial villages and rustic boarding houses, which were blindingly white, sterile, and stuffy, to Manchester's big, mad melting pot. I hadn't been out of the house since I arrived, and on the way to town, I experienced a cultural awakening. As we walked to the bus stop, a mist of alien aromas emanating from a row of colourful Balti houses and Caribbean takeaways assaulted my nostrils, and we weaved past people from a multitude of ethnicities, chatting and bartering away among the chaotic homeware stores, whose wares lined the pavements in precarious stacks. A barber in the old Oasis market buzzed off my bushy mop and shaved a lightning bolt from my temple to my crown. To complete the new look, Brenda bought me a pair of silver slip-on trainers and a baggy black shirt with a neon dragon sewn from the breast pocket to the hem. I looked like an especially unstylish darts player.

At the turn of the twenty-first century, Manchester was a diverse, progressive, optimistic and exciting city. It was also deprived, violent and dangerous. Guns, gangs and drugs were so rife that the city earned the unwelcome nickname 'Gunchester' as a result. Longsight was at the heart of this crime belt, which stretched down the road to neighbouring Moss Side and Hulme. The off-licences, newsagents and post offices held the biggest clues to this criminality; gunmen robbed them so often that nervous shopkeepers hid behind bulletproof plexiglass and handed customers their groceries through letterboxes.

I thought I was a tough kid. In reality, I was a cocky kid who'd always been able to rely on adult protection. Not here. The rules were different, but no one bothered to tell me. The first time I tried out my schoolyard bravado on an older lad Brenda was fostering, I learned the new rules the hard way. Brenda had bollocked him for something or other, and he'd told her where to go. 'Hey, don't talk to her like that!' I shouted to him as he walked past me on the landing. I didn't care that he'd mouthed off to Brenda; this was all about posturing. He strode over to me and, without any warning, squaring up or threats, nutted me on the nose, which burst open like an exploding strawberry. When he'd had enough of sharpening his boxing skills on my face, I staggered to my feet. My head felt like it had a boom box in it. I screamed and screamed as I washed the blood from my face in the bathroom sink, but I got no sympathy from Brenda. 'It's yer own fault for being a mouthy twat,' she said.

If I'd had any doubts after that beating that people didn't fuck about in Manchester, they were gone completely after an outing at Crowcroft Park one afternoon. I'd gone there with Rick, another kid Brenda was looking after. Rick was my age, only he was a lot more streetwise and seemed like an adult to me. He taught me how to shoplift, and how to sneak on buses and into cinemas. Rick and I were having a kickabout when two men walked into the park, one of whom was brandishing a large meat cleaver. They walked over to a group of men playing football nearby and started shouting at them, but Rick and I were too far away to make out what they were saying – I'm guessing it wasn't friendly. The man took his cleaver and began to hack at one of the bikes lying on the sidelines. We didn't hang around.

I was captivated by Manchester's vibrancy, rough and ready charm, funny accents, and spectacular arrogance. The foster family introduced me to Bruce Lee and seventies reggae, and taught me to make West Indian cuisine, including jerk chicken, fried dumplings and rice and peas. I even learned how to blag a few quid from match-goers at Main Road, which involved promising Man City fans that I'd 'look after their car' for a quid or two (which meant 'Give me some money and I won't key your car' in Manc).

However, moving to Longsight didn't correct my behaviour, and the onset of adolescence only exacerbated things. Brenda was a rough diamond who usually made pleasant company, but she could also be cold and strict. 'Bedtime!' she would bark out like an angry bar lady at last orders as soon as the clock struck 9pm. I found her irritating, too. She had this infuriating habit of adopting different accents depending on who she was talking to. This was not a simple matter of softening one's accent in formal company. When Jim or other West Indians came around, she would speak in Jamaican patois, then revert to angry Manc when her white pals were there. I would mouth off, skive off and regularly do runners.

Brenda threw the towel in after eight months, so social services moved me to Mumpshill Road, a children's home in Oldham. I stayed there briefly, before moving to another foster placement, this time in Hulme. While in Hulme, I encountered

Rick again, who by now had bleached his jet-black hair to a bright platinum blond, had several facial piercings and was openly gay. The last thing I heard about him was that he'd had an overdose. I never saw him again and, like many of the kids I grew up with, never found out what became of him.

The constant displacement had been going on for a long time by this point, but I was about to become a human pinball – and I'm still bouncing around the world to this day. If you want to understand why so many children who experience care end up homeless adults, just look at the pitfalls within the system. Kids who follow the paint-by-numbers guide to growing up usually live in the same household, attend a couple of schools, a sixth form and a university, and during this time they form a strong network of relatives, friends and co-workers they can rely on in hard times. Many care-leavers don't have the same support structures. They don't have responsible parents or close friends to bail them out when things go awry.

In 2002, I was moved back to Oldham, this time into Nelson Avenue, a children's home. Oldham is small yet sprawling. One of the integral veins of the northern textile industry, it was key to the Victorians' prosperity. These days, though, it's a town on the brink: dour, deprived, fag-stained and rough, tinged with grey even on a clear, bright summer's day. It was to be my home for the rest of the 2000s.

The home at Nelson Avenue was inside a huge red-brick Victorian building. The bars on the windows and almost sterile interior made it clear that this was an institution. The home housed up to six kids at once and had an emergency place for an extra child in an annexe adjacent to the main building. I was greeted at a big, sickly green door by a young, burly ginger-headed man (let's call him Bouncer) and a gangly, saturnine middle-aged woman (let's call her Joyless), with eyes so close together that they almost met.

'Don't look so nervous,' said Joyless, in her thick Oldham brogue.

'I'm not. I've been in a kids' home before,' I replied defiantly.

'OK, well this isn't a "kids' home". We don't call them that any more. It's a Young Person's Unit.'

After a few more pleasantries, Bouncer escorted me to my room, where he rifled through my bag looking for drugs and weapons. As I tossed and turned in bed that night, I heard shouting coming from downstairs. The other kids had returned to the unit, and were demanding that staff let them into the kitchen. They carried on yelling abuse into the early hours. For the first few days, I barely left my room; at night, I cried into my pillow. I even moved my bed so it was against the door, scared someone might try to break in.

In my experience, rules in children's homes are applied inconsistently. This is partly because the staff are undertrained, underpaid and often clueless. For every competent member of staff, there was a rule stickler, a wind-up merchant, or a complete pushover. You never knew where you stood. On one shift, staff might let you stay up until midnight; you'd get away with smoking at the front door and were allowed to watch a film with an eighteen certificate. Then, on another evening, you'd get reprimanded for doing the same things.

After a few weeks, I started to come out of my shell. I made friends with two of the lads staying there. Carter was tall, skinny and domineering; Lloyd was tall, skinny and sycophantic. Lloyd stuck to Carter like glue and always emanated a vague whiff of cheese. Carter was the star of the unit. He had a magnetic personality and seemed like he had lived several lives already. He was off the wall, exciting and sometimes frightening to be around, as he was prone to violent outbursts. I first met him in the kitchen one evening. I was having a cup of tea when he burst in, high as a kite, with a broad smile fixed to his face.

'Where's me skran?!' he demanded as he marched haughtily into the walk-in pantry. He spent the rest of the evening laughing hysterically into a bowl of Coco Pops.

Bouncer was on duty that night, and was making futile attempts to get Carter off to bed. Bouncer was a hulking, intimidating Scouser. Years after I left the system, I saw him manning the door of an Oldham nightclub, so he could handle himself – and could certainly handle us if push came to shove. Still, Carter wasn't scared of anyone: 'Nah, mate. Fuck off. *You* go to bed.'

I instantly warmed to Carter in that moment. *I can't believe he said that and got away with it*, I thought.

'This is my gaff, ye!' Carter continued, as he poured himself another bowl while staring unblinkingly into Bouncer's eyes.

We did eventually manage to convince Carter to go to bed before things got out of hand. The next day, there were no consequences for him. He was fourteen, had stayed out long after his curfew, and was clearly under the influence, yet the day unfolded as if nothing had happened. All this taught us was that we could do what we wanted and there would be no penalties – until things got so out of hand that the police had to be called. Then, instead of an early night, a grounding or a dock in pocket money, we earned a criminal record.

Most of us had nothing to do during the day. I'd been expelled from Dippydale before I arrived at Nelson Avenue. My behaviour had become so unmanageable that even a special school couldn't cope with me. Imagine that: I got expelled from a school for naughty kids for being *too* naughty; that's surely an achievement of sorts. By the end, the school had separated me from my classmates; I was doing all my work from a meeting room near Headmaster Cue Ball's office, and was only allowed to mix with my other classmates at home time when we were getting into our buses.

During my last year there, entries in my logbooks state that I frequently remarked on how much I hated being at Dippydale. The logs say that I was abusive to pupils and staff; that I arrived at school without eating breakfast; that I had bite marks on my arm, holes in my jumper, and was generally dishevelled and unwashed. The author of this entry dismissed it as 'attention-seeking'.

According to my logs, I was in trouble every day during the last few months at school. One entry reports how I became abusive 'almost immediately' when confronted about my hygiene. The entry claims that I threatened the member of staff and began kicking furniture. 'Eventually, he had to be held to prevent him from hurting himself and carrying out his threats to staff and damaging property.' The entry goes on to state that I showed 'no remorse' after I had calmed down and 'continued verbal abuse of staff.' This entry demonstrates why children should have an opportunity to correct the records kept on them, because this is not how I remember this incident. I recall being chastised about my hygiene by this staff member in front of the rest of my class. I felt humiliated and angry, so I shouted and swore and threatened and kicked furniture; I was folded in half and stretched as a result.

And no, I wasn't sorry. I'm still not.

As I said, I had nothing to do during the day at Nelson Avenue – that is, until Lucy arrived at the unit a few weeks after me. I was completely enamoured with her. She was an incandescent ball of energy and quickly became my disruptive partner in crime. Actually, I was more of a disciple of hers, as she quickly took over from Carter as the trouble-causer extraordinaire. Carter, Lucy, Lloyd and I were in similar financial positions and came to the collective conclusion that causing trouble was the best way to entertain ourselves. This was when drugs made their first appearance in my life.

Friday was pocket money day at the unit, and we'd combine our funds to 'get on the sesh'. We'd travel to a collection of decaying tower blocks in nearby Werneth and order some pills from a gangly lad with a walkie-talkie. He'd radio to his colleagues, who were hiding somewhere in the block. A couple of minutes later, we would hand our cash to another bloke and pick up our wares from under a brick. Lucy and I were too anxious to partake in the drugs, so we would just swig from a bottle of alcopop while the others popped MDMA pills with Mitsubishi symbols on them. I'd watch as their jaws clenched, and they became all mushy and sentimental. Nearly every care-leaver I've met over the years is struggling with or has had to overcome an addiction of one kind or another. These issues begin on lazy days like these. Drug-taking escalates among care-leavers, especially during the transition to independence, for a variety of reasons. Many find it difficult to manage their own homes; they don't have strong family ties, and thus have no support network, and they often have emotional, psychological and behavioural problems that make them vulnerable to starting or continuing a drug habit.

I didn't need drugs. If you were to take a snapshot of the unit, though, you'd assume that I was the big user. Unfettered ADHD had me bouncing off the walls. When I wasn't causing trouble with the rest of them, I was flipping, kicking and punching around the place, imitating the intricate kung-fu choreography I'd seen in Hong Kong action movies. Jackie Chan, Sammo Hung and Yuen Biao were my heroes, and I wanted to follow in their footsteps and become a stuntman. The idea of throwing myself around for a living really appealed to me.

When there were no drugs, we got our fix from fucking with the staff, something I was more on board with. The lack of con-sequences for bad behaviour led to us pushing the limits as far as they could go. We were usually asked to go to bed at 9.30pm, but we didn't feel like it one summer night. Bouncer was on duty with Joyless. Both of them were about as tactful as a famished lion in a zebra enclosure. We refused to go to bed, and blocked the TV in the living room so that they couldn't turn it off. The staff cut the power – no more TV. So, we (except Lloyd – he always bottled it) decided to throw our wardrobes and bed frames down the stairs. We even broke off our wardrobe doors and sledged on them down the staircase, shouting abuse at the staff the whole time. Bouncer tried to grip me, but Carter and Lucy got in his face, and he backed off. The staff had completely lost control, and retreated to their office to call the police.

'They've called the Five-Oh,' Lucy said. 'Yo, come 'n put this baby oil on. If they put the cuffs on us, we can get out of it.'

I said nothing. The police and their handcuffs were completely new to me.

Lucy got her baby oil and we squirted it all over our hands and feet. When the 'Five-Oh' turned up, Carter continued to mouth off. Two burly officers twisted him up and bundled him into their van, while another two advanced on Lucy and me. I'd had little issue with giving the staff as much shit as I could muster, but I went as quiet as a mouse when the police turned up. A tall officer told me to face the wall, and I obliged. He cuffed me and led me outside to their van, where I could hear Carter continuing his tirade.

'Yes, Danny!' he shouted to me from inside the cage in the van. 'Give 'em bare shit, man!'

'What, him?' the tall copper said. 'He's been as good as gold.'

I looked up sheepishly at Carter as the officer guided me into the van's fixed steel cage; when our eyes met, I noticed that he looked disappointed. Even though I was a mixed-up teen with a bad attitude, I knew where the line was and when to keep my mouth shut; Carter had no such awareness. When we got to the local station, Lucy and Carter – who hadn't managed to slip off their cuffs, despite the globules of baby oily they'd smeared on their hands – continued to give the cops dogs' abuse. They must have trotted out every pig-related epithet known to man before they got processed.

I was led into a cell. 'Try and get some sleep,' the desk sergeant said sarcastically, as the blindingly bright fluorescent light ignited in the ceiling, revealing an austere, cold and windowless box with flakes of plaster clumped around the skirting boards. And then, clink: I was shut in. My eyes were itching to shut, all I wanted to do was sleep, but the mucky cushion on the cell's narrow bench was far from inviting, so I just paced, shadow-boxed, and paced some more. After a few minutes, I heard the sound of heavy footsteps screeching heavily on the waxed floors outside my cell, mixed with intermittent thuds and muffled groans.

'Fuckin' get off him, you bastards!' That was Lucy's voice.

'What's going on!?' I shouted, but no one answered.

Eventually the kerfuffle died down. I didn't find out what happened until we were released the next morning. Apparently, the coppers had grown tired of Carter's big gob and decided to give him a 'rough walk' to his cell. Lucy received a caution and Carter had to go to the magistrates, while I – because it was my first offence – was given a warning.

It was remarkable how fast the staff were willing to involve the police to mete out discipline at the unit. Aside from exhaustion, police intervention was probably the only thing that would have stopped us that night, but a 999 call could have been avoided if the staff weren't so incompetent. I ended up in handcuffs on several occasions after that, on a few other nights of mischief – and once for breaking a mug. Often, the police would come just to make sure we went to bed at night.

This was two decades ago, but criminalisation is still common in the care system. Government guidelines say: 'The police should not be used for low-level behaviour management or matters a reasonable parent would not have called the police over.'[1] Yet children in care homes are criminalised at ten times the rate of other children,[2] and that figure is probably an underestimate, as it only counts children who have been in continuous care for at least twelve months. According to a *Guardian* investigation, children in care are still being arrested and taken to court for trivial offences that would earn most children a stern word and a grounding. In August 2019, 128 youngsters passed through Greater Manchester's youth court. Seventeen per cent of them were in care.[3]

It's not surprising that up to 27 per cent of the prison population is comprised of care-leavers when practically everyone I lived with in care had a criminal record.[4] Even though Carter, Lucy and I didn't know it yet, our mischief would shape our future, and make a life embroiled in poverty, the criminal justice system and destitution increasingly likely.

If we'd had little respect for the staff before that incident, we had none after it. Our dissent only intensified. It was me, Carter and Lucy against the world. We'd go everywhere together, and sometimes cram into the same single bed to protect ourselves from restraints. Rebelling against the staff had almost become a cause.

This all came to a head on one sunny summer afternoon. Hamza, Lucy's eighteen-year-old boyfriend, had visited the unit and was hanging around with her on the front doorstep. Lucy wanted to come back into the unit for a drink, but the staff told her she couldn't come in if Hamza was still on the premises. He refused to go, and Lucy shouted obscenities through the letterbox: 'Let me in, you fuckin' dick 'eds; it's my house, yeah,' she said, cackling. 'Yo, Danny! Carter! Let us in, man!'

Not wanting to miss out on the fun, Carter and I interrupted our gaming session and headed to the front door to let her in. Two male staff members were on that day, along with Joyless, who was manning the office. Let's call them Gramps (he had a white beard) and Titch (he was tiny). They stopped us in our tracks.

'Hey, pack it in, lads,' Gramps said. 'Don't get involved in this.'

'What are you on about?' I said. 'We're just going out.'

'Oi, you can't keep us in, you muppet. So fuckin' move!' Carter shouted.

Titch put his hand on the door, but Carter managed to over-power him while Gramps was still blocking my path. When Carter got the door open, Gramps rushed over to shut it, giving me enough space to slip past him and through the threshold. The staff locked the door behind us and shook their heads in disgust as we flipped them off on the other side. Austin Powers was a big deal at the time, and, because I've always been a sophisticated chap, I opened the letterbox and unleashed a tirade of verbal bile in my best 'Fat Bastard' impression, while Carter and Lucy cheered me on. Hamza distracted me from tormenting the staff when he produced the gun he'd brought along. I don't know if it was real, but it looked real enough, and Hamza certainly got nervous when we turned the barrel at Titch and Gramps through the window. Things went on like this for a while until we'd grown bored and wanted to come back in.

The staff insisted we enter one at a time, but as soon as they opened the door for me, Carter and Hamza attempted to force their way in. An almighty scuffle broke out. Gramps had Hamza in a chokehold, and Carter held Titch in a tight clinch while thrusting his knees relentlessly into his face until he crumpled to the floor. Carter then rushed outside and attempted to pick up one of the boulders lying on a flower bed close to the entrance.

'Why aren't you doing anything, you pussy?' he shouted to me as I stood there, frozen.

He couldn't lift the boulder, so instead went for a fire extinguisher near the door. Fortunately for Gramps, Hamza had managed to turn the tables on him before Carter could put the extinguisher to use. A flurry of punches and kicks followed. Then sirens. Carter, Lucy and Hamza scattered and ran past me. I was still rooted to the spot, staring in disbelief at the unconscious, bloody bodies of Gramps and Titch.

'C'mon!' Carter shouted as he dragged me away.

I found my feet and sprinted after the rest of them. The whole atmosphere had been polluted with deafening sirens, and they were for us. We ran as fast as we could, for as long as we could – longer than we'd ever run before. When we stopped – when we could no longer hear sirens – it felt like my whole body had become engorged and my tongue was made of copper.

'Stop, stop!' Hamza said, breathlessly. 'Me mate lives up 'ere.'

We had run non-stop for at least four miles, and were on the other side of town. 'Youse wait 'ere. He don't know you. I'll ask him if you can come, yeah?'

Carter and I watched Hamza and Lucy make their way up a long, dark street with red-brick terrace houses on either side.

They stopped at one near the end and were invited in after a brief chat at the front door. Hamza looked at us and shook his head apologetically as he crossed the threshold with Lucy. It was getting dark now. The affectless uniformity of the red terraces under the ugly orange streetlamps were the perfect backdrop for our bleak circumstances.

'We could go to my gran's house,' I suggested to Carter.

'Yeah, where does she live?' he said.

'Greenfield,' I said.

Carter managed a laugh. 'Nah. Mission, that.'

'What are we gonna do then?' I asked.

'Go back,' he said, and started walking.

'If we go back, we'll get lifted,' I said.

'*I'll* get lifted. Fuck all's gonna 'appen to you,' he said.

'How do you know?' I asked.

'Because I know! You didn't do owt, did you?' he said.

'They could say I did,' I said.

Carter just sucked his teeth and carried on walking back to the unit. After hesitating for a bit, I caught up with him. We didn't talk much on the way home. The adrenaline that had kept us on our toes for over four miles had since sapped from our bodies and left cold reality in its wake. We both knew Carter had ruined his life, and the slow march home felt like a funeral procession. We arrived back and I knocked on the door, while Carter took a seat on the bottom rung on the railings that ran along the steps, the same place where all the drama had begun, only it felt like a different world now.

Joyless came to the door with Biker (he rode a bike from Halifax to get to work), a stout thirty-something care worker who no one had much time for. Joyless was wearing a look of revulsion. 'Just you,' she said to me.

I looked back at Carter.

'Told you. Go on,' he said.

I didn't see Carter again until a year later. I heard that he'd been detained in a young offender's prison. He called for me at the unit a few times, but we realised that we didn't have much of a friendship. We had little in common; the only thing uniting us when we lived together was rebellion. We soon lost touch.

What began as defiance of the rules, broken curfews, midnight pantry raids, and abusive tantrums escalated to criminal damage and grievous bodily harm in a matter of months. It didn't have to be this way. When children go into care, it's invariably because their family situation has broken down. After this happens, the state becomes the parent and is responsible for the child's welfare. A reasonable parent would not allow their child to spend a night in a police cell and receive a life-altering criminal record for something as trivial as a broken wardrobe door. If you're working in a children's home, you will do well to understand that dialling 999 might provide you with respite, but it won't help you in the long term. All it achieves is the alienation of the kids under your charge, and the alienation of yourself. I resented the staff who'd had me locked up and I showed them nothing but contempt in the aftermath. It doesn't help anyone, and there's a real human cost. The kids I grew up with in care – Carter, Lucy and Lloyd – were tearaways coping with terrible traumas; they could be obnoxious, abusive and defiant, but they were far from a lost cause. They were bright, funny and capable. If social services hadn't criminalised them at such an early age, then maybe they could have gone on to lead productive lives. Who knows who they would have become; what they would have achieved. I never found out what happened to Carter; I hope he became a multi-millionaire and moved to some exotic, far-away land. When we ask ourselves why it is that so many care-leavers end up destitute and on the street, the failure to properly cope with mixed-up kids like Carter is a big part of it.

Lucy returned to the unit three weeks later, after the police caught up with her and Hamza. She was pregnant, and remained with us until she gave birth to a baby girl, after which she left the unit. Lucy was fourteen, and social services decided that she couldn't look after her daughter, so she was made to give her up for adoption. There was no social media back then, and I couldn't afford a computer or a mobile phone, so we lost touch and I didn't see or hear from Lucy again for fifteen years.

We were both a little wider and more melted when we were reunited, meeting in the food court at the Arndale Centre in Manchester in 2017. Lucy was twenty-nine by then, and had had four more children. Despite suffering from bipolar disorder, she was holding it together and was a great mum: all of her kids were in school and were well cared for. 'I want to make sure that my kids have a better life than we had,' she said. Out of the few kids that I managed to reconnect with, Lucy was the only one who agreed to speak to me on the record.

'Some of the staff were horrible, but we were little bastards, to be fair,' she told me as we wandered through the city centre. She was still the wild child I remembered. We'd only been reunited for ten minutes before we were racing around a discount store, buying cheap booze and butties before handing them around to the homeless in Piccadilly Gardens. Lucy told me everything about her life after care – her kids, her relationship woes – but she got cold feet about me getting it all on the record: 'I don't like to think about it that much. It just makes me depressed,' she said.

We stayed in touch over the years, and she gradually opened up, allowing me to flip on my tape recorder over long phone calls at all hours.

In summer 2020, she called me completely out of the blue in tears, telling me she'd just split up with her boyfriend. 'I never used to cry, but I never stop now,' she said.

I tried my best to comfort her and steer the conversation on to more cheery pastures, but we ended up talking about that gun incident.

'Was Hamza's gun real?' I asked her. This was something I'd always been curious about.

'It was real, but the barrel had been soldered shut, so you couldn't actually put a bullet in it. But it was originally a real gun, yeah. I don't even know where he got it from – it just appeared,' said Lucy.

It wasn't surprising to hear the gun had been real. Lucy told me that Hamza was now serving time for gun trafficking. He was eighteen when he was seeing Lucy, and she'd been fourteen. Nelson Avenue had been aware of this. How could they not be? We were. Yet I don't recall staff lifting a finger to prevent Lucy, or other girls I knew in the system, from leaving the unit and getting in the cars of older men. For those of us who'd been in the system and witnessed this, sexual abuse scandals like the one in Rochdale didn't surprise us at all.

'Danny, in my social services records, they admit they knew I was having sex from the age of eleven and still did nothing. *E-le-ven!* I was ELEVEN!' she said.

I thought that Lucy had become pregnant while she was on the run with Hamza, but she said she'd been keeping it secret for a few months before that. 'I think it was actually Cat [a Nelson Avenue staff member] who got on to it, because I kept eating pickled onions and drinking Ribena. Do you remember I used to eat jars of pickles?' she asked.

'I just knew you were off your head, so I probably didn't register it, Luce,' I said.

'I was that kid that you didn't want your kid to play with,' Lucy said, in hysterics.

I'd always wondered what became of Lucy after she left the unit. It turns out that social services thought it wise to return her to her mother, even though she'd been taken from her on a full care order when she was eleven. Lucy's mum used the family home for sex work to fund her addiction to hard drugs.

'They [social services] said in records that they let me move back with my mum because at least they knew where I was, but little did they know I was sitting in brothels while she was prostituting herself out. Me and my brothers were still exposed to crack and heroin.' She tells me she came home one day to find a middle-aged man injecting heroin into his thigh in the kitchen, while her two younger brothers were in the lounge. 'My brothers had walked into the kitchen and caught him, but luckily they didn't see the needle. I'd always hidden drugs from them,' she said.

As well as exposing her to drug abuse, Lucy's mum would

ridicule her and call her a slag, an epithet that still upsets her. 'When you're just told that your whole life . . . it's even in my social service records. My mum had said to the social worker: "Oh, she's just a little fuckin' slag." Well, maybe that's because I witnessed you prostituting yourself,' Lucy said. We were both laughing now.

'Were you ever homeless after you left Nelson Avenue?' I asked.

'Fuckin' hell – many times! After I'd gone to my mum's, I had nowhere to go and she kicked me out or she wasn't there. Fuckin' 'ell, I've slept in bin sheds and all sorts. I just looked around for somewhere that looked warm, and I'd just get in there till it was like morning or summat.'

'What was going through your mind at the time?' I asked.

'Do you know what, Danny? I was so hard-faced back then, and I'd been through so much, that I don't think it phased me. I think I just got my head down and was like, "Whatever." I didn't even cry back then. When I lost my baby, it changed me. I was cold. Cold. I had no fear. I mean, I had *no fear*. I didn't like anyone; I was angry at the world.'

I felt guilty that while I was tucked up, cosy in bed at Nelson Avenue, she was huddled in a bin shed on her estate. I foolishly asked her why she didn't return to the unit, with the empty promise that I would've let her in and provided sanctuary.

'Those people gave up on me. They took my baby off me. Do you think I was gonna go back to them?' she said.

Lucy had just successfully sued Oldham Council for neglect when we spoke. She won a hefty cash settlement, but she wasn't finished with them yet – she didn't feel like she'd won justice.

'It's sad – more than anything – that it's still happening. And this is why we've got to do something. We really have, Danny. Together, we'll bring them down!' she said.

We debated how we would change the system. I told her that I have no problem if the care homes feel like an institution if they're consistent with the kids under their charge.

Lucy disagreed. 'Nah, I don't like that; that's where they're going wrong. They need to make it feel like it's their home,' she insisted.

'But they can't make it feel like home,' I protested, a little too passionately.

'They have to,' Lucy said, mirroring my indignation. 'If a kid's coming from a place that's never been a home, they need to show a child what a real home should be like. Otherwise, that child is never gonna know how to form relationships, how to have a real family life.'

It's a strong argument, and all I can offer is: 'You get all them rich kids who go to boarding schools, and they're regimented, aren't they?'

'Yeah – and half of them are dickheads or paedos or summat! They've got no common sense and they wouldn't last a day in the real world. I say that to people: "Listen, I might not have GCSEs, mate, but chuck me and you on the street; I'll fuckin' survive longer than you!"'

Point Lucy.

Even though we met in a hopeless place, I'm glad I know Lucy. I know we'll always have each other's backs.

'We all just became like a family at one point. Even if we didn't agree with what each other was doing, we followed each other, because we had no one else. We didn't have anyone else; we had each other,' she said.

Maybe we would have had someone else if the staff knew what they were doing. In Nelson Avenue, we all adored Penny, a tiny and gentle woman in her mid-fifties. She would allow us to get away with murder, and often undermine other staff's disciplinary decisions. That's because she was the unit's cleaner and didn't have a duty of care to us. However, Penny would regularly be called upon for shifts during staff shortages. Luckily, we all respected her, and would usually follow her orders on the rare occasions that she gave them out (typically when paired with a more officious staff member). There were temporary staff working at the unit, who were completely out of their depth. Some of them would retreat into the office in tears when things got fraught; others would become angry and lash out at kids.

I managed to track Penny down. Some of these staff, she agreed, should never have worked with kids; she told me she even gave up the job in the end because of the attitude of her colleagues. 'Too many of them saw how little [money] they were making, so they came in and went home and that was it,' she said. Penny told me she saw staff 'winding up children', as well as physical abuse at Nelson Avenue. On one shift, she witnessed a brutal restraint perpetrated by two male staff members. 'They sat on his chest, and I'm thinking: "My God – this lad is going to die if they don't get off him."' She was later interviewed about it by the manager. 'They said: "Are you sure it was his chest? Are you sure it wasn't his stomach?" And I told them that they shouldn't have even sat on his bleeding stomach. I felt as if I was in the wrong because I was complaining,' she said.

Lucy is the only person I'm in contact with from my time in the system and I must have met hundreds of kids from various homes around Greater Manchester. People living well-adjusted lives don't just drop off the map. Things haven't changed much for looked-after children in the town. Children in care are more likely to leave school with fewer qualifications than children who remain at home; they are also more likely to be unemployed, to have mental health problems and to enter the criminal justice system.[5] When you meet homeless people, especially entrenched rough sleepers, you'll invariably find that they're struggling with at least one of these issues. It's almost as if the care system is training children for this life. In September 2018, social-care inspectors found that children from a privately managed care home in Oldham would regularly abscond, were involved in 'county lines' drug running and had 'minimal engagement' with education.[6] This negligence often continues for kids as they transition from care to independence.

When I turned sixteen, social services moved me from Nelson Avenue into Hawthorn Crescent, a semi-independent unit on Fitton Hill, a large housing estate in south Oldham. Unlike the children's homes I'd lived in and visited, Hawthorn blended in with the other nondescript houses at the end of a tucked-away cul-de-sac on the estate. The idea of a semi-independent unit is to prepare the young people living in it for a life of independence. We had our own keys and could return to the unit when we liked, as long as we notified staff that we'd be staying out. We had an allowance of £40 per week, and had to purchase, prepare and cook our own food. Hawthorn also expected us to pursue gainful employment and education.

The other teens at the unit were from children's homes or foster placements around the borough. I knew most of them, or had heard of them at least. During my first six months in the cul-de-sac, there was little done to encourage me into anything productive. I spent my first six months preparing for adulthood by chonging copious amounts of weed and slurping black lager at the back of dilapidated allotments on the estate; the rest of the time, I'd veg in front of screens.

When I speak to people who were in the system at the same time as me, I realise that I was lucky to receive the help I did when I turned sixteen. My experiences may seem challenging to the uninitiated, but I promise you they were a cakewalk compared to the ordeal that some of my peers went through. Even though the support I received was threadbare and inconsistent, I was given a care grant for furniture, and I had key workers visiting me on a semi-regular basis.

When Sunita turned sixteen, she left her children's home in Manchester and was placed in a flat with nothing but a sofa bed.

I met her on a bitterly cold winter afternoon in February 2020. The harsh Manchester rain flew at me horizontally while I waited for her to buzz me into her ground-floor flat. She met me huddled in her doorway and beckoned me to 'Hurry up!'

Sunita's pretty direct like that, and not afraid of telling you to fuck off, which she did when I teased her that she's a Manchester City fan living next to the main thoroughfare that Manchester United fans take to Old Trafford football ground on match day. Sunita is slight in stature and has bright purple hair to match her bright purple top. She flitted between outrage and teary resignation as she described the many issues that had kept her up at night over the last few months. She showed me into her living room, which, superficially at least, looked like a lovely space. It was well decorated, glitzy and modern; it boasted an expensive L-shaped sofa, a giant flat-screen telly and laminate flooring. However, the windows were draughty and cracked, mould was growing in the bathroom, the appliances were either breaking or broken, and she told me that it looked even worse the previous year.

Before Sunita removed the carpet, it was rotten and riven with mould; the walls were damp, and mushrooms, which looked like melted human ears, had sprouted on her old sofa. Sunita thought this was due to a leak that had sprung from the flat above her five years before, and a dripping radiator she'd had replaced earlier that year. Her landlord had refused to contribute to repairs, even after she was rushed to hospital in May 2019 because the mould had caused her serious breathing difficulties. She showed me a video of her wearing a nebuliser, the same video sent to her landlord as evidence. He didn't budge and all the repairs came out of her own pocket. Sunita bought the new furnishings and flooring from a buy-now-pay-later catalogue and, as a result, was now £4,000 in debt.

She handed me a letter that detailed her illnesses, which included a pulmonary embolism on her lung, scoliosis of the spine and mental health problems. Sunita only remained in her flat because its location in a gated community made her feel secure, but she admitted that it was making her health worse: 'When I'm sleeping, I'm waking up and coughing, coughing and coughing, and I've already got problems with my lungs anyway.'

If anyone deserves stability, it's Sunita. We're the same age, and our early lives followed a similar road, marked by early trauma and school exclusions. We both ended up in special education and bounced around Manchester's care system in foster placements and children's homes; we both spent nights in police custody and ultimately became homeless. Despite the similarities, after listening to Sunita's story, I feel embarrassed even to raise a murmur of complaint about my own experiences. Sunita was placed in care when she was born. She's in touch with her mother now, but she was understandably reluctant to talk about their relationship in great detail. She said she endured serious abuse during her early life.

'They kept taking me out of care, putting me back in care, taking me back out, when he was doing what he was doing. So, even though we had the full care order, they just kept pissing me about.'

Sunita said that social services felt it was important to maintain family ties, even after she told them about the abuse.

'They knew about it because I told a man [in the children's home]. He was a residential social worker in Broom House,' she said.

'Is that a kids' home?' I asked.

'Have you never looked into Broom House children's home in Didsbury?!' she asked incredulously. 'Read about it. There's been loads of articles in the *Evening News*.'

I did read about it. I discovered that Broom House was one of sixty-six children's homes in Manchester to be involved in the systematic abuse of dozens of young boys in care. In 1997, Greater Manchester Police launched operation Cleopatra, an investigation into historic child abuse, after they received forty-eight separate allegations, one dating back as far as 1958. When the investigation wrapped up in 2002, pay-outs were made to 168 victims who'd been abused in children's homes in Manchester throughout the 1960s, 1970s and 1980s.[7] Broom House was in the headlines again in 2014 when it was revealed that Ronald Hall, a former warden at the home, who was sentenced to eleven years in 2002 for his involvement in the abuse scandal, introduced children in his care at Broom House to Jimmy Savile.[8] Sunita never met Savile during her time at Broom House, but she said that Rolf Harris was invited to an event the home was running.

From Broom House, Sunita was bounced around the system to over eighteen different placements, where she was subjected to violent abuse from staff and other children. At one of the homes, she was attacked by a male staff member because she refused to go to bed.

She told me, 'I said: "I'm not going to bed," so he started shouting in my face, and I said: "Your breath stinks of coffee, move from me." And then he grabbed me up by my arm and he kept pushing me. He's pushed me that hard, he's knocked my front teeth out.'

'Did he get in trouble; did they do anything about this?' I asked.

'No, nothing! It's like they were allowed to abuse you! They knew you weren't going home to your mum or your dad; they had the authority, they could do what they wanted with you, they didn't give a shit. They didn't care.'

Sunita talked about how care staff in a children's home in

Wythenshawe ignored her complaints about bullying; she told me about the time a foster family took a day trip and locked her in the house without any food; she describes her many encounters with the police. She was in tears after explaining these events. All I could offer her in return were conciliatory grunts, 'Oh dears', and 'fuckin' 'ells'.

When Sunita left the care system aged sixteen, social services placed her in a flat in Gorton. She experienced serious abuse before that, but for legal reasons it cannot be discussed here.

All care-leavers are entitled to a Leaving Care grant (now a Setting Up Home Allowance) to help with furnishing and appliances.[9] Moreover, according to the Children's Commissioner's website, care-leavers have a right to a needs assessment before they leave care: 'This report should include your views and wishes. It should consider your independent living skills and ability to manage your own finances.'[10] I received the grant, but I don't think my assessment was done properly, as I wasn't ready to live independently. At least I had the grant, though. Sunita had to fend for herself: 'I was supposed to get a Leaving Care grant, and I never. [I went] Straight into a flat with nothing in it. Oh, sorry – they got me a sofa bed. Nothing else: no support, nothing – they left me.'

After a short time in the flat, Sunita got into a relationship with an abusive man ten years older than her. 'The police had to come in with riot shields because he was beating me, and he threatened to throw boiling hot fat on me.' Sunita explains she couldn't cope in the flat after that. She left to live on the street, deciding to bed down at Piccadilly station, where the security cameras made her feel safe.

I wondered if we should pause. I was piling misery on top of misery, but the impulse to stop was due more to my own discomfort than her lack of resolve. It wasn't the first time I'd had to turn off the tape, but Sunita is tough – and if she went through all this, the least I could do was listen.

'What was the first night like?' I asked.

There was a long pause.

'Scary, cold, dark, lonely,' she said, eventually.

'Did you have a blanket?'

'I don't think I did at the start. I used my coat on my knees.'

'How did you sleep?'

'You never do. You sleep with one eye open. You never have a good sleep. You feel weak. You've got no energy. Some days, you don't want to be here no more.'

Sunita went to live in a refuge, but she only lasted a night. There were no beds available, so she had to bed down on a sofa, but she couldn't get any sleep because a hysterical resident was setting all the fire alarms off. 'I thought: "Y'know what, I'm no better in here than out there."'

Sunita went to the council for help. They told her that she had made herself intentionally homeless and was, therefore, not entitled to their assistance. Sunita claims they weren't interested in the domestic abuse that precipitated her rough sleeping, so she went back to Piccadilly station, where she had to rely on shoplifting and random donations from strangers to survive.

'I was always rubbish at shoplifting. I was always too scared of getting caught,' I told her. 'Were you any good at it?'

'I was shit! I was really bad at it,' she said. She told me she would stuff multi-bags of crisps and blocks of cheese down the band of her pants, but it would often slide down one of her trouser legs and give the game away.

'One day I robbed PG tea bags, because the box had a little [toy] monkey at the top,' she explained.

'How're you gonna make a brew on the street?' I asked, somewhat naively.

'Nah, I could sell 'em, but keep the monkey and keep my Tetley tea men. When people walked past me, I used to ask them [what they wanted], and then I stopped because people were asking me to get this, get that. And then they'd turn up the next day and I didn't have it because I didn't have the courage to go in again,' she said.

Sunita slept rough for a year, and only made it off the street because of a chance meeting with a stranger. A woman called Leanne would frequently visit her at the station. 'I used to talk to her and tell her about my life and what I'd gone through. One day, she said there's a job going at a call centre. I said: "Yeah, right, like I can get a job; look at me." So, she said to me, "I'll bring you some clothes."'

Leanne gave Sunita a smart blouse and shoes to wear to interview for a job in telecoms – cold-calling people to complete surveys. What Sunita didn't know was that the woman was the manager of the building, so she got the job.

Sunita would arrive in the early morning before anyone else got in, then get washed and changed in the office toilets. She'd stay until 10pm, when everyone else had already left for the day, and would then go back to Piccadilly station to sleep rough. One afternoon, Leanne approached Sunita and instructed her to meet her in the car park. Sunita thought she was in trouble.

'She's having a cigarette in the car park, and I'm shitting it, thinking, "I've lost everything now, what am I going to do?"' Sunita said.

A man pulled into the car park. Leanne handed him an envelope in exchange for a piece of paper, which Leanne asked her to sign. The man told Sunita that he was here to give her keys to a new apartment. Leanne had been holding back some of Sunita's wages and used it to set her up in a flat.

'I said: "Can I go back to Piccadilly station? I've got my bag there; it's got bits in." She said, "You don't need nothing like that no more. This is the start of your life. That's all rags to you now."'

When I spoke to her, Sunita was still facing challenges with her housing and was still struggling with the trauma of her early years. However, she refuses to be a victim. 'I see myself as a survivor, if that makes sense. I won't be a victim to social services; I won't be a victim to a government that's failed. I will always now be a survivor. I can turn around and say: "Y'know what? I'm a survivor of your abuse. I'm a survivor of your failings."'

Sunita's life seemed like it had careered relentlessly from one harrowing incident to another. It was overwhelming to listen to, almost surreal. One might find themselves asking: 'How could so much shit happen to one person?' I would struggle to believe it if I hadn't experienced and seen similar things myself; if I hadn't watched girls like Lucy getting into the cars of older men while care staff looked on with apathy; if I hadn't experienced the restraints, the bullying, the displacement and abuse.

Sunita's journey to the streets, and the fact that she only escaped due to a stranger's kindness, who gave her a job and saved her money in secret to get her a place of her own, shows just how broken Britain's care system was. Today, the outlook for over-sixteens is still bleak. After a decade of austerity, the provision for kids transitioning to independence has been stripped to the bone. I was lucky that Hawthorn Crescent was a regulated home run by Oldham Council, and had experienced staff on duty twenty-four hours a day. Three-quarters of these homes in England are now in the private sector.[11] Teenagers in care are discarded in unregulated accommodation, sometimes a hundred miles away from home, with little to no supervision.[12]

In 2019, BBC's *Newsnight* reported that 'the number of looked-after children aged sixteen and over living in unregistered accommodation in England has increased by 70 per cent in a decade.'[13] Like the accommodation Jake Humm had in Brighton, these homes avoid inspection from Ofsted and are able to self-regulate because they provide 'support' instead of 'care'.

A 2019 report conducted by the All-Party Parliamentary Group for Runaway and Missing Children and Adults found that children over the age of sixteen are being placed in a 'frightening, twilight world of unregulated semi-independent homes'.[14] The report stated that young people living in this accommodation are easy targets for sexual exploitation and drug running. Is it really a surprise that the next step for these kids is the street?

Even if a care-experienced kid grew up in a stable environment with conscientious care staff who ensured they steered clear of drugs, avoided crime, and completed their education, it could still go pear-shaped during the transition from care to independence. Once they reach a certain age – usually eighteen – people in care are expected to fend for themselves, regardless of whether they're ready or not. Compared to Sunita and Lucy, I was mollycoddled when I left the system – but I still think I was set up to fail.

Chapter Four

Independence

Autumn rain had soaked the mossy stone wall that my brother Ollie was preparing to hurl himself from on a vaporous late morning at Greenfield cricket ground. The practice nets opposite the pavilion had been removed for the season, leaving an enticing metal frame for hyperactive adolescents to swing from. It was late 2004, and I was on the cusp of moving out of Hawthorn Crescent. I had visited Grandma and she had sent Ollie and me on a shop run. We decided to make the journey more interesting with a bit of ill-thought-out parkour.

'Nah, it's too slippy, that,' Ollie said of the rain-sodden horizontal bar running along the top of the frame.

'Move. I'll do it, then,' I said impatiently.

Ollie leapt off the wall, tapped the bar with his outstretched fingers and landed nimbly on the balls of his feet on the synthetic turf below.

I scaled the wall and saw what Ollie meant as I surveyed the bar in front of me. This wasn't a good idea. But just because my little brother didn't have the 'courage' to perform gymnastics on a slippery sixteen-foot-high bar didn't mean I had to bottle it, too. I leapt forward with feline moxie, grasped the bar with my soaking gloves, swung violently up into the air and plummeted to the ground like a rock. I landed neck first, and my legs shot over my head as the momentum of the fall spun me 180 degrees to face back towards the wall I'd just jumped from.

'That did not look good,' Ollie said. Understatement of the century.

The result of my terrible Kōhei Uchimura impression was a couple of nights in hospital, a cracked vertebra on my lower spine and months of physiotherapy. This is how I began life as an independent adult – and it wasn't the worst choice I was about to make.

I was seventeen and still unemployed, without qualifications or prospects, but at least I knew how a gas hob worked when I left Hawthorn. A private care management company took over from Oldham Council, and they moved me from the cul-de-sac into my own place, a two-up, two-down terrace on a small housing estate outside Oldham town centre.

By this time, I'd been in a combination of special boarding schools, foster homes and children's homes since I was ten. These places could be terrifying at times, but the presence of others had always been reassuring, especially at night. I went from this to living alone. Six schools and eleven different addresses had left me without a strong support network. I felt a need to plug the loneliness, and my new home quickly became a doss house, where other teenagers from the estate could drink, smoke weed and act out away from grown-ups.

I had also become crippled with neuroticism. I was twelve

when I had my first panic attack. As I was retrieving a bottle of blackcurrant cordial from a cluttered cupboard in my parent's kitchen, I sent a bottle of calamine lotion tumbling to the stone floor, where it burst open like a water balloon. Silver spots danced in my peripherals, and then the room blurred and spun like a supersonic washing machine. 'What's happening?!' I screamed, running furiously on the spot as if I could stamp the sensation out of my body. Mum took me to hospital and stayed with me overnight on the children's ward. An electro-cardiogram, encephalogram and other tests followed over the next fortnight, until the doctors decided that what had happened was all in my mind.

From then on, I started experiencing acute anxiety regularly. I became a hypochondriac. A mild headache became a brain haemorrhage, a stomachache was stomach cancer, and any bump, lump or blemish was fatal. The onset of my anxiety coincided with the epiphany that many adolescents have about their appearance. This epiphany is either good news or bad news. For me, it was bad news. Before puberty, the relentless jibes about my prominent incisors were bothersome, but not soul-destroying. When I finally discovered that I liked girls – and that my face would not win any of them over – I began to detest my teeth. I used to punch my mouth to try and force my teeth back, but I refused to wear braces, as I didn't fancy the insults that came with them, either. Even though I was slender and over six feet tall when I entered early adulthood, I would wear baggy clothes, big overcoats and woolly hats to hide from the world. If being one's own worst enemy was a sport, I'd be a Hall of Fame world champion.

This anxiety peaked in my new home. I was so paranoid that someone would invade the house that I spent several hours checking and re-checking that my windows and doors were locked. I even began looking in the cupboards to check if a burglar had stowed themselves inside one. The fact that said burglar would've needed to be a circus contortionist to hide in there didn't stop me in my tracks, but that's the thing about irrationality: it's irrational. When I turned nineteen, I wasn't entitled to any more aftercare support, but I still wasn't ready to stand on my own two feet. Before the care provider withdrew their services, I had weekly panic attacks and there were several trips to A&E.

In the beginning, my key workers would visit me on most weekdays to help me manage my home. They supervised my job-seeking and further education; they ensured I kept my house clean and tidy, and that I was eating properly. Within the first few months, I'd got into Manchester City College on a filmmaking course, I was managing my bills and coping reasonably well.

Even if there's a clear and open road expanding into a rosy frontier ahead of you, you're going nowhere if you can't drive. Despite the house, the benefits, the course, the world at my feet, I didn't have a clue about how to get on in life and how to live independently. By the time I left the terrace in 2006, visits from key workers had dwindled to one or two a week, usually for cinema excursions, grocery trips and Job Centre appointments. I'd dropped out of college; I was only getting £45 a week from my Jobseeker's Allowance and I was struggling to budget. My cupboards were often empty; the pay-as-you-go electric and gas meters were constantly depleted, often leaving me cold and in darkness. I was still unemployed and unemployable.

The care management provider was paying half of the rent, but there was no way I could hope to make up the difference, so social services moved me across the borough into a block of council flats – a typical late-sixties eyesore in Glodwick. Glodwick was at the heart of Oldham's race riots, which had kicked off over three days in 2001. Oldham was, and to a large extent remains, segregated along racial lines.[1] The riots were the culmination of years of racial tension between the communities. Despite this, Oldham social services still thought it appropriate to move a nineteen-year-old white care-leaver with learning difficulties and an anxiety disorder into a flat on his own in the middle of the Asian community.

It would be just as – if not more – dangerous to move a young Asian man with a similar background into a predominantly white area. Because when it comes to racial abuse, the British Asian community have borne the brunt of it in Oldham and continue to do so. I grew up around some of the most racist people you'll ever meet: classmates who bragged about the windows they'd broken at the local mosque over the weekend; taproom bores reminiscing about beating up Asians in the seventies like it was a sport; and doddering old sods at bus stops, grumbling about Asians taking jobs, benefits and England. I can understand why young Asian males might want to seek retribution on young white males when they've probably heard about the horrific abuse their older relatives suffered when they first came to work in Oldham's mills after the war.

I'd only been living in Glodwick for a month when my skin

colour got me into trouble. I was hiking back home from Oldham town centre after pawning some of my DVDs at Cash Generator on a rare day of pure sunshine and cloudless skies. I was on the dole, always skint and my modest DVD collection functioned as an emergency fund of sorts. As I turned on to Glodwick Road, a group of Asian teens confronted me from across the road.

'Oi, you Gora [white] bastard, what're you doing round 'ere!' one of them shouted.

I ignored them and carried on walking. A large rock whistled past my right ear and skidded along the pavement in front of me. I looked back and saw the group had crossed the road, and were hurling more abuse and rocks my way. I got on my toes and legged it towards my block. I had just enough of a head start to keep them at a safe distance, but I still had the obstacle of opening my security door, a fiasco even when I wasn't trying to evade a kicking. Luckily, a taxi driver spotted the chase and pulled up to obstruct my would-be assailants, buying me enough time to make it inside my block. When I got into my third-floor flat, I looked out of my bedroom window and saw that the group had shrugged off the taxi driver and were pelting my building with stones. This prompted a shirtless and tattooed skinhead to come rushing out of the adjacent block. 'Hey, fuck off, you little bastards!' he bellowed, while wielding a cricket bat around his head. They scattered. 'You all right, lad?' he shouted up to me.

'Yeah,' I said.

An elderly woman who lived on the ground floor opened her window and asked Skinhead what was going on.

'It's all right love. Just a bit of trouble with the local Pakis,' Skinhead said casually.

This racist cretin is going to get me killed, I thought as I closed my window.

When the late Black Panther and writer Darcus Howe visited Oldham in 1999 for his Channel 4 documentary *White Tribe*, he looked stupefied after interviewing white racists on the doorsteps of their Fitton Hill homes. Howe said his experiences in the town 'substantially' changed his view of England. 'Maybe Britain is a racist society,' he lamented, looking utterly dejected as he leaned on a grey Oldham lamp post.[2] Reflecting on the programme in an article for the *New Statesman*, Howe said he left the town with a feeling of dread: a sense that bloodshed was on the horizon.

> I talked extensively to poor, very poor, whites. They were preparing for bloodshed, they told me. This is a stronghold of the fascist group, Combat 18. A young woman terrified me. She talked herself into a frenzy about Pakistani filth, about their personal habits. I wince as I write . . .
>
> Her neighbour joined us. Hundreds would die, he said. And wherever I went, I heard similar forecasts which, I suspect, are being pushed by right-wing groups. I can see how it might come about. A riot is provoked between Pakistanis and young whites and the marksmen, the assassins, move in. It is easily done.[3]

I watched the documentary in 2020, and Howe's reaction to the doorstep fascists really put things in perspective for me. The appalling views aired in the documentary weren't particularly surprising; I'd heard them all my life. But the documentary finally made me understand why so many Londoners and others in metropolitan bubbles were left flabbergasted by the Brexit vote: they didn't – and still don't – understand provincial communities and just how ingrained racism is in parts of the north.

Most of the time, I could walk through Glodwick and experience no problems, but that chase wasn't my last experience of harassment. Sometimes I'd get caught and have to absorb a few blows before it got broken up by a passer-by, sometimes I had to turtle up on the ground until they lost interest, and sometimes I managed to wriggle away. It got so bad that I became scared to leave my flat: only I had to if I wanted to remain there any longer.

I was still entitled to some form of aftercare support until I was twenty-one, but it was all but removed when I lived in Glodwick, save for the odd phone check-up or casual visit. After a few months there, Oldham Job Centre became wholly unimpressed by my commitment to job-seeking. I had no skills, no qualifications, no experience and no connections – what did they expect? The Job Centre referred me to an agency that loaned me out to the local mills in the area. These behemoths of the old textile industry had been transformed into customs warehouses, where grunts like me strapped on hi-vis vests and loaded and unloaded shipping containers. The longest stint I did for the agency was during the run-up to Christmas 2006, at a crumbling Victorian textile mill in Coppice, a small housing estate on the outskirts of Oldham town centre.

The mill was capacious yet claustrophobic, dank, dusty and cold. *This is where people come to die*, I thought as I arrived at 6am on a grim autumn morning for my first ever day of proper graft. After a few shifts, I understood why byssinosis – a chronic lung condition caused by prolonged exposure to cotton dust – had afflicted many of the tenders over the years. I'm pretty sure that you shouldn't be able to *chew* the air. We weren't weaving cotton any more, but the mill was poorly ventilated and thick with dust. At the end of shifts, I'd fill tissues with black snot, and when I stood under my shower, black water would run from my scalp and pool under my feet.

The people I worked with brought me the most misery. I was the youngest and least experienced on-site; I still hadn't grown out of my adolescent body or my ADHD, and was an easy target for the boorish lads who had full-time contracts. Gaz, a gangly six-foot-five-inch meathead, was the ringleader. One morning we were picking pallets containing boxes of socks from the second floor to load on to trucks in the afternoon when Gaz ordered me to go to the reception and ask for a 'long stand'. It was early, I was bleary-eyed, and I didn't even consider what a 'long stand' was when I approached reception on the ground floor.

'Can I have a long stand?' I asked the greying middle-aged bloke at the reception counter.

A peculiar smirk creased his face.

What's up with him? I thought.

'Yeah, no problem. Just stand there, will you?' he said as he walked into the office behind him.

Ten minutes went by. I became restless. 'Have you got it yet, mate?' I shouted.

The man emerged from the office moments later. 'So, was that long enough then?' he asked.

'You what?'

'You wanted a long stand. Was it long enough?'

The penny eventually dropped.

This wasn't the worst of it. The real misery came when I revealed my non-existent sex life while bragging about my sexual prowess. It was break time on one rain-sodden morning, and we were all perched on pallets inside a truck we'd half loaded, puffing on roll-ups and swigging from polystyrene cups of instant coffee, while the rain hammered on the metal container above us. The conversation veered towards women. I was in the middle of a fictional story about picking up girls in the town centre when Karl – Gaz's spindly right-hand man – interrupted me mid-flow.

'Are you a virgin?' he asked. The others sniggered into their cups.

I could feel my cheeks reddening with embarrassment as the rest of the group shifted to the edge of their pallets in anticipation of my response. 'Nah. I do all right, me, mate,' I said.

'Where's the clit on a girl then?' Karl asked, inducing more sniggers around the truck.

I've got you here! I thought. 'It's above the vagina, underneath the clitoral hood,' I answered triumphantly, but this didn't have the effect that I thought it would. The sniggers transformed into belly laughs.

Karl stood up, took his roll-up from the corner of his mouth, pointed at me with it and bellowed: 'You read that in a textbook. You're a fuckin' virgin!'

From that day on, I was known around the mill as Virgin, or Virg for short. When Madonna's 'Like a Virgin' came on the radio one afternoon, the lads blasted it out at full volume over the tannoy in my honour. Bastards.

Agency work is commissioned ad hoc, and the work soon

dried up after the festive season in 2006, leaving me in financial strife. I was soon in arrears and back on the dole. This was before the gig economy came to dominate the low-skilled sector, but it was beginning to creep in, and zero-hours contracts produced the same disruptive uncertainty in one's life then as they do now. An agency worker is on call every day, and is expected to say: 'How high?' when told to jump. You don't turn down work for fear that it won't be offered again; when the phone doesn't ring, you can't enjoy the respite for the same reason. There are no 'days off'.

It's not just the lack of security inherent in these contracts that plunges people into arrears and ultimately causes them to lose their homes. They can also prevent people from getting homes in the first place. Private landlords often see zero-hour workers in the same way as they see Dole-ites, and are reluctant to give them a rental agreement. Some private landlords see people on benefits as more desirable than zero-hour workers, as at least the money they receive doesn't change from one week to the next.[4] A 2016 King's College London study found the ex-homeless working on casual contracts brought home an average income that was less than that of the unemployed.[5]

The following two years were a maelstrom of displacement. During this time, I moved home seven times, lost four jobs, and ended up with debts that are still blighting my credit score to this day. I simply wasn't equipped to look after myself. I was aimless and anxious, angry with the world and everything in it. I don't want to use ADHD as a crutch, but I wasn't medicated, and was still making disastrously impulsive decisions.

Down and Out

I fled from the block in Glodwick in late 2006 when I returned home one evening to find my front door smashed in and my few possessions stolen. I reported the incident and the harassment I was suffering to Oldham Council, who moved me on to Higginshaw, one of the town's most deprived council estates.

The flat in Higginshaw was bare, and I couldn't afford to transport my furniture from Glodwick to my new pebbledash dwellings. All I had was a donated mattress, which I laid on the concrete floor of my bedroom. Just after turning twenty, when I'd been there less than a month, I was roused from my mattress one evening when a cinder block crashed through my kitchen window. Why? I don't know. The only explanation I can offer is that the flat was empty for a while before I moved in. It was dilapidated, with graffiti plastered on the interior and exterior walls, and the culprits probably assumed they were vandalising an empty property. I couldn't muster this rationalisation at the time. I called the police, and a pair of officers arrived several hours later to scribble on their notepads and offer indifferent shrugs. The impression they gave was that this was the norm in Higginshaw. I left that night for my grandparents', where I stayed for the next few months.

Even though I wasn't qualified for anything other than menial labour, I used this period of relative stability to secure a job as a part-time shelf-stacker with Sainsbury's in Ashton-under-Lyne. While the work wasn't as physically taxing as warehouse packing, it was monotonous and just as unrewarding. The metronomic act of placing tins on shelves requires a robotic level of concentration, and there's not a Ritalin tablet on the planet that could give me that. The only silver lining in this dull cloud was the entertaining customer queries I was confronted with on a daily basis.

'Do you know where the pharmacy is?' a flustered shopper asked me on one slow afternoon. 'I've been up and down this place!' he groaned, while standing underneath a ten-foot-long, three-foot-wide banner with 'PHARMACY' plastered on it in giant green capital letters. On another day, a customer asked me if we stocked ASDA's own-brand butter – no, really.

Nevertheless, I had guaranteed hours and there was plenty of overtime available, providing me with just enough cash to pursue my ambitions in the evenings. I still hadn't given up on my dream of becoming Manchester's Jackie Chan, and continued to throw myself around martial arts dojos and gymnastics centres with the hope of qualifying for the Equity stunt register. This frenetic routine entailed antisocial working hours. My grandparents were well into their seventies, and if I wasn't home by 11pm, they were in bed, lights off, comatose, unable to hear me, no matter how firmly, persistently and repetitively I rapped on their front door. They didn't trust me with a house key, so I was left to lumber around the streets for the night. After growing tired of this miserable routine, I stole a key and had it copied. This wasn't appreciated. Grandma refused to have me any longer, so I returned to my parents' house for the first time since I was twelve.

As much as I love my parents, we can't live together. The working hours I kept frustrated them even more than they'd frustrated my grandparents, so tensions were high from the start. I also refused to contribute a penny of board. They owed me a childhood, I reasoned. 'You lot paid for fuck all when I was a kid, so *you* owe *me*!' I would shout at Mum whenever she broached the subject. I was still the same petulant six-year-old, only instead of books and a staircase, I had manipulative guilt trips to bully her with. I lasted there for about five months before it all went tits up. I was relaxing in front of the telly one afternoon when Mum burst in and announced: 'Danny! I've found you a bedsit and you're going there!'

'Wha—' I began to say.

'You just can't stay here any more!'

'What are you on about? You're kicking me out again?'

'No, you just can't stay here. You're keeping me up all hours; you're not paying your way. That's it!'

'You've never paid *your* way. You pay for fuck all!'

Ollie was also living in the care system by this point, and I took the opportunity to remind her of how bad a mother she was.

'Is it Ollie's fault 'n' all? Bit of a pattern here, Mum. Doesn't that tell you something? It's not all our fault, but you won't 'fess up to nowt!' I boomed at her as she attempted to leave the room.

I followed her and continued on a raging tirade, browbeating her until she had no choice but to blank me completely. With the benefit of hindsight, I realise that the awful things I said to her were hideously unfair, but I meant them at the time. And she meant what she said: I was out, and back to Oldham to live in a cramped bedsit.

While living with my folks, I had transferred to a Sainsbury's store closer to home. After six months there, I lost my job. I'd worked for the company for eighteen months in total (still my longest term of employment). Lasting that long was a minor miracle. In the beginning, I'd concocted all manner of scenarios to stifle the unrelenting tedium of the work. Sometimes I imagined my roll cage was a munitions trolley that I was wheeling to the front line of a historical battle, and that the tins I was stacking on to shelves were shells being loaded into a cannon.

By early 2008, I'd exhausted my imagination and patience, and did everything except what I was supposed to be doing. For every half hour I worked on the shop floor, I spent an hour reading in the locker rooms. This didn't go unnoticed for long. After one skiving session, my line manager (let's call him Mr Stickler), a short, wiry jobsworth type, who had everything in order, from his military haircut to his perfectly fitted suits, angrily, and very publicly, confronted me about my frequent absences.

'Where are you going all the time?' Mr Stickler barked as I strolled back to my post on the homeware section.

'I just went to the loo,' I protested.

'Have you got a bladder problem? If you have, you need to disclose it.'

My wellspring of anger poured from me just as readily as ever. 'Shut up, you dickhead. I'm allowed to go to the fuckin' toilet!' I shouted.

Stickler ordered me to join him in his office, where he continued to give me a dressing down, and I continued to tell him where to go.

'Sit down, Daniel,' he ordered. Stickler was standing behind his desk; I was standing stubbornly on the other side.

'Nah, mate! Don't fuckin' tell me what to do! You sit down, innit,' I retorted.

I then told him I was *his* boss and it was my shop; I even

challenged him to a fight after my shift. What a petulant tit I was. They sacked me.

After that, I got a gig on the checkouts with the Co-op, where I lasted for three months until they sacked me. I hadn't done anything wrong this time. I was a model professional. I turned up on time, did everything they asked and didn't offer to fight anyone – honest. Essentially, Sainsbury's sacked me again. They decided to send my reference (why I decided to cite them as a referee eludes me to this day), which amounted to a character assassination three months late, so the Co-op sacked me for being sacked from Sainsbury's.

Everyone is entitled to make mistakes when they're young, but the consequences can be life-destroying for independent care-leavers. A few weeks later, I was skint and I sank into rent arrears. My bedsit was inside a featureless and foreboding three-storey, red-bricked shit hole, which could have been a rectory in the past for the derelict parish church next door. There were five of us sharing the place, all blokes, predominantly middle-aged, and, for the most part, just as skint as I was. After a few months on the unemployment line, I ended up on the breadline; only there was no bread at the end of it, so I stole it from my housemates. Before, I could have called my social worker, who would arrive with a food parcel to tide me over to my next Giro payment. Not any more.

I packed in the thievery when I got caught red-handed by one of my housemates one cold winter evening. I'd just wolfed down two slices of cheap white bread I'd stolen from the communal kitchen when my bedsit door began booming. I opened it and found my balding neighbour standing there with his hands balled into fists, looking like a purple balloon that was about to burst.

'Did you steal my bread?!' he shouted.

'No, why?' I lied.

'Yeah, you did. I just opened it and there's two slices missing. I know it's you because you've been robbin' other people's shit 'n' all.'

I couldn't believe this was happening. 'What sort of person keeps track of how many slices of bread they have?' I asked myself as he continued to chew my ear off. 'Why would I rob your bread when I've got my own?' I lied again.

'Show us, then!' he demanded.

I hadn't seen that coming. 'No, why should I?'

'Exactly!' he shouted victoriously. 'If you do it again, I'll break your fuckin' jaw! I don't care how big you are. I know bare heads who'll come round here and sort you out, pal,' he shouted before marching back to his room.

I'd shaken off the timidity I'd carried around with me during adolescence and was willing to stick up for myself in these situations. Yet I knew I was in the wrong, so I said nothing and closed my door.

By this point in 2008, I had racked up over a thousand pounds of arrears and began playing cat and mouse with my landlord. It was just as well that I didn't pay. Just before Christmas 2008, a Section 21 eviction notice was delivered, informing all residents that the owners were selling the building and we had a month to find somewhere else to live. Section 21 of the Housing Act 1988 – a wonderful idea concocted by Margaret Thatcher – allows landlords to evict private renters on short notice for no good reason.[6] At the state opening of Parliament on 19 December 2019, the Queen's Speech announced that the Renters' Reform Bill would abolish no-fault evictions and 'provide greater certainty for tenants and make the housing market fit for the 21st century'.[7] At the time of writing, this promise has still not been met by the government. When I asked them about it in early 2020, a Ministry for Housing and Local Government spokesperson did not confirm if the government still intended to abolish such evictions, but stated that the Renters' Rights Bill would deliver 'radical change for tenants' and 'drive out poor landlords'. I won't hold my breath.

Luckily, social services had picked up my case again when the eviction notice came through my letterbox. My re-referral illustrates just how disorganised the council was. Earlier in 2008, I'd been manning the tills at the Co-op on one humid summer afternoon when I served a former social worker of mine. I don't know if she sensed I was down or if she was just curious, but she asked if I was still receiving support. I told her I was on my own. A few weeks later, another social worker from the council's vulnerable adults team visited me. By that time, the Co-op had sacked me, and if it weren't for that chance encounter at the supermarket, I would have been on the streets that Christmas, because I was penniless, I wasn't speaking to my family and I had nowhere to go.

When the hammer fell on the flat, I was placed in a bed and breakfast on Saddleworth Moor over the festive period while my social worker tried to find a permanent solution. I spent that Christmas alone, skint and hungry, contemplating the dismal direction my life had taken. Most of my peers were either in higher education or beginning their careers; they had sex lives, social circles, relationships, holidays and love. I had failure stacked on top of failure, self-pity and self-loathing.

In the new year, my social worker found me another funded flat, this time with Regenda, a north-west based housing association. The flat was a one-bedroom maisonette in Glodwick, two hundred metres from the block I had fled two years earlier. I was incredulous, but what could I do? If I raised objections, I would've been deemed to have made myself 'intentionally homeless' and refused assistance.

Despite making the same mistake as their predecessors by moving me back to Glodwick, Oldham Council's vulnerable adults team made amends for the failings of aftercare. My needs were properly assessed, and I was referred to a disability support group, who helped me apply for a concessionary bus pass and Disability Living Allowance (DLA). I was also assigned a diligent employment support worker, who helped me apply for jobs and training at a job club in Chadderton every Friday.

After months of CV-writing and completing job applications at Friday's job club, I won a place on Oldham Council's horticultural trainee scheme. The scheme was a two-year placement for people with learning difficulties. It was like being at Dippydale all over again. The support staff heavily monitored every move I made on the project. They directed the day's tasks, which mostly involved running a Dutch hoe through flower beds to excavate thistles, hairy bittercress, horsetail and other stubborn weeds.

I shared the trainee scheme with people with severe learning difficulties, all of whom had completely different support needs.

This is the state of the provision in England: if you tick a box, everyone is lumbered in with everyone else who ticked that box, irrespective of their actual issues and needs. There's no room for nuance.

The job got old quickly, and, just like I had at school, I began to amuse myself at other people's expense. I'd start arguments about religion and politics, and try to make people feel silly by using obscure words I'd swallowed from the dictionary. I became an insufferable sesquipedalian, which turned me into an even more insufferable ultracrepidarian and occasional mumpsimus (How do you like them *Malus sieversii*s, Will Self?).

I'd had an excuse at Dippydale – I was a mixed-up kid – but now I was a twenty-two-year-old man who was acting like an arsehole. If this were any other job, I would've been shown the door, but the council persevered. After lasting a year on the scheme, I finally used my improved vocabulary for something other than intellectual pretence. The adult literacy and numeracy lessons supplemented an Access to Higher Education course I attended in the evening. I passed the course, and won a place at Manchester Metropolitan University to study for a bachelor's degree in history.

I'm often asked how I managed to get to university. Well, it certainly wasn't due to any inspiration from Oldham social services. A study conducted by the Rees Centre at the University of Oxford found that 13 per cent of care-leavers in England had entered higher education, compared to 49 per cent of the general population.[8]

In 2019, the Centre for Social Justice, a centre-right think tank, found that care-leavers in the UK are 'more likely to end up in a prison cell than a lecture theatre'.[9] I'm convinced that the reason I made it while the kids I grew up with in care didn't is that my parents went to university; my grandparents were teachers. I had role models. The kids I lived with in care had no such examples to follow, and saw higher education as an abstract concept – beyond their reach and capabilities – whereas I knew it was possible, and that's why I had the audacity to try and get there. Education is vital for social mobility. If we want to mitigate the appalling social outcomes for care-leavers, to stop them from heading to prison and the streets, we must do more to let them know, as I did, that higher education is a realistic proposition.

If a child is taken into care, it is usually because their family is incapable of looking after them, so the idea is that the state should do a better job. A 2017 research paper published by Centrepoint, a homeless charity catering to fifteen-to-twenty-five-year-olds, showed that more than one in four care-leavers have sofa-surfed, and 14 per cent have slept rough.[10] There are several reasons for this: the quality of aftercare support varies from region to region; privatisation has fragmented services, making them less accountable; and some care-leavers refuse help once they're old enough to stand on their own two feet. They may want, as I did, to be free from a system that did so little for them while they were caught in it. Finally, managing finances is a skill that many care-leavers have not been taught, so those who are less resourceful often fall behind with their rent and bills.

Why should care-leavers be treated differently from other children? Many people leave home at the age of twenty-two[11] and receive long-term support from their parents well into adulthood. In 2017, the government passed the Children and Social Work Act. According to the Department of Education, the legislation obliges councils to 'provide Personal Adviser (PA) support to all care-leavers up to age 25, if they want this support'.[12] This is a positive step, but the government haven't backed it up with more funding for social care,[13] and the policy falls short of what is required. Care-leavers should receive support for as long as they need it, and even if they've gone without it for years, they should be able to access it again, in just the same way that non-care-leavers will occasionally need to lean on their parents in times of difficulty, throughout adulthood.

If social services had handled my transition to independence more competently, if readiness rather than an arbitrary age determined when I stood on my own two feet, maybe I would have done better. I wasn't ready, and was still making hair-brained decisions about my future. The incoming student loans and grants convinced me to sever ties with Oldham social services, end my traineeship, and give up my socially rented housing association flat for private digs in Mossley, which I perceived to be safer than Glodwick. That's three social homes I left in the space of three years.

When thinking about housing in Britain, and the millions of people languishing on social-housing waiting lists, I feel guilty about those decisions. Getting accepted on a local housing register is hard enough; getting a socially rented home is like winning the lottery – and I gave up three winning tickets.

Chapter Five

Fighting the Housing Crisis

The word 'crisis' is bandied around far too readily by the main-stream media and its constituent commentariat, but when it comes to the nation's housing, I think the fictional character Edmund Blackadder summed it up best: 'This is a crisis, a large crisis. A twelve-storey crisis with a magnificent entrance hall, carving throughout, twenty-four-hour porterage and an enormous sign on the roof saying, "This is a Large Crisis!"'[1] It's the crisis constructed by Margaret Thatcher, and its foundations were put in place merely a year after she led her Tories to victory in the 1979 general election.

The Thatcher era presided over the greatest heist in modern history, a heist perpetrated under the guise of giving people a stake in public assets they already had a stake in. When Maggie's Tories won power, they passed the Housing Act in August 1980, giving council tenants the 'Right to Buy' their council homes.[2]

Why someone would want to buy a home they could occupy until death anyway would be beyond my comprehension if I didn't understand the British public's susceptibility to the politics of aspiration. Across the pond, they call it the American

Dream, and as the late comedian George Carlin pointed out, 'You'd have to be asleep to believe it.'[3] But who could blame the public for being hoodwinked by the golden carrots dangled in front of their faces? Councils offered their tenants 100 per cent mortgages and generous discounts on the market value of their homes, which began at 33 per cent and rose as high as 50 per cent for tenants who'd rented their homes for twenty years.[4],[5] It was terrific news for a generation of social renters who were able to transform their modest dwellings into piggy banks, and great news for Mrs Thatcher, who benefited from their trips to the ballot box at subsequent elections.

It was bad news for poorer tenants, who ended up footing the bill after steep hikes in rent. The average weekly rent for a council house in 1979 was £6.40;[6] by the time John Major took office in 1991, it had risen to £30 per week, an increase of approximately 370 per cent.[7] The average weekly pay rose by only 180 per cent for the average full-time manual worker over the same period,[8] which means the proportion of income spent on rent by those workers had increased by roughly 68 per cent by 1991.

Even though the government made billions from Right to Buy, they didn't reinvest the cash in the system. A study published by the *Journal of Housing Economics* found that after 1990, local authorities could only access '25 per cent of the capital receipts' and the rest was 'treated as "reserved receipts"', which could not be spent on new council housing. And they could only spend the quarter of receipts they did recoup on maintenance and renovation of existing properties.[9] By the mid-2000s, 2.8 million council tenants had bought their homes under Right to Buy, making up approximately 50 per cent of the council housing stock that existed in 1980.[10]

This has proved disastrous for generations of renters, who now languish on protracted housing waiting lists for decades and have to depend on the private sector for housing that is often insecure, overpriced and overcrowded. Part of the problem is that it's too easy for private landlords to evict tenants. In 2019, the BBC reported that no-fault evictions had risen sharply since 2011, and that in 2018 '10,128 repossessions were carried out by county court bailiffs in England using the "accelerated procedure" (which doesn't require a court hearing).'[11]

When private tenants find themselves without a home, they're forced into a misery contest for housing and, unless they tick every box on the misery checklist, will probably find themselves in a box in a converted office block or container. Far from home. Forgotten. Others fall completely through the net and end up on the street. The situation has become so bad that some are taking the law into their own hands to mitigate this growing crisis.

Stuart Potts, or 'Pottsy', was in shorts and shirtless when we met on a sweltering day on Deansgate, central Manchester, in June 2019. Stuart runs the Saving People Shelter Project, a squatter's network that occupies abandoned buildings in order to house homeless people around Greater Manchester. He's a tough, funny, compassionate rogue. I first became aware of Stuart when I read about him in the *Manchester Evening News* under the headline: 'The homeless people living on the banks of the Salford Canal – and fishing for their food.' He was snapped in the same clobber: shorts, shirtless, and sporting shit-kicker boots while fishing from the canal. He'd taken to living there after he was evicted from his flat, and had transformed the bank into an outdoor living room, complete with leather couches, bookshelves, a television and a bed. It was a big fat Manc 'fuck you' to the council and anyone else who didn't like it.[12]

We walked down Deansgate to chat at the nearest bar, a swanky glass box opposite John Rylands Library, but a haughty waiter ordered us to leave before we could sip on our lemonades because Stuart refused to pop his shirt back on. 'It's bar policy,' the waiter insisted. We downed our lemonades and settled on some nearby steps instead, agreeing that the waiter was up himself and the 'policy' was a load of bollocks.

Stuart was thirty-eight when we met, a dad of five who had struggled with mental health and addiction. He appeared to have been through the wars and I couldn't help but notice the scars on his torso.

'What happened there?' I asked, gesturing to a deep scar on his side.

'I got stabbed at my girlfriend's. I lost three pints of blood,' he said.

Stuart told me his assailant was his girlfriend's stalker. 'We were upstairs having a bit of nookie; he came into the bedroom and said, "What's going on here?" I said, "What do you mean what's going on here – get out!" He started fighting with me. I got him down the stairs, then next minute he smashed a bottle and stabbed me in the side there, and almost took my ear off. Could have died,' Stuart explained.

Stuart took the law into his own hands after getting evicted from his flat in Eccles. He was evicted because he took in a homeless man off the streets and got him back on his feet. One of his neighbours told his landlord that Stuart had taken in a lodger. 'I got a phone call when I was at church [from the landlord]. "Who's this druggy you've got back home, this homeless druggie?" he asked me. I said, "He's not a druggie. I got him off the drugs." He said, "I don't care, mate. Get him out of the house – and you're going as well." I didn't argue with him 'cause he's a boxer, you know what I mean.'

Stuart left but not before the neighbour gave him an abusive send-off. 'As I was moving a few bits out and putting them in a taxi, the neighbour came out from over the road and said, "Haha, he's kicked you out, has he? See that smackhead. You're gonna be in the gutter with him. I can't fuckin' wait." He just made me really mad. No compassion or anything. I wanted to hit him, but I didn't.'

Stuart had helped the homeless man get clean and finally start thinking about his future. But a fortnight after the eviction, the man died of a heroin overdose. Stuart went to live on the canal.

'How did you end up on the canal with a couch, a bed and bookshelves? Were you taking the piss?' I asked.

Stuart threw his head back and cackled. 'Part of it was taking the piss,' he said. 'I was a bit further down the canal, where nobody could see me. Bollocks to this, I thought. I'll do it so everyone can fuckin' see me. I did it right in their fuckin' face, and then the police kept coming down, saying, "You can't stay here. It's public land." I said, "Well, I am a member of the fuckin' public, mate."'

'How did the telly work?' I asked.

'It was plugged into the lamp post.'

'What, you plugged the telly into the lamp post?' I said, impressed with the audacity of it all.

'No, *I* didn't. That's illegal. *I* must have been at the shop when that happened,' Stuart clarified.

'Was there a point to it, though?' I asked.

'Of course I was making a point. Obviously. Nobody should be sat there in that position. Why should I hide under the carpet because that's what they wanted me to do? I can't hide that I'm homeless because I am fuckin' homeless. What do you want me to do, hide in a fuckin' bush?'

'What happened in the end?' I asked.

'Police came down and gave me a forty-eight-hour dispersal notice not to camp anywhere within the Salford area within the next forty-eight hours. I asked, "Where can I go? I've got no roof over my head." They said, "Go to Manchester." I said: "I don't want to go to Manchester. I slept with my phone down my bollocks in Manchester and another homeless guy tried to take it off me while I was asleep."'

As a former locksmith, locked buildings didn't present much of a challenge to Stuart, and he decided to research squatting. Section 144 of the Legal Aid, Sentencing and Punishment of Offenders Act 2012 made squatting in a residential building a criminal offence,[13] but Stuart avoids police evictions by choosing commercial buildings to occupy. Still, after setting up his first squat in a decaying mansion in Eccles, he's been forced to move on from several abandoned buildings in the area, including a former vet's surgery and a disused chemist's shop. Stuart handed me a leaflet for his shelter with 'Helping homeless change lives' emblazoned across the top. 'We can sort many issues out . . . No red tape, we get things done,' the leaflet bragged. In these temporary squats, he has roughly fourteen adults with him at any given time. Stuart must stay one step ahead of the police, who have evicted him on several occasions. Stuart said bailiffs visited their squat at the vet's one evening and told him, 'There's no telling what can go on at night time.'

'What did you say?' I asked.

'I said, "If that's some sort of threat, mate, I've just told you how many people we've got here, and what kind of issues they've got. I can't guarantee your safety. You might end up in the canal at the back."'

I wondered what Stuart says to residents when they really do have to leave. 'Do you have to tell them that they're on their arse tonight?' I asked.

'I say: "Don't worry, everything is in hand."'

Stuart said he had made connections with a local taxi firm that will send a 'fleet' of drivers out when the time comes to flee a squat, and others will lend a hand when he puts a call out on social media. 'Everyone goes, "Yeah, OK, Potts, bang, bang, bang, bang. We'll be there, don't worry about it. Everything's free,"' Stuart explained.

Ironically, the police began referring homeless people to Stuart's squats. 'We got a phone call from the police the other day,' he said. '"Hi, is that Mr Potts?" I said, "Yeah." "We've got a young vulnerable lady here. She has just come out of Meadowbrook mental health unit, and she's got nowhere to go. I was just wondering if there was any room at your shelters?"'

'What did you say?'

'I said, "Are you mad? You are the ones who are kicking us out, mate."'

We laughed at the absurdity of it.

Stuart pointed out another irony: the first time the police evicted them, Manchester's mayor Andy Burnham was announcing his 'A Bed Every Night' scheme, which aimed to guarantee all rough sleepers a bed and additional support to get into secure housing.[14] In January 2017, Burnham promised to make ending rough sleeping in Manchester by 2020 one of his 'top Mayoral priorities' if he won the election.[15] It was a bold, frankly ridiculous promise, but he stormed to a landslide victory in May 2017, winning 63 per cent of the vote. He promptly donated 15 per cent of his £110,000 salary to the Greater Manchester Mayor's Charity, established to address social concerns, with homelessness as a priority. 'Rising homelessness is the issue that has defined this campaign,' he said. 'The fact it is barely getting a mention in the [2017] general election campaign tells you something about our dysfunctional political and media culture. But walk out of this building tonight and you will see the reality behind the election slogans.'[16]

Stuart tells me he had a meeting with the mayor around Christmas 2018 in a café in the city centre. Stuart claimed that Burnham assured him that the Bed Every Night scheme was successfully housing people. 'I said, "Not really, mate. You're putting people in places like Narrowgate, yeah. None of them want to go in there."' The Narrowgate is a notorious Manchester hostel that provides emergency accommodation just outside the city centre for up to thirty-five men and women from various age groups and backgrounds. They are crammed together on dozens of single beds in the same room. Stuart, the consummate straight talker, didn't hesitate to let the mayor know exactly what he thought about the place. "'You're sticking vulnerable adults in there from, I don't know, sixteen to eighteen to as old as they get, girls and males in one room,'" Stuart claimed to have told Burnham. 'You've got some people there with drug issues, some people there with alcohol issues, some people with mental health issues and some with combined issues. So, I said, "The ones that haven't got issues, by the time they've come out of there, they're drug users, drinkers. You're making the problem worse by doing that.'"

Stuart said he told the mayor that within the last forty-eight hours, he had housed eighteen people in a functioning safe space. 'We had on-site support; we had food in the cupboards; it was staffed. I said, "We've got no money. You've got all the money in the world and all the resources in the world, and you can't even do it.'"

'Fuckin' hell,' I said. 'How did he respond to all that?'

'He said: "I've got red tape, you haven't." I've got red tape! Well, fuck that shit. Solve the problem!'

In September, I met up with Stuart again on a more typical windswept and wet Manchester afternoon. As he welcomed me inside the Unicorn, a pub that had recently closed in Eccles, he told me he had been evicted from two squats since we'd last met. The pub's bar area had been transformed into an ad hoc storage facility for donated clothes and other items. I followed Stuart upstairs, where I was greeted in the lounge by other residents. I chatted to Paul Doyle, who was parked in an armchair watching Sky on a big plasma telly. Tara, his big white staff-akita cross, was mauling me with sloppy kisses as I tried to flip my tape recorder on. Paul had been homeless for several years, and had been bunking up with Stuart for months when I met him. He wasn't at all complimentary about A Bed Every Night and the Narrowgate.

'You don't get proper food,' said Paul. 'Now and again, Greggs donated. But sometimes we'd just have a bowl of soup at night.'

Stuart said he 'wouldn't put a rat' in Narrowgate, likening it to a 'refugee camp' in which 'thirty to thirty-five people are bunked up'.

Throughout my brief visit, the atmosphere was relaxed. Stuart said they all share household chores, but things can get hectic. He'd had to bounce a frying pan off another resident's head in self-defence a few months before my visit.

I met with Andy Burnham in his plush corporate city centre offices a few days after I'd left the Unicorn. I put some of Paul's claims about A Bed Every Night to him.

'I think the quality of accommodation is quite variable [and] more single-room provision would be good,' Burnham conceded. 'There are some people who really like the sort of company or camaraderie of being in a big space. Others would rather turn the key, wouldn't they?' He said that almost all the locations they operate separate women from men, but admits that there needs to be at least the option of single-room provision for women.

On the whole, Burnham considers A Bed Every Night a huge success, even crediting it with Greater Manchester's first decline in rough-sleeping numbers in eight years. The 2018 snapshot recorded 229 rough sleepers, compared to 278 the previous year. The statistics available at that time, however, told a more complex story than Burnham suggested. The number of rough sleepers in Greater Manchester had decreased, but the number of rough sleepers in *central* Manchester had climbed by 31 per cent, indicating that the problem had merely migrated to the city centre. Moreover, Burnham launched A Bed Every Night in November 2018, and the decline he cited was based on a one-night snapshot taken in autumn 2018.[17] The 2020 snapshot (the most up-to-date snapshot at the time of writing) recorded a 25 per cent decline in rough sleeping on a single night in autumn.[18]

Predictably, Burnham did not live up to his pledge to end rough sleeping in Manchester by 2020. Did he regret making it in the first place?

'I wasn't making what you would call a traditional target,' the mayor said. 'I issued my commitment to make it more of a wake-up call to the system. And I think it has had that effect.'

Burnham's advisors had told him to tone down the pledge, but he resisted. 'The team here said I should have said: "End the need for rough sleeping," because you can't force people into a shelter if they don't want to because they have a concern about it. In retrospect, if I had said "end the need for", that probably would have been a wiser thing to have done. But I wasn't in the space of wanting to play semantics with it. Honestly, I don't regret it. I feel in spirit I'm meeting it by creating four hundred places every single night from October until the middle of June.'

Burnham won the 2021 Manchester Mayoral election by another landslide. His stock rose during the pandemic when he publicly challenged the government's Covid restrictions. He said the government treated Greater Manchester like a 'sacrificial lamb' when the region was placed in one of the highest Covid tiers in 2020.[19] Burnham even got #KingoftheNorth trending on Twitter with his stand. As soon as the re-elected mayor took office, he launched a new homelessness prevention strategy and announced plans to build 30,000 social homes.[20] Even though I'm dubious about the efficacy of A Bed Every Night, I like Burnham. He seems to be a decent man who has his heart in the right place, and I think he is serious about his commitment to tackling poverty in Greater Manchester.

The government made the same promise for the whole country during the first lockdown; it's doubtful they were as sincere as Burnham, as their approach was akin to tackling a raging fire with a water pistol. After a whip-round, the Treasury coughed up £3.2 million of emergency funding to eliminate homelessness during the pandemic.[21] But when spread among the estimated 25,000 people to have slept rough the year before, it amounted to £128 per head – more an act of contempt than a serious attempt to protect the homeless.

During lockdown, I was housebound in south London and, like everybody else, prohibited from travelling outside except for exercise. But outreach workers in Manchester told me the situation was dire in the temporary placements given to rough sleepers. I heard that some were left to their own devices while drug dealers equipped with better PPE (personal protective equipment) than some NHS staff lingered outside, shotting baggies behind face masks and plastic gloves. After the government splashed out their peanuts, approximately 25 per cent of the homeless sheltered in Manchester's hotels during lockdown (roughly 47 out of 200) had left their placements, either after having been evicted due to antisocial incidents or leaving voluntarily after struggling to adapt.[22] According to one outreach worker, who wanted to remain anonymous, the city centre came to resemble 'God's waiting room' in the aftermath. He told me that dozens of rough sleepers were living on the streets, strung out on drugs or paralytic on cheap booze, unable to wash and change clothes.

On 9 October 2019, the police evicted Stuart and his squatters from the Unicorn. Stuart live-streamed the eviction on social media before moving on to the Albert Edward, another pub in Eccles. A month later, he made national headlines after disrupting a Remembrance Sunday event held at Eccles cenotaph, just over the road from the pub. 'A yob ruined a Remembrance Sunday memorial service in honour of fallen servicemen by launching a firework into a crowd of war veterans during a two-minute silence,' the *Sun* newspaper reported.[23] Stuart said the fireworks were a tribute intended to mimic a twenty-one-gun salute; many in attendance didn't see it that way when the fireworks exploded over their heads. A mini riot broke out, part of which was captured on video. Stuart can be seen on the roof of the Albert Edward, dodging traffic cones hurled up at him by furious beret-wearing army veterans. At the same time, other incensed memorial-goers grappled with police officers in an attempt to break into the pub.

If Stuart wants to run a legitimate hostel one day, this incident did nothing to further that ambition. The furore became known among locals as the Battle of the Albert Edward, and the *Manchester Evening News* reported that one Salford local decided to auction one of the cones thrown at Stuart for charity.

The man told the paper that he did it to raise money for the 'genuine homeless' and 'ex-servicemen.'[24]

The angry mob continued their attack on Stuart and his squatters online. One commenter wrote underneath a news article: 'Any sympathy I had for this group has gone. Let them sleep on park benches this winter. Nutters.' Others on social media posted comments that ranged from petty insults to more violent fantasies. Some hoped Stuart would get beaten up in prison, 'lynched', and even 'sent to the Tower of London'. One person wrote: 'I hope someone puts a rocket up his arse.'

As a nation, I feel we take Remembrance Day, the national anthem and those parasites in crowns far too seriously, but Stuart's actions were undoubtedly daft. He was arrested and later appeared in court. Salford Magistrates judge Mark Hadfield didn't buy Stuart's explanation for setting off the fireworks.

> Even if it is correct that you were handed them by another person, nobody in their right mind would think that letting them off in the middle of the ceremony shows a mark of respect. On the contrary, it shows a lack of respect. I have heard a statement from someone who served in the armed forces who was attending this event. He thought it was gunfire. This has had a detrimental effect on him, and many others like him would have been shocked.[25]

The *Sun* were on hand again to bask in the jingoist outrage, smearing Stuart with more typical red-top epithets while making sure they contrasted his actions with the tears the Queen shed at the cenotaph in Whitehall that afternoon.[26] Stuart got sixteen weeks.

Stuart and I reconvened a year later, on the last day of a scorching heatwave at the tail end of summer 2020. He had called me a week earlier to tell me about Louis, a young man he'd put up throughout the coronavirus pandemic. Stuart said that Oldham Council had instructed Louis to sleep rough at the bus station and pose for photographs to prove his homelessness after applying for assistance from them earlier in the year.

Stuart was again shirtless and as animated as ever when I greeted him outside his flat in Bury. After his sentence, he'd lost a flat he was renting in Salford and had been bounced around squalid, drug-infested hostels throughout lockdown before settling in Bury. He was still running the Shelter Project. A month before we met, he'd sent me a short video of him, Louis, three women and a man sporting a neck brace having dinner around a table on the roof of another building he'd occupied. They got kicked out by the owner before we met, and he was now scoping out other properties to occupy. He had a few in mind, but said he won't make a move 'until the moment's right'.

Sixteen weeks inside hadn't dimmed Stuart's rebellious streak. We got talking about the pandemic, the lockdown, conflicting regulations, government incompetence and all that goes with it. Stuart was not convinced by the efficacy of wearing face masks, which were mandatory accessories at the time. I shared much of the scepticism around masks, as I didn't think it was prudent to create a warm and moist house for germs in front of your gob while a killer virus was on the prowl (as many studies have shown, I was wrong about this). Nevertheless, like most people, I swallowed my reservations in return for an easy life. Not Stuart.

'I got on the bus the other week. I was in Middleton,' Stuart told me. 'Three people got off with no masks on, and I got on and the driver went, "Where's your mask?" I said, "You've let three people off with no mask; they must have got on with no mask. You never said nothing to them." He said, "You need one." I said, "Well, even you haven't got one on." He said, "I don't need one." So, I said, "Why do I then?"'

Stuart went to a local pound shop and bought himself a balaclava. He went to get on the next bus and had a barney with another driver. 'The driver said, "You can't get on with that!" I said: "It's a face-covering, innit; it's covering my face." He said, "It's not covering your mouth." I said, "No, it didn't say anything about that. It just said wear a face-covering."' The driver let him on.

As we walked towards his ground-floor one-bedroom flat, I asked him about the 'Battle of the Albert Edward' and if he regretted it.

'No!' Stuart said unequivocally. 'I didn't do it to upset anybody.' He explained that there were a couple of Harley Davidsons making just as much racket, and pointed out that he'd set the fireworks off before the silence and that the veterans were the ones kicking off during it. 'On VE day, they set millions of fireworks off. Same thing, innit!?' he said, cackling.

'Why did you plead guilty? Wouldn't you have got a trial?' I asked.

'No trial. It's only a magistrate's decision. That's fair that, innit?' he said. He played out what he thought would've happened if he'd pled not guilty. '"I'm not guilty!" "Yes, you are! And if you appeal this, we'll give you more. We'll take you all the way down to the courts in London and start your sentence again when you get there." So, you're bollocksed, aren't you?'

We filed into the living room. Louis, eighteen, was perched on a leather couch. He had a pale baby face topped with messy black hair; the rest of him was hidden underneath baggy sports gear. If you'd told me Louis was fourteen, I would've believed it. In February 2019, a week before his eighteenth birthday, he'd left his parents' home after a scuffle with a family member.

'What happened?' I asked.

Louis shifted uncomfortably in his seat and spoke at the ground. 'I think I was just getting really pissed off with something, and I tend to punch stuff. I think he's just gripped me up and said: "Don't do it." He had me by the throat. I didn't like it, so I headbutted him. I shouldn't have done that . . .' he said, trailing off, staring into the distance. Louis was visibly nervous and was constantly wringing his hands at the beginning of our conversation.

'There's lots of things we shouldn't do,' Stuart reassured him, as he tucked into a cheese toastie.

Like me, Louis had been diagnosed with ADHD when he was young, and had left school with no qualifications and as many job prospects. After his mum kicked him out, he visited Oldham's Civic Centre to seek help with his housing, and there he participated in *Pauper Idol* – officially known as a homelessness application. Louis's audition wasn't good enough for the judges.

'I told them my situation and they basically said to me, "[You're] not a priority." And they wanted to know what bus stop I was staying at, and they were going to take pictures of me for three nights in a row staying there,' Louis explained.

I looked aghast at Stuart. 'Can you believe that?' I said.

'There's nothing I don't believe any more,' Stuart said, his mouth full of cheese toastie. 'Nothing fazes me any more.'

When I heard about Louis's ordeal with the council, I felt even more guilty about the three social homes I had given up when I lived in the town ten years earlier. Things have got worse in that time. Oldham Council chopped 20,000 people from their council housing waiting list in 2019 to prioritise the most in need.[27] 'Most in need' is quite a broad term, but the council defines it as those who live in homeless households, people with serious medical conditions and high-risk victims of domestic violence. You'd think, after going to sleep rough on the streets at the age of seventeen, that Louis would have satisfied their criteria. As is the case with many local authorities, it's never clear how homeless one needs to be in order to get help.

Louis doesn't know if the council came to photograph him, as he didn't stay in one place during his time on the street. He moved around, roughing it on a roundabout outside Oldham town centre, in a field and on friends' sofas.

'How did you feed yourself?' I asked.

'Luckily enough, it was my birthday, so I was just able to get what I needed. Got my food for the day. I got a Maccy breakfast in the morning, and then I'd go and get a pizza at night. And if I didn't eat all that pizza – instead of throwing it – I'd just put it back in my suitcase or something and save it for the morning.'

Louis got very little sleep while on the street, and spent most of his time roaming the length and breadth of the borough.

'I was on one of the bus stops further down the road. It was getting cold up at the top, so I thought if I come back down to the city [Manchester], it's gonna be a little bit warmer, but I didn't want to go into the city. I didn't feel safe there,' Louis said.

He spent a night underneath his coat in a field outside his aunt's house. It was the middle of a bitterly cold February, and I wondered how anyone could sleep in those conditions, but Louis just about managed it: 'All you've got to do is close your eyes and fight through, and eventually you'll end up dropping off, but you'll wake up at three in the morning, freezing, going, "Fuck this!"'

'How many nights on the street in total?' I asked.

'About a week in total, but it wasn't for a whole complete week. It was sort of here and there.'

So many of Louis's experiences echo my own. We're both from Oldham; we've both been diagnosed with ADHD ('this imaginary thing', as Louis describes it); I share his lack of confidence; and I too used to hide underneath a mountain of baggy fabric. We spent a similar amount of time on the street. Like Louis, I probably spent a week rough sleeping over three weeks or so, but at least I had a tent, and it was in sleepy Saddleworth in the middle of spring. By the time I was in that tent, I was twenty-six years old and had just graduated from university; Louis was a seventeen-year-old kid sleeping rough at the height of winter in one of the roughest towns in the country.

'Did you think you were going to be stuck in this position, or did you have hope?' I asked.

'I just thought, you know what, this is life now. I've just got to get on with it and keep my head down.'

Louis eventually approached his aunt for help, and she housed him throughout the lockdown. He contributed £200 a month from his Universal Credit to her. But his aunt was pregnant, and Louis had to leave when she was about to give birth. He went into temporary accommodation and accessed Night Stop, emergency overnight accommodation provided by volunteers who host young rough sleepers in their houses.

'I didn't really like it,' Louis told me. 'I'm a very nervous person. I felt like I was intruding on the people I was staying with.'

'Have you always been nervous?' I asked.

'Yeah,' admitted Louis.

'Where do you think that comes from?' I asked him, doing my best impression of a therapist.

'Err, just lacking in self-confidence. It was all right. I'm thankful for the people who put me up.'

The conversation turned back to the council and the lack of help they've provided. Louis claimed to have a social worker, but said he'd never heard from them or social services. He said he was still not registered on the council's waiting list for social housing, and thought it wouldn't do him any good anyway.

'It would be all right if I walked in there with my hijab on . . .' Louis said.

'That's not even the case. They get turned away, mate,' Stuart interrupted.

'Really? Wow,' Louis said incredulously.

'Yeah, yeah, really,' said Stuart.

'It's a myth, that, you know,' I said.

'It is a myth,' Stuart agreed. 'And, like I said to you, that's just to make you argue, "It's his fault, it's her fault."'

Fleet Street, the commentators who scribble for them, and

even government ministers regularly disseminate the well-worn prejudice that minorities and migrants are prioritised over white Britons by housing services, the welfare system and employers. The fact is, for migrants to qualify for social housing, they need to have settled status, be a European Economic Area worker or a refugee – and the same goes for accessing benefits. Most migrants do not qualify for social housing, and there's not a shred of evidence that local authorities give them favourable treatment.

We talked a bit more about Louis's hopes for the future. He wasn't sure about the way forward. When we met, in the middle of the pandemic, the economy was haemorrhaging the kind of low-skilled jobs that Louis was barely qualified to do, and Brexit was about to make life even more uncertain. I couldn't help pitying him. Here was a young man who was more than capable of getting on in life. He wasn't dependent on hard drugs or alcohol, and there was no serious illness holding him back. Self-belief was all that was lacking. The right encouragement, proper housing and support was all he would need to make progress.

In response to Louis's claims about being told to pose for pictures at his bus stop, an Oldham Council spokesperson said:

> We do not comment on individual cases. However, we can confirm that this is not Oldham's [sic] Council's response to a young person presenting as homeless. There are a number of protocols in place to ensure that we are compliant and provide the best possible customer service. We do not take photographs of anyone sleeping rough – we are here to support anyone in Oldham that finds themselves homeless or at risk of

homelessness. For any young person (anyone under the age of 18) presenting as homeless, we would undertake a joint assessment with Children's Services and a homelessness assessment would be carried out to understand the person's needs and which options are available for them.

I'm in two minds about Louis's story. Claiming that a council told you to pose for photographs at a bus stop to prove your homelessness is just the kind of thing that a mixed-up adolescent would make up. However, it's not that far-fetched. Stuart said he'd heard that story from at least four other homeless people he'd worked with; I've heard similar stories from homeless people all over the country. And I spent a night on the street after a housing advisor told me I wasn't vulnerable enough.

I said my goodbyes to Louis and walked with Stuart to my bus stop.

'Do you think he'll be all right?' I asked.

'Yeah, we'll get him sorted,' Stuart said.

Stuart has been doing this for nearly five years, and as well as putting up Louis and a few others, he's about to jump back into the cat-and-mouse game with the police.

'Do you ever get tired of doing this?' I asked.

'A little bit. It's like hitting a brick wall, innit.'

'Does it make you wanna give up? I think I would've jacked it in by now.'

Stuart laughed. 'No, no, no. The end result does get people re-housed. Even with all that fuckin' mayhem with the firework incident and all that.'

Stuart and I parted ways at the bus stop. We've kept in touch, and he rings me now and again to provide updates. The last time we spoke, in January 2020, five more people had crammed into his flat and Louis had moved to Wales with his girlfriend.

I admire Stuart for his audacity and compassion, but he shouldn't have to be doing this. The fact that people like him are squatting in abandoned buildings to house homeless people shows how decrepit housing in the UK has become, and it's only going to get harder for people like Stuart to help. In their 2019 manifesto, the Conservatives pledged to crack down on squatting, promising to give the police 'new powers to arrest and seize the property and vehicles of trespassers who set up unauthorised encampments'. They also pledged to make 'intentional trespass' a criminal offence.[28]

As well as criminalising the homeless, the government are committed to making it even harder for them to secure housing. In 2012, the ConDem coalition raised discounts under the Right to Buy scheme after sales slumped following the financial crisis in 2007–8. The coalition assured the public that there was no need to worry, as they committed to replacing homes sold under Right to Buy on a 'one-to-one basis' with new 'affordable' rental properties.[29] Predictably, the government didn't meet their commitment. Per the government's own figures, local authorities have sold 94,093 social homes under Right to Buy since 2012; over the same period, only 33,238 'affordable' properties have been acquired.[30] This looks like a shortfall of 60,855 homes. Well, it does to any rational person, but the government built a fudge into these figures from the beginning. The Tories only committed to replace housing stock that exceeded the Treasury's projection for homes sold *before* the rise in discounts. As a result, they claim to be only 10,576 homes short of their replacement target of 43,814.[31] So, theoretically, if the Treasury projected 5,000 house sales in a year without the rise in discounts, and then 5,001 homes were sold, the government would only need to build one additional 'affordable home' to live up to their one-for-one policy. Of course, the homes the government builds are not one-for-one at all, as these 'affordable homes' can charge up to 80 per cent of local market rents;[32] the average rent for a two-bedroom socially rented property can be 30 per cent cheaper than 'affordable' rents.[33]

In 2021, the government announced plans to enable councils to use 40 per cent of receipts from Right to Buy sales on new affordable and social housing.[34] This doesn't nearly go far enough. The National Housing Federation claims that the number of people in need of social housing in Britain has reached 3.8 million (1.6 million households).[35] Nothing short of a radical and nationwide social-home-building programme will plug this gap and stop people like Stuart from having to break into abandoned buildings to secure a basic human right.

Solving homelessness is about more than putting a roof over someone's head. As well as building homes, we must integrate them with the relevant social care and support services. The country saw the efficacy of this approach during the pandemic. After a poor start, the government passed the Everyone In scheme, emergency measures to house rough sleepers during the first UK lockdown. Local authorities and an army of volunteers from various homeless charities mobilised and helped 37,430 people into temporary places in budget hotels, delivering them hot meals and support from a secure and settled base. In January 2021, the government reported that the scheme had helped 26,167 people move into permanent accommodation.[36]

Everyone In was effectively the UK's most comprehensive trial of Housing First to date. Housing First prioritises providing homeless people with a home in the first instance, and then wraparound support tailored specifically to their needs. The policy has been highly successful in tackling, if not eliminating, homelessness in other countries. Everyone In provided more evidence that Housing First is the correct approach. The chronically homeless – rough sleepers and people entangled in the emergency hostel system – often have acute mental illnesses and suffer from addiction; simply giving them a bed for the night will not solve their problems.

Chapter Six

Dependency

When I got accepted at Manchester Metropolitan University (MMU), I believed I could finally escape all the chaos and instability of my adolescence: leave it in the past, move on and plot a clear path. Even if I wasn't conscious of it, the baggage I thought I'd left behind had travelled with me to Mossley – and it was going to bring me down.

Me and booze didn't hit it off from the start. I was fifteen and living in Nelson Avenue when I first lifted a bottle of white shite to my lips. Carter was rumoured to be in a young offender's prison by then, and I don't know what had become of Lloyd. A fresh cohort of mixed-up misfits eventually replaced them. I had become the long-timer at the unit, and had taken over from Lucy as the ringleader of mischief. As part of my new role, I decided to recruit Peter, a pockmarked fifteen-year-old who had enough bum fluff and pluck to convince the shopkeepers in the area that he was of age, on a booze-buying mission. I'd had a tipple in the past, but only the odd luminous alcopop. Now I wanted the real deal.

Peter took to the booze mission with alacrity and, after a few attempts at different shops, he managed to get his hands on a couple of two-litre bottles of White Lightning. We had one each and competed to see who could swig from theirs the longest. This was less a test of oesophageal elasticity than of one's gag reflex. The acidic bile, with its acrid chemical flavour – which was supposed to approximate apples, but didn't come close – tasted so bad that a toilet would bring it back up. Still, it did the trick. I was spinning around in circles, chugging that putrid shite – until, very quickly, my head started spinning all on its own. I got so drunk that I blacked out on a Chadderton pavement and woke up in the early hours of the morning on a gurney in the A&E department of the Royal Oldham hospital, where an irritable nurse was monitoring my blood pressure.

What began as a fairly typical foray into adolescent drinking with friends quickly descended into a solitary pursuit of pain relief. This habit really took off when I experienced my first break-up. I was in a relationship with Michelle, one of the new girls at Nelson Avenue. The relationship lasted about ten minutes, but she was my first girlfriend and I believed I was in love with her. I even lost my virginity to her, a trembling, anxious fumble one night in her bedroom on a rickety single bed, which was interrupted several times by her giggling fits. 'You look like you're wearing the *Scream* mask,' she said during one interlude. As bad as the sex was, it made me feel like we'd last forever; she didn't feel the same. Michelle was far more experienced than me, and my clinginess and saccharine gushing were about as attractive as a plastic magnet. She ended up with Peter, my drinking buddy. Usually, when you break up with someone, you don't have to carry on living with them; you certainly don't have to hear them sleep with one of your close friends every night in a neighbouring room.

I quickly learned that, although it didn't cure the pain of rejection and failure, alcohol pushed negative feelings to the fringes of my mind. I experienced failure so often that solo drinking sessions became a consolatory ritual throughout my time at university. When I enrolled in 2010, at the age of twenty-three, I hadn't been in mainstream education since I was ten. I'd written essays on the Access to Higher Education course, but the assignments weren't as demanding or as stringently marked as they were at university. During one introductory seminar, I can recall my professor informing the class that 'it's called reading a degree for a reason' as he presented us with a dauntingly extensive reading list. At that point in my life, I had scarcely read a book from cover to cover – apart from *Harry Potter*.

Feeling alienated among one's peers isn't a unique experience. Still, I felt like a square peg being thrust violently into a round hole when I was around my fellow undergrads. They seemed well-rounded, stable and put together, while I was all scuffed with sharp edges. Adding to the ostracisation I felt was my own inverted snobbery. Social class, what it is and where I fit into it, is something I have torn my hair out over my entire life. Both of my working-class grandparents ascended the social ladder when they became schoolteachers; Mum was educated at a posh prep school where my grandad taught, and my dad is a lawyer and a part-time judge. All of these things put me firmly in the category of the middle class. However, I spent my early years in poverty and my teens in care; I lived on council estates in the most deprived areas in the country, and have been skint for most of my adulthood. All of these things would earn me a working-class badge. So, I'm in class limbo, fitting in with everyone and no one at the same time.

I resented middle-class people: their well-spoken tones, the easy ride I perceived they'd had and – to put on my 'woke pants' for a moment – their privilege. As I advance further into middle age, this prejudice is steadily leaving me. I have no right to assume that someone's had an easier time than me because they went to a fancy school, use fancy words and wear fancy pants. Nevertheless, this is how I felt at university. I found myself isolated because of it and, on the whole, was left to deal with the pressures of higher education on my own.

My grades in my first year were mediocre. Compounding my miserable experience at university was my imploding personal life.

Grandma had moved out of the north-west before I enrolled at MMU, and she'd relocated to Birmingham, where she'd lived in a warden-controlled bungalow. When I'd visited her, she had still been the same old Grandma, only frailer, with fewer marbles rattling around upstairs. She had been hospitalised in the spring of 2011 with a renal infection and developed bed sores due to negligence. These became infected, causing her to become fatally ill. She was moved into a hospice, which may as well have been called God's Waiting Room.

A few months later, I was high on endorphins during the middle of a hike on Saddleworth Moor when I got a call from Mum.

'Grandma's about to die. Can you make it to Birmingham?' she said.

That brought me back down to earth. Her death was something I had prepared for, but that didn't soften the impact.

When I visited Grandma's room to say goodbye, she registered my presence, but I'm not sure she knew who I was. She was skeletal and couldn't speak. I found it too painful to look at her, so, along with Mum, my uncles, aunties and cousins, I went and crammed into a small room, where we watched the 2011 London riots rage on rolling news coverage and waited for the inevitable. Grandma died, and then my grandad died a few months later. I was very close to Grandma. I rang her at least once a week, and she was always the first person I leaned on and asked for guidance in times of need. Now, I can scarcely remember her face and I can't bring myself to look at pictures of her.

Ten years after her death, as I was sifting through the mountain of my social services records, I came across a four-page letter written in elegant handwriting that was unmistakably Grandma's. She had written to the education authority in 1999 to ask that I be removed from Dippydale and placed in a school that adopted a non-punitive approach to my behaviour. She wrote about how the school placed too much emphasis on early traumas and failed to deal with my underlying neurological condition. She argued that confrontational behavioural modification made my behaviour towards authority figures worse; the school was punishing me for behaviour I couldn't help, which made me confused about my identity and made me feel like a failure.

'Any one individual who has taken care of Daniel on a round-the-clock basis can understand his inner confusion and turmoil of emotions – hurt and bewilderment [at] other people's reaction to him; ashamed [of] his own reaction to them; frustrated and angry because he cannot relate to other people's judgements,' Grandma wrote. She added: 'To send him to an EBD [Emotional and Behavioural Difficulties] school is on a par to denying glasses but offering a hearing aid to a poorly sighted child. It is not acceptable in a civilised society to be punished for having a disability, and Daniel is being denied rights which should not even be brought into question.'

I found myself pausing many times as I read her words. Of all the many things that were said about me in the voluminous stacks of records, this letter was the only thing written in my defence. Then this line finished me: 'Even at the age of twelve, Danny asks at the end of the day: "Have I been good today?"'

I broke down in tears. I have an ADHD brain that is constantly bombarded with impulses to interrupt, blurt out and fidget, and I was constantly in trouble for it, being told ad nauseum that there was something wrong with me and I needed to change. I was obsessed with my behaviour. I wanted more than anyone to correct it, but this was a battle that only the passage of time could win. Grandma understood this. She understood me. I haven't confronted her death, but reading her letter made me realise how much I miss her. I'll never see her again, but I know she was there for me.

Even though I can't point to the loss of my grandparents as the key reason for my ending up with nothing, their deaths seemed to trap me in the dysfunctional maze that was my life at the time. After they passed away, I drank, and drank, and drank some more. I didn't stop for months. Ollie, my brother, had just turned twenty-one. He was homeless at the time and bouncing around Oldham's hostel system. He was already teetering on the edge of sanity before Grandma died; her death sent him over it. He came to live with me for the rest of summer 2011, and for the next two months it was like we were in a self-destructive drinking contest with each other.

Ollie and I are brothers, but you'd never know it from appearance alone. I'm tall and broad-shouldered, with hazel eyes and a long face topped with uncooperative mousy-brown hair. Ollie is slight, with brown eyes and soft features framed by jet-black hair. I'm uncomfortable in my own skin, scared of my own shadow; Ollie is completely unfazed and incapable of embarrassment. But spend any time in our company and you'll soon figure out that we hatched in the same nest. Our voices are identical; we have the same sense of (or lack of, depending on your perspective) humour; we share similar interests; and have developed such specific colloquialisms that we almost speak to each other in our own language. We are close, is what I'm trying to say. We've faced similar challenges, too. We were both diagnosed with neurological disorders in childhood; we both attended special-education schools; we've both lived in semi-independent supported accommodation, struggled with dependency and ended up homeless.

I wouldn't know if I was in the grips of depression when Ollie came to stay, because I didn't bother going to the doctors to find out, even though my local surgery was less than a hundred yards down the road. With the benefit of hindsight, I think depression would have been an easy diagnosis for a doctor to make. I drank myself into a stupor most days from my bed, which I seldom left. Ollie and I had fallen into a dreadful sleeping pattern. We'd binge-watch TV or game until our eyes closed around dawn, then wake up at dusk to repeat the whole cycle. It's not that I didn't want to get up and get on. I physically couldn't do it. It was as if my subconscious was hibernating and had dragged my body along to somewhere that my conscious mind – the part of me that just wanted to get on with it – couldn't escape.

Even if I had visited the surgery, my GP would probably have fobbed me off with some happy pills and a referral to a specialist, which could have taken the best part of a year to materialise. According to the Royal College of Psychiatrists, 64 per cent of patients wait more than four weeks for an appointment after initial assessment, while 23 per cent wait over three months, and 11 per cent wait longer than six months. Other patients suffering from depression, anxiety, and suicidal ideation could be left waiting for four years for treatment.[1]

I was Ollie's only source of income at the time, and because of this I had even fewer reasons to rise from my pit, as he sat at my beck and call for shop runs, launderette trips and takeaway collections. He was the pissed-up Manc Jeeves to my pissed-up Manc Wooster. This involved trusting our kid with my bank card and PIN – a mistake, because Ollie is about as trustworthy as a magpie left in charge of a jewellery store. We were soon at each other's throats.

Ollie is simultaneously a brilliant and terrible liar. Brilliant in the sense that he tells his tall tales, porkies, fibs, cock-and-bull stories, mistruths and half-truths with unblinking conviction and forthrightness; terrible because they're spectacularly il-logical and obvious lies.

Ollie had a habit of buying himself booze on top of the other groceries on the shopping list. He clearly had an inflated idea about how much money I had, and thought I wouldn't notice the odd tenner missing from my balance.

'How come you spent forty quid?' I asked him after one shopping trip. I knew he had withdrawn an extra tenner from the cash machine because I saw the withdrawal on my statement, but I played dumb in the hope that he would confess.

'That's how much it cost,' he lied.

'Odge [his nickname], I know you've nicked a tenner. It's on my statement,' I said, turning my phone around to show him.

'No, I didn't!' he insisted furiously.

'Yeah, you did. You've nicked it to buy beer! I can smell it on you!'

We continued like this until Ollie got a temporary place in a hostel in Oldham that October. At least, that's what he told me at the time.

Ollie had been sober for five years when I caught up with him at my parents' house at the end of spring 2021. He's a lot more coherent these days, looks after himself well and is devoted to Hershey, his gorgeous black-and-chocolate-brown Alsatian-collie cross.

When Ollie left my flat in 2011, he hadn't left for a hostel after all. He'd somehow got his hands on a fat wad of cash, and had gone on a bender in London.

'I was just fucked out of my head. I spent about five hundred quid in one night,' he told me. Ollie went on a solo pub crawl in the capital, which left him penniless and hungover the next morning. A bender like that would leave me incapacitated for days, but Ollie could just crack on with the hair of the dog.

'What's the most you could put away, back in the day?' I asked.

'About twenty or thirty cans,' he said.

'Fuck off! Really?'

'Yeah. Twenty pints, probably. If I wanted to.'

'Were you paralytic in London?'

'Nah, I never get like that, no matter how much I've drunk. It was just another drink, like coffee.'

Even though he could put them away, it doesn't explain how he frittered away £500 in one night. But Ollie can't remember all the details; there have been many benders since then. When he noticed his empty pockets the morning after, he realised he had nowhere to stay, so he walked into a police station to try and get arrested.

'I said, "I'm wanted,"' he told me. I was doubled over in stitches – I'd never heard this story before.

The police didn't oblige him, so he marched across the street, found a brick, and hurled it through a shop window. They still wouldn't nick him. Ollie then spent five days in London, wandering the streets and using his concessionary bus pass to sleep on the night services.

'I was really thirsty, and I hadn't had water for a day or so. So, I went outside London. I had to get into this hospital and sneak into the bathroom to get a drink of tap water just to rejuvenate myself. And then I would steal the odd Lucozade or something from the shop,' Ollie said.

That made no sense. Why bother sneaking into a hospital for refreshment if you're going to steal a soft drink afterwards? He didn't know.

'Why didn't you try to get back home?' I asked.

'I just felt out of it. Lifeless. I can't imagine being homeless in London, though,' he said.

'Well, you were for a week.'

'Yeah, but imagine long term. Them people begging.'

'Were you not worried that you were gonna smell?'

'I didn't give a fuck. My head was blank.'

Instead of begging, he carried on stealing sustenance from shops to keep himself going. My brother doesn't wear his heart on his sleeve as much as I do. He's gentle, but tough, and doesn't like to think of himself as vulnerable. I imagine he sees his time on the street and in hostels as an embarrassing period of weakness.

'I didn't really play victim,' he said, when I asked him if he considered himself a homeless person. He managed to sneak on to a train back to Manchester when Mum rang him to tell him he'd got a place at an emergency hostel in Oldham. He stayed there for a few months in early 2012 until he found his own place, a council flat outside the town centre.

'I got my own house. Fuck all help from social services! I went out every week and looked,' he said.

Ollie carried on drinking heavily for three years, and graduated to hard drugs, including coke, speed, ketamine, psychedelics and anything else he could get his hands on (except for crack and smack). I remember visiting him during this period of excess. His face was bulbous and purple, and it sounded like he was snoring even when he was awake. I thought he was going to die. Then one day, he just stopped. By then, he had fallen into similar social circles to the one I had in Mossley: predominantly middle-aged drunken men at his local pub and twenty-something tearaways on his estate. They were broken, always in crisis, and their lives revolved around their next fix. Ollie said he saw his future in them and was scared sober.

Nearly all the former addicts I've spoken to throughout the years have achieved sobriety after a turn of fortune or a moment of clarity. I rarely hear that social services or the health system guided them there. In Ollie's case, this is shameful. Social workers visited him multiple times a week during the first few years he spent on his own; they saw the same dishevelled, vulnerable young man that I did, and yet, as far as I can tell, they functioned solely as a chauffeur service to my brother. They'd collect him at his flat and ferry him to appointments, to the launderette and to buy groceries, but failed to see the walking crisis in front of them and get him the help that he really needed.

I had already missed a month of my second year when Ollie left, but I forced myself back to MMU's lecture halls. Despite all the chaos and grief, I was still determined to complete my degree and finish something for once in my life. I tried to buckle down with my studies, but my ballooning body would soon cause me to relapse.

Months of idleness had led me to pile on extra and unwanted flesh at an alarmingly rapid rate. Ever since I'd given up on my dreams of becoming a stuntman, my body had grown steadily sideways, but by Christmas 2011 I had become an out-and-out bloater. I wore layers upon layers of baggy clothes, but this only increased the amount of flop sweat welding my soggy fringe to my purpling forehead, so I couldn't win. The shame kept me inside. I missed most of my lectures and seminars, yet, somehow, I managed to scrape together a 2:1 at the end of my second year in 2012. I even received a few firsts on some assignments. But for every first, there was a Desmond just around the corner. I responded to both grades in much the same way: If I scored a first or a 2:1, I'd go out – usually on my own – on a celebratory bender followed by a week of inertia. A lower grade would result in a consolatory bender, definitely alone, with harder stuff and even more inertia.

In summer 2012, my mum suffered multiple organ failure. I'm ashamed to say that when Dad rang to tell me the news, I felt no sense of alarm or sadness. By this time, my life felt like fiction; like I was a discardable character in a bleak William Golding novel. *This is the part where my mum dies*, I thought when I got off the phone. I was throwing booze and all manner of processed junk down my gullet on a daily basis, had completely neglected exercise, and avoided social situations like the plague. I had a tendency to blot out my pain with alcohol; when I lost consciousness, I thought I wouldn't mind if I didn't come back around. The truth is, I didn't care about myself or anybody else.

I should have been studying for my finals and preparing for my future as a graduate; instead, I was, unwittingly, preparing for a life of homelessness and social exclusion. I had a social life of sorts by the time I entered my third year in 2013 – but instead of dating, attending parties or enjoying nights on the town with my peers, I was mixing with heroin addicts and middle-aged alcoholics on my estate.

I met Walter and Rover at around this time, although I don't know exactly how – probably on a drunken walk back from the off-licence at the end of my street. Walter would ultimately intro-duce me to Emmaus Mossley after I fled my flat, but before that, our friendship mostly revolved around binge-drinking while binge-watching shite daytime telly in his living room across the road. Walter mixed in a large social circle comprising a motley crew of interesting misfits who filed in and out of his living room throughout the day. There was Steve, a talented graffiti artist who made a score or two for personalising people's wheelie bins in the area; Bruno, a Guinean chef whose signature dish was salt, salt and more salt with a hint of meat; two obnoxious German men, who were tolerated but not particularly liked; Ron, an ageing punk who always told you the same tall story about the time he 'snuck into Glastonbury'; and a few other supporting cast members who had occasional cameos. When Walter was sober, or only one litre of cider deep, he was fun to be around, but he would become belligerent – borderline tyrannical – when he'd supped two or three litres.

'You don't know fuck all about life,' he spat at me one evening. This came completely out of the blue, as we'd been happily lis-tening to *Dub Side of the Moon* just moments earlier.

'What are you on about?' I said.

'Ye, see you're fuckin' ignorant, man. Y'know what I fuckin' mean.'

'I'm just sat 'ere,' I protested.

'You don't know fuck all about life, man!' he repeated. 'I'm a fuckin' welder, a fuckin' working man. Y'know what I mean. When have you had to fuckin' sleep outside your fuckin' missus' house 'cause she wunt let you in?'

'I haven't. Why, have you?'

'Ah, get the fuck out of it, man!'

I'd usually steer him on to another topic, placate him with more booze or make him laugh before it escalated any further.

I spent more and more time on Walter's sofa instead of in MMU's libraries and lecture theatres. I missed so many months in my second and third years that some of my classmates were convinced I'd dropped out – yet I still managed to collect enough of my senses to complete assignments and attend all my exams.

My dysfunction, just like everything in my life up to that point, wasn't consistent. It was broken up by intermittent periods of mental clarity and dedication, which allowed me to complete my degree. After my finals, however, I was finished mentally. It had long been my default state for paranoia to be whispering in the recesses of my mind, but by the time I was due to graduate, every synapse was screaming with it. Not only was I checking my cupboards for phantom burglars, I was also filming myself do it. I did this so that if a pang of fear propelled me out of sleep in the middle of the night, I could reach for my phone and watch my crazed security check for reassurance. I had spent the last of my student loans and grants; prioritising drink and takeaways over rent left me in thousands of pounds of arrears. I was in no fit state to get a job. I could barely maintain eye contact with a stranger without breaking out in nervous sweating episodes, let alone attend an interview.

I wish I had a more sensational story to tell about my descent to the streets. I don't even have any interesting drunken escapades to speak of, as most of my bingeing took place alone, in front of a screen, during the early hours of the morning. Then, one afternoon, I just left with my tent. The only contact I'd received from my landlord at that time had been a few polite reminders to pay off my debts. I could've stayed, contacted my landlord and arranged to pay him instalments to cover my outstanding rent. I could've reached out to Tameside social services, the Citizens Advice Bureau and other agencies for support. I probably could've gone back to live with my parents. I did none of those things. Instead, I went to live in a tent and on random sofas for a few weeks, before voluntarily moving into a modern workhouse.

Homelessness isn't a uniform condition, yet when looking into the lives of homeless people, you'll often find mental illness and substance dependency. This dependency may have been the *reason* people were homeless, or it could have developed while they were on the streets. Of course, not everyone who becomes homeless has drug and alcohol problems, and not every homeless person abuses drugs and alcohol. However, Crisis reported that levels of drug and alcohol abuse are relatively high among the homeless population. At first contact, 60 per cent of Crisis Skylight clients report a history of mental health and drug and alcohol problems.[2]

Austerity has crippled addiction and mental health services. The lack of funding can leave people waiting for up to four years for their initial assessment, making it more likely they'll deteriorate, lose their jobs and relationships, and end up on the streets or in the hostel system. It looks like things are only going to get worse. In 2020, the Royal College of Psychiatrists said psychiatrists were expecting a 'tsunami of mental illness' after the pandemic,[3] and a public health analysis by the College found that high-risk drinking had almost doubled in the UK population, from over 4.8 million people in February 2020 to 8.4 million in September 2020. According to the National Drug Treatment Monitoring System, the numbers of people seeking help for opiate addiction are also on the rise. Over 500 new cases were reported in April 2020, compared to data recorded in April 2019 – a rise of 20 per cent.[4]

I had problems with drink and mental illness, and had made myself homeless. I had a tough ordeal, but it was an easy ride compared to the struggles of some. I avoided the sharp end of poverty because my bingeing was inconsistent and was subject to my mood, which could swing from the top of Everest to the Dead Sea. Because of this, I was able to bounce back relatively easily from rock bottom. Others must struggle for far longer.

I hadn't seen Noel for four years when he picked me up outside a train station in rural Derbyshire in the middle of a scorching heatwave in May 2020. I first met him in Emmaus St Albans in 2015. I had assumed he was a staff member when I greeted him inside the community's second-hand furniture shop on my first day. Noel was well-spoken, self-assured and intelligent, all of which lent him a commanding presence. I was shocked when I learned he was a Companion, and even more shocked when he told me he had been a drug addict for over half of his life.

I warmed to him straight away. We are both northern, and have similar backgrounds and interests. We both support

Manchester United, and we viewed Emmaus in a similar light. We also inspired each other to make changes in our lives. We would spend hours on the local playing fields, kicking a ball to one another while discussing and dissecting our pasts, making sense of things – as much as one can make sense of something so warped and disjointed – and trying to figure out a way forward.

Noel left the community before Emmaus launched me for putting my fist through that van window in early 2016. He had left to take a job with an engineering firm in Buckinghamshire and appeared to have put his life back together. A few months later, though, he went off the radar. He didn't answer calls, texts or emails. I didn't have contact details for any of his family or friends, so I couldn't confirm his well-being. I was starting to fear the worst until he contacted me out of the blue one afternoon in late 2016. It turned out things had broken down in Bucks, and he had gone to live at a Christian rehab to finally kick methadone.

Looking back at our time in St Albans, there were clear signs of his suffering. His skin was pale, and he always had to keep a towel handy to mop up the pools of sweat that collected on his brow – a side effect of methadone use. But when we reunited in 2020, as the first lockdown restrictions were eased in England, Noel was a man transformed. He looked healthy and full of energy; colour had returned to his cheeks, and there wasn't a face towel in sight. He had three years of sobriety under his belt, had a top job in electrical engineering and was in a happy relationship.

As I entered his house, I was met by Frankie, his soppy and

ultra-hyper Staffordshire bull terrier, who greeted me like a long-lost brother. At forty, Noel was finally settled, but before beginning his new life here, he'd abused all manner of drugs for the last two decades. He'd served two stints in prison, got married, got divorced, all while flitting from job to job across the length and breadth of the UK.

After catching up, we decided to take Frankie for a walk across the clusters of thickets and unkempt fields that lie beyond his spacious back garden. It's never easy to transform a cosy catch-up into a deep discussion about drug abuse. Even though Noel is open and frank about it and was more than happy to discuss it with me, a conspicuous recorder or notepad can put off the most gregarious of people.

So, I held off until the right moment, which came right after dinner, when Noel invited me into his shed for a spliff. I hadn't touched cannabis for at least five years. Every time I smoke it, I feel like my heart will beat out of my chest. Noel said I was probably putting too much weed in my joints.

'I only sprinkle it lightly on top of the baccy,' Noel said, as he did just that.

After the joint, we settled in front of Netflix in the living room. Noel was right. I had no palpitations; I wasn't even sure if it was having any effect on me at all, as I sank into one of his deep-cushioned settees while giggling at nothing in particular.

I pulled out my recorder and held it aloft. 'Let's talk about drugs!' I announced.

'Yeah, why not?' Noel said.

'When did you start taking them?' I asked.

Noel explained that he struggles to remember dates, as much

of his life is a blur, but he said he thought he'd first dabbled in weed in his early teens, before graduating to speed after leaving school during the Happy Hardcore scene in the early nineties. Before that, Noel had been a dedicated student and a decent athlete; he'd even had trials at Norwich City while growing up on the east coast. He'd moved to Chesterfield with his family during his last year at school, which had disrupted his secondary education and crushed his football dreams.

'How do you go from taking speed at raves to taking heroin?' I asked.

'I had a car crash when I was about seventeen. I chopped my eyelid off and went through the window of a car,' he said.

'Fuckin' hell, who was driving?' I asked.

'My mate. My mum said, "Don't get in that." Anyway, I jumped in the car and we shot off, and he was flying. If some fucker had stood out in front of him, they'd be in trouble.'

Noel's friend had lied about getting his licence, and his inexperience, coupled with high speeds, caused him to lose control and career off the road. The only thing Noel remembered from the accident before everything went black was veering towards a lamp post at ninety miles per hour.

'I just came round outside with a guy with his arm around me. He said I was talking for ages, but I can't remember.'

Noel's friend came off a lot worse in the accident – he shattered all the bones in his legs – but Noel came away with a deep laceration on his face, which, he said, left him looking like the Elephant Man. He'd since had two operations to conceal the damage.

I was beginning to connect the dots in my mind: Noel suffered a traumatic accident that left him scarred and in chronic pain; this must be where the heroin came in. 'So, you started on the gear to numb the pain?'

'No,' Noel said, unequivocally. 'In rehab it's all about finding *why*. I honestly don't know. I could have every excuse: "Oh, I smashed my head, I'm a bit mental, and that's what did it."'

'Did it?' I asked.

'In a way, but at the same time, all the fucking people I was hanging about with ended up doing it. What do you think would have happened, anyway?'

'Were you not worried about the stigma that comes with heroin use?' I asked. I told him that taking heroin was taboo when I was growing up, that the people I knew treated users like pariahs, so I wondered why he gravitated towards it.

'Heroin was the drug of choice around here. I could look at a photo from school and go: "He's on it, he's dead, he's on it." The girls were on it as well. Even in the nice areas. It was everywhere.'

Noel was flying in the clouds on a speed binge, from which he came crashing down to earth a few days later at a house party. Some of his mates were smoking 'Brown' and he took a few tokes.

'I didn't even know it was heroin. I was that naive. I didn't twig heroin was Brown,' he said.

Speed made him feel invincible, and he would binge on it for days without sleep until everything became trippy and a gut-wrenching comedown set in. Heroin made the hangover feel like a non-entity. Pretty soon, smoking it had negligible effects on him, so he found a friend who used needles and followed their lead. 'As soon as I did that . . . game over.'

'How often did you take it after that?' I asked.

'Oh, every day. You've gotta have it every day. You can't miss a day,' he said.

Heroin is a seductive monster, the kind that cradles you lovingly in its arms on the honeymoon, then dominates every moment of your life, going to war with every cell in your body if you try to leave. People who attempt to kick opiates will look forward to months of vomiting, diarrhoea, severe trembling, profuse sweating and chronic pain. Noel would have to battle this monster for the next two decades.

The next day, Noel and I picked up from where we'd left off during a drive across the Peak District towards the spa town of Buxton, Derbyshire. The heatwave had broken, and there was a chill in the air as we took turns launching Frankie's drool-soaked tennis ball for him to chase across Buxton Park. When I had the ball in my hand, Frankie stared at it like it was the only thing that existed in the world.

'He'd chase that all day if you let him,' Noel said as Frankie pounced on the ball about fifty yards from where we were standing. 'You see how fixated he is on that ball? Well, that was me and drugs,' he said.

Just like Frankie and his ball, nothing would stop Noel from getting his fix. He was living in Barrow-in-Furness in the early 2000s when he decided, arbitrarily, to drive down to Liverpool to score drugs with another user he'd just met. As he pulled up near his dealer's house, he saw a young boy produce a gun from his jacket and watched him unload a clip at his drug dealer, who was standing idly in his doorway. Somehow, the gunman managed to miss the dealer and the would-be assassin scarpered. However, the attempted murder didn't deter Noel.

'So, rather than think, "Oh, fuckin' hell, there's been some gunfire right outside," [we thought,] "Nah, fuck it, we've come all the way to Liverpool to get some drugs, so we'll go in."'

Noel had started an electrical engineering apprenticeship soon after his accident. Despite his drug use he rose quickly through the ranks and, before turning twenty-six, was managing complicated engineering projects. This was when his double life began. In front of colleagues, friends, his wife and family members, he was the charming and sophisticated man I'd met on my first day in Emmaus. When they weren't around, he would be out on the other side of the country taking extraordinary risks to get his fix. Noel said his ability to live a double life stemmed from all the upheaval in his childhood, which had constantly forced him to adapt to new environments.

'So, if I'm in a room with loads of businessmen, I can be business-like, then go from that to a smack or crack den and [I can] be with them – there's a skill to that,' he said.

I share that skill to an extent. I moved around so much in my childhood and adolescence – from Pennine villages to kids' homes and council estates – that I had to adapt to new environments constantly. Still, I don't have Noel's poker face.

Heroin is an expensive habit, and Noel's work was mostly provided through agencies in his early twenties, resulting in a fluctuating income. To solve that problem, he became an expert shoplifter.

'What would you nick?' I asked. We'd left the park and were driving through Bakewell, a market town on the Derbyshire dales.

'We used to go into a garage with a holdall. Grab all the bacon, all the cheese, and walk out.'

I was laughing. 'Cheese. Where would you sell that?'

'In the pubs. It would go like that. In the pubs back then, if you took bacon and cheese in, it was gone.'

Every rough 'n' tumble pub I've ever known has a character like Noel frequenting it with a bulging bin liner of ill-gotten wares, but I wouldn't have pegged him as one of them. This routine earned him enough to fuel his habit until he inevitably got caught. The way in which his cheese-and-bacon business came to an ignominious end could have been lifted straight from a bad sixties comedy: *Carry on Junkie*.

On one visit to the garage, the clerk spotted Noel stuffing several packs of cheese into his holdall. After hearing the clerk's angry cries, Noel sprinted for the door, frantically tossing packs of cheese behind him. When he reached the threshold, he thought he was in the clear, but a burly man emerged from nowhere and rugby-tackled him to the ground. As they waited for the police to arrive, Noel noticed that he'd left one packet of cheese in his holdall; when the clerk and rugby-tackling motorist were distracted, he dispensed it surreptitiously into a bin that he was fortunate enough to be standing next to. If he had no cheese on him, he couldn't be accused of stealing any, he reasoned. Unfortunately, after the cops lifted Noel, the clerk found the discarded cheese and called the police, who discovered Noel's fingerprints.

'They got me done for one bar of cheese,' Noel said.

I was in stitches. 'How long did you get for that bar of cheese?'

'Three months.'

By now, we were both laughing at the madness of it. I reminded Noel that when we were living at Emmaus, I'd shoplifted a bottle of pop from the local off-licence, and had spent the rest of the afternoon badgering him for reassurance.

"'Will they check the cameras?'" Noel said, imitating me. We agreed that I'd make a rubbish thief.

A year before the botched cheese heist, Noel had done three months for getting into a wrestling match with a pair of coppers during a stop-and-search. Far from being a rehabilitative institution, prison is a conduit to recidivism and homelessness.[5] Noel avoided this well-trodden path – at least at first.

During this first entanglement with the law, his growing drug dependency was addressed, and Noel was introduced to methadone. Methadone is a synthetic opioid used to treat addiction and withdrawal by binding to the same receptors in the brain that heroin and morphine do, only without the accompanying euphoria. It's an opiate used to wean people off opiates – only it can be just as addictive and destructive.[6] Noel said the only thing methadone gave him was another habit to kick. 'You could get up to a hundred-odd mil quite easily, which is a lot. If *you* drunk that, it would probably kill you. I don't think they realise how addictive it is.'

We were back in his shed by now, puffing on another joint while Frankie chased his shadow in the garden. Noel told me that out of all the drugs he's had to get off over the years, methadone was the hardest to beat.

'That's what I was on for twenty-odd years. So, from nineteen, all the way into rehab, I've been on methadone. When I say they gave me another habit, it's because what I used to do was binge on heroin, save the methadone up – so at the end of that I wouldn't feel shit.'

Noel still struggles to understand what triggered his drug binges. 'I'd be doing really well and go off, get a job, do really well in the job, and for whatever reason, something would set me off and I'd go off on a bender,' he said.

I understand his confusion. I still can't explain my own triggers and precisely why I fell apart – which is frustrating, because I'd like to prevent it from happening again if possible.

Things really started going off the rails for Noel in his mid-thirties, when his ability to bounce back from heavy sessions was not as robust. Noel began to abuse Valium. He bought hundreds of pills at once, thinking that he could spread them out and moderate his use.

But that didn't happen. Instead, he took as many pills as he could until they were all gone.

Valium obliterated his senses, and he'd lose days. 'A few times, I'd come round and there'd be blue tablets on my desk at work. I was like, "Fucking hell, they could have been there for ages." That's when it all came to a head. I was getting divorced; she [his wife] was working at the same place. It was just a horrible time. My way of coping was getting off my head, which then was making it worse.'

After Noel got divorced, he took a job in St Albans.

I'd moved to St Albans because the Emmaus community there was the furthest one from the north of England that had available spaces. I thought if I could escape my familiar environment, I could escape from my problems – but they followed me anyway.

Noel's problems followed him, too: 'It's like big circles that get smaller and smaller, because you just end up at the same point again,' Noel said. 'I moved away. It's like you're trying to escape from the problem, but the problem *is* you. So, no matter what you do, you don't get away from your problem.'

'How did you end up homeless down there?' I asked.

'Just the amount of using. St Albans isn't cheap. It's hard, because a lot of it is just a blur,' Noel explained.

I told him that I have a similar problem recalling the last few months I spent in Mossley. I'm sure I was out of my mind, because the decisions I made, including taking to the streets when I didn't need to, make no sense at all.

'This is how I ended up in Emmaus,' Noel continued. 'It had got really bad. Going in stealing DVDs had kicked in bad. St Albans is not a big place, is it? So, if you start hitting a place like that, it soon gets on top.'

Noel had no job or flat when he eventually got caught for stealing. He was either spending nights in his car or on friends' sofas. He had a plan when he got arrested: he made sure to tell the police from the beginning that he did it because he wasn't getting any help with his addiction. He told me he thinks this may have saved him from returning to prison. Instead, Noel was given probation and ended up in Emmaus, spending just over a year there before moving on.

Noel shared some of my views about Emmaus. Like me, he'd welcomed the sanctuary the community provided in the beginning, but after a few months, his views had changed. He told me he'd felt like he was walking on eggshells throughout his stay. 'You could wake up in a bad mood one morning, tell someone to fuck off or do something equally stupid, and that's it – you're back homeless again.' Like me, Noel had found that the rules were applied inconsistently in the community: 'I think a lot of it is, if your face fits, and if the staff like you.' He also said that the meagre allowance is not enough to help Emmaus residents make a quick transition to independence. 'How long would it take you [. . .] in somewhere like St Albans, where you need a grand for the rent, and another grand for the deposit?'

If Companions find a job, Emmaus allows them to continue living in the community for up to three months, and will help them furnish their new accommodation with donated furniture from its charity shops. An Emmaus spokeswoman said they take 'great pride' in not forcing anyone to leave before they are ready: 'Those who are looking to move on are given support to do so.' The spokeswoman added: 'No Companion should feel they need to "walk on eggshells", and we work hard to ensure we are consistent with people. As a charity, we do work with people with complex and varied needs, and it is important we ensure we can be adaptable to these needs wherever possible.'

Noel could not get well at Emmaus. It can take three months to get over the methadone hump, and Companions are expected to lug heavy furniture around and work with the public forty hours a week: impossible if you're rattling. However, Noel said there were positives at Emmaus. 'One thing: I met you, which was a good thing. I needed somebody else who was maybe in the same situation. Although we were both in this mess, we had very similar views; we could talk a lot, so that made it a lot easier.'

When Noel took his new job in Buckinghamshire, he fell into a familiar self-destructive pattern. After six months, his employer didn't renew his contract, and he was left in Bucks with a £600-a-month rent bill, no job, dwindling savings and a renewed drug habit. 'So, rather than try and get a job, I'd just use. I met this couple on the next road up. They were using, and then, for what must have been three weeks, I was around there, and we were using all the time. Heroin, crack – proper doing it.' A month later, he arrived at his drug-counselling centre looking worse for wear. His counsellor was concerned and referred him to a Christian rehab clinic in Leicestershire.

Noel was fortunate to get into rehab: as with housing provision, demand far exceeds supply. Austerity has left its mark on drug and alcohol services. Since 2013, residential rehabilitation and detox services in England have been cut by a third.[7] Moreover, just like homeless provision, addiction services are run mainly by the private sector and charities, who all have their own treatment ideas, ranging from the empirical to the absurd.[8]

The pandemic brought the consequences of a decade of austerity into sharp focus. In 2020, the Royal College of Psychiatrists (RCP) warned that the number of people addicted to opiates seeking help in April was at its highest level since 2014, and stated that 'years of cuts mean addiction services are ill-equipped to cope with the pandemic surge'.[9] In 2021, the government announced a £148 million funding package to tackle drug-related crime and addiction.[10] The investment is welcome, but it falls well short of the £900 million the government's drug tsar Professor Dame Carol Black recommended to ministers in December 2020.[11] In an open letter to the government published in the *Guardian*, Dr Adrian James and Professor Julia Sinclair of the RCP said the government's investment would do 'little to reduce the record numbers of drug-related deaths, or to support the thousands living with addiction'. They argued that the government should take their own drug tsar's advice seriously, invest £374 million a year in adult addiction services, and return clinical treatment to the NHS. They added that 'more lives will be lost to this treatable health condition unless the government takes decisive action'.[12]

Of course, luxury rehabs offer treatment based on the latest research, along with fine linens, swimming pools, saunas and gourmet cuisine; the only snag is that you need to have a spare twenty grand lying around. Tackling drug addiction is not as straightforward as addressing the fundamental problem of homelessness – not having a home. Nevertheless, we should treat mental illness and dependency in the same way we treat physical maladies. I concede that there's no cure for addiction, and many addicts attest to this. They will often say they are never cured; they just learn to abstain. Moreover, there is no consensus about what addiction is, let alone how to treat it in all circumstances, and that's a conversation we must continue having with each other. However, it is clear that addiction is a health issue, and it is high time we treated it as such.

If a GP suspects that one of their patients has cancer, they will refer them to an oncology department, where they will be assessed and prescribed the appropriate treatment. The same goes for broken limbs, burns and diseases. The standard of care varies throughout the country, but overall, NHS patients will encounter the same approach to their illnesses in Inverness as they will in Truro. The NHS should provide all drug-counselling services, residential rehabilitation and aftercare services.

Doing this would mean those services can be closely monitored, accountable to the fourth estate and driven by scientific research instead of the whims of do-gooders trying to curry favour with St Peter.

There was nothing scientific about Noel's time in rehab. From the get-go, they told him that Jesus and the Good Book would cure his addiction.

'The way they look at it is, if you believe in Jesus and give your life to Jesus, you won't feel any pain; you're not an addict any more; you're a child of God. These are the things they tell you, so if you're in pain or feeling rough, it's like you're not believing, because Jesus will take that pain away,' Noel explained. The only problem was, Noel is an atheist. 'We had the Christian Channel on all day. I found it difficult just to sit. Like a cat on a hot tin roof.'

Noel saw a lot of broken people coming in and out of the place. A lot of the residents arrived straight from prison, hostels or the streets. On Noel's first day, he learned about the rehab's regime: phones and computers were prohibited, and attending church was mandatory. Some of the rules were just bat-shit crazy. Coming off methadone was exhausting, and all Noel wanted to do was sleep in the beginning, but the rehab staff wouldn't allow forty winks. 'One time, they made me stand up and start writing things on the whiteboard to keep me awake.'

'Were they trying to get you into a proper sleeping pattern?' I asked.

'They didn't really give a reason. I don't know.'

Presumably, if the health service ran rehabs, they would be required to explain procedures to patients. If a doctor is about to stick you with a needle and you ask them to explain why, they won't say, 'That's for me to know and you to find out.'

Once Noel completed his detox, it wasn't long before he got another job – which, he said, irked the staff at the rehab. 'I was doing [the job] for a while, but it didn't fit in with what they wanted, so they made it difficult. They said things like, "We think you're rushing it; you're working too hard."' Noel pointed out that he was only working fifteen hours per week, while other residents at the rehab were volunteering for twenty-five hours in their food bank. Noel thinks the difference was the other residents were doing something for the rehab, and they didn't like the fact that he wasn't wholly reliant on them. 'A lot of people who have taken drugs have fried their brains. They can be manipulated; they may be anxious; they may have hang-ups about themselves. But I'm not like that. People who call you a drug addict assume you live on the street, you have no money, you've got nothing. [That's] not necessarily the kind of drug addict that I was. And yet people had these preconceived ideas. I wouldn't let them take advantage. I've lived my own life. I'm not an idiot. I've done stupid things, but I'm not a fucking idiot.'

There was a high turnover of people at the rehab. Some weren't ready to kick drugs, others couldn't tolerate the withdrawal, and some just couldn't get to grips with the religious regime. Noel persevered through all the scripture readings, church outings and condescension; he got clean, got a job and got out.

As Noel and I sat in his living room, watching football and reminiscing, we had reached the end of our homeless journey. We were both in the privileged position of looking back at the chaos of our formative years as an abstract, slightly amusing blur – almost like a bad dream we'd now awoken from. Again, I can't adequately explain why I deteriorated so dramatically in Mossley, or how I hoisted myself from ruin. Still, I'm confident that the latter had nothing to do with the nation's safety net.

Noel, like me, just avoided the sharp end of poverty. A mental breakdown and terrible choices saw me on the street, but dependency didn't keep me there. For Noel, twenty years of dependency and terrible choices ended in homelessness, but his mental toughness and drive saw him avoid the worst of it. When it comes to mental illness and dependency, one usually begets the other, and for those suffering from both, homelessness can be a death sentence.

In 2019, three years after I left Emmaus St Albans, I returned to Manchester to investigate how drugs had blighted the city's homeless community, and to tell the life stories of those who had died in the city. As I spoke to rough sleepers about their lives and outreach workers about the degradation they witnessed every day, I thought about how lucky I was. It could've been me on the street with no hope, clutching a paper cup: ignored, frightened and alone with the knowledge that my death would be nothing but a whisper in the wind.

Chapter Seven

Dying Homeless

In 2019, the Office for National Statistics (ONS) reported that homeless deaths in England and Wales in 2018 had increased by over a fifth from the previous year. Seven hundred and twenty-six homeless people died in England and Wales that year, the highest year-to-year increase since the ONS time series began.[1] For the same year, the National Records of Scotland reported an estimated 195 homeless deaths, a rise of 19 per cent from the year before.[2]

The statistics were horrifying, but they were just that: statistics. Cold, indifferent numbers. My friend and mentor, journalist Simon Hattenstone, and I decided we wanted to tell the stories behind those numbers. And we wanted not just to tell the stories of their deaths, but the stories of their lives. We wanted to speak to those closest to them about their childhoods, dreams, interests and flaws. We intended to tell as many life stories as possible, from as many major UK cities as possible, and to explore a different theme for each city we covered.

All the people we interviewed had demons. Many had suffered abuse; some were self-destructive or had mental illnesses; all were dependent on alcohol or drugs. This wasn't a huge surprise: the ONS found that two in five homeless deaths recorded in England and Wales in 2018 were related to drug poisoning (294 deaths), an increase of 55 per cent since 2017.[3] In Scotland, a similar picture emerged, with 53 per cent of homeless deaths linked to drugs.[4]

We could have chosen any city to focus on drugs, but we landed on Manchester, 'Spice City', our home – and home to the walking dead. Spice, Dawn, Bliss, Black Mamba and Bombay Blue are some of the many names for the psychoactive synthetic cannabinoids (fake weed) that flooded Manchester's homeless community in 2017.[5] Spice is usually sprayed on to plant matter and smoked, usually with rolling tobacco in a spliff. Even though it's described as imitation weed, it's nothing of the sort. It's far more potent than your average joint, and the chemicals in Spice can be lethal.[6]

Spice has caused chaos in British prisons. It's an ideal drug for inmates: it's easily smuggled, and it doesn't register on most drug tests.[7] Spice, known as Bird Killer[8] among users, can make years feel like months – perfect for when you're doing hard time, and perfect for the homeless living in cramped, drug-infested hostels, tent cities and doorways.

Spice's origin story is tragically ironic. John W. Huffman, a Clemson University chemist, was studying drug abuse and how cannabis receptors work in the brain when he synthesised the compound JWH-018 in 1993.[9] Somehow, Huffman's compound was leaked from his lab and made its way to our streets in the early 2000s.[10] It was sold legally in retailers known as 'head shops' until the Home Office intervened in May 2016 with the Psychoactive Substances Act, forcing the drug on to the black market.[11]

Researchers have estimated that up to 95 per cent of the homeless community in Manchester use Spice.[12] Like most cities, homelessness has always been a feature in Manchester, but after a decade of crippling austerity, it has consumed the city. Rough sleeping is visible everywhere. You can see it in almost every doorway, bus shelter and subway. It's at the centre of the city's politics, leads the front pages of the local papers, and everyone, from shop workers to volunteers at the cathedral, has an opinion about it. Spice brought the problem into sharper focus. The drug induces catatonia, causing users to become rooted to the spot, or to stagger in aimless circles until they fall flat on their faces. An unpleasant sight, but it makes for shocking photographs, so in summer 2017 the world's media flocked to the city to snap and shoot the 'Spice zombies' straining Manchester's emergency services.[13]

Most of the coverage was surprisingly commendable and vital. There was also rubbernecking *Schadenfreude* from the red-top tabloids, culture zines and YouTube channels, who descended on the city to scribble and shoot their poverty pornos, making the place resemble something from a bleak John Cooper Clarke poem. What drew particular ire from Manchester's front-line homeless workers was the 2019 Channel 4 documentary *60 Days on the Streets*, which was criticised by some for ignoring the alleged progress being made in the city. British explorer Ed Stafford, who holds a world record for walking the length of the Amazon River, decided to test his record-breaking endurance on Britain's streets over the course of three hour-long episodes. Stafford filmed the first episode in Manchester. When I tuned in, I was expecting another exploitative hour of poverty safari along the lines of *Benefits Street*. What I saw was an unflinching, unsanitised record of life on the streets. Its only flaw was that Stafford didn't go deeply enough into the precursors and politics.

When I arrived in Manchester in April, a month after *60 Days* aired, I encountered an almost comprehensive reluctance from the city's charities to help me find the friends and relatives of those who'd died, and some cited the documentary as a reason for not speaking to me. Trawling the social media profiles of relatives and friends of those who had died was also proving fruitless, so I decided to take to the streets, armed with a list of the names of homeless people who had been reported dead by the local press.

The trees had begun to flourish on a dry and warm May morning in central Manchester. There were plenty of rough sleepers in the city that day, and each one I spoke to could cite a location where someone had died, yet no one recognised the names on my list. Frank, a middle-aged beggar, was sitting with four of his mates underneath the Arndale shopping centre, slurping from cans of black lager and puffing on roll-ups when I approached him. He explained that the term 'homeless community' was a misnomer.

'We don't all know each other or get together and chat about the latest developments,' he said derisively, as he swayed on the spot about six inches away from my face. 'Everyone's in their little cliques,' he explained.

I'd been at it all day; my feet were sore after walking the length and breadth of the city, and I'd got nowhere. 'Do you know anyone who would know any of these people?' I muttered, expecting that no helpful answer would be forthcoming.

'You could try St Anne's. They held a service there for all the homeless who'd died over the years,' Frank said.

Why didn't I think of that? I thought.

'Nice one,' I said. I handed him a fag (my currency for a chat) and made for the church.

Moments later, inside St Anne's, I approached a balding and robed rector – or he may have been a vicar. Whoever he was, he had a dog collar on and looked like he was in charge. I asked him about the service, and if the church could help me find friends and relatives of those listed on the memorial. Mr Church Man said he couldn't give me the names, but suggested I contacted the charity that arranged the service.

My hopes weren't high when I dialled their number. I managed to get through to their CEO, let's call them Roadblock. When Roadblock came on the phone, I put my foot in it straight away. I was so eager to get going on the story that I abandoned any hint of sensitivity or discretion. I divulged that we weren't only looking to tell the story of a dead homeless person, but one who had specifically perished due to drug abuse – ideally Spice abuse.

'We can't help you with this,' Roadblock said. 'There's enough people calling Manchester "the Spice capital" as it is!'

Another brick wall.

I became pessimistic about finding a story in Manchester, as the whole issue of homelessness there was, and remains, intensely sensitive. Then I received a call from Sarah, a city outreach worker. Sarah said she'd be happy to help me with the story, and we arranged to meet at a coffee shop the next day in Piccadilly Gardens.

Sarah was short and stout, and had short hair. She was friendly and direct. She told me she was living in temporary accommodation after being hospitalised on the acute stroke ward a few months earlier. 'I've been from pillar to post, but it just shows you that everyone's one pay cheque away from that happening. And just because I work for homeless charities doesn't mean that I automatically know what to do or who to contact,' Sarah said.

'You're looking after homeless people while living in a homeless hostel?' I asked.

'I've been homeless in the past; I've been in prison in the past. So, I can relate to the clients we work with.'

Sarah went to prison for a year after she was caught selling Class-A drugs in Manchester city centre. Many of her clients have been inside, too. 'It's that revolving door thing. So, they'll come in, they'll come to town and breach their order, or not get back on time, or something like that, and they end up breaching; back to prison for twenty-eight days.'

We were sitting underneath the pavilion which connects to Manchester's 'Berlin Wall', a dreary and dystopian hunk of concrete that connects the gardens to the bus terminal. It's a hotbed of drug-dealing, drug-using and rough sleeping. Sarah said she'd spotted three Spice dealers during the brief time we'd been chatting. I'd noticed them, too: young men in tracksuits with small bags thrown over their shoulders, walking up to strangers on rows of benches in front of us, exchanging a few words and moving on to the next person. They couldn't have been more conspicuous if they were advertising their wares through a bullhorn. I had also clocked a couple of plain-clothed coppers who looked especially vigilant, dressed in their customary black fleeces.

I told Sarah I'd upset Roadblock by suggesting Manchester was becoming the 'Spice capital'. Sarah said it was 'too late' for that. 'Y'know, there's no point denying it. It's not very nice. When we had the Gunchester label – it's not very nice to have that title, but it's true. I could probably go and get a gun in an hour. Where we're sat now, easily.'

I didn't know if Sarah was right about that, but there had certainly been loads of guns knocking about when I'd lived in Manchester twenty years before, and it was easy to get one if you knew the 'right' person. Sarah told me she believed that Spice was contributing to deaths on Manchester's streets. I read her the names on my list. She recognised some of them, and agreed to try and put me in touch with friends and relatives before we parted ways.

I texted Sarah a couple of months later in July and told her we were thinking of telling Daniel Smith's story. Daniel's death was senseless and horrific. He was rough sleeping in a disused workshop under railway arches in Salford when two men beat him to death during the early hours of 20 January 2016.[14] His corpse was then set on fire by those who had murdered him. He was twenty-three years old. The press reported that Smith's murderers and their accomplices were high on Spice at the time. Sarah knew Daniel. I asked if she'd talk to me about him and if

197

she could put us in touch with Smith's friends and family. She replied a few days later: 'Daniel's case was a massive mess and Spice was the main factor in Daniel's death. It's something you would have to handle very delicately. It's not just a story when you see the pain it caused with so many of our clients, who have always had fuck all anyway.'

At the end of September, I returned to the city with Simon to interview Oliver Sutcliffe, a chemist at Manchester Metropolitan University (MMU) and his research partner Rob Ralphs, a criminologist at MMU. The pair had recently teamed up to study Spice and its effects on users. Oliver was running late, so we chatted with Rob first at the back of a noisy coffee shop on Oxford Street. Rob looked bookish and sounded a bit like Professor Brian Cox.

'What impact has Spice had on the homeless?' I asked.

'It's a perfect prison or homeless drug. That's why it's popular in those settings. People would say, "It makes a two-year sentence feel like months. Or I smoke it and the next minute I wake up in my cell. It's the only thing that gets me to sleep at night. It takes the bars away. It's a head shift." If you're in that situation, you just want to forget about your environment,' Rob explained.

'We've spoken to many rough sleepers in the city and around the country; they say it's lethal,' I said.

'At the end of the day, Spice isn't killing people,' Rob said.

This was a surprise, as almost everyone I'd spoken to about the drug had said the opposite.

'If you look at the drug-related deaths, two-thirds of them are heroin,' Rob said.

We suggested to him that the absence of Spice on death certificates may be because coroners were missing it. Before we'd headed to Manchester, Simon and I had covered the case of Gyula Remes, a Hungarian man who had died while sleeping rough outside the Houses of Parliament. Remes had been sleeping in a passage in Westminster underground station that led into Parliament Square. His death, the second in the same underpass in under a year, made national headlines.[15]

The inquest concluded that he had died of a heart attack and acute alcohol poisoning. However, his homeless friend Gabor Kasza insisted to us that a stranger had handed Gyula a cigarette. After he'd inhaled it, he convulsed on the ground and lost consciousness. Gabor was convinced it was a Spice cigarette that had killed Remes, but the toxicology report presented at the inquest stated there was no sign of Spice or morphine found in his body. According to the coroner, he had enough alcohol in his urine to be three times over the drink-drive limit.

Oliver joined us and weighed in on the topic: 'It's not the testing that's the problem; it's the compounds. The compounds are broken down by the body very, very quickly. So, they dissipate from the samples and tissues very quickly.' Oliver told us the research MMU have done has shown that the body can break down some of the cannabinoids in Spice in under fifteen minutes.

The chemical compounds of synthetic cannabis are constantly in flux. When the government cracked down on legal highs, amateur chemists tweaked their formulas to stay ahead of the legislation.[16] The Psychoactive Substances Act curtailed this, but now Spice is in the hands of criminals, and there's no way of ensuring the safety of the compounds. Also, more evidence is emerging that the drug can become more dangerous when combined with alcohol and other substances.[17] This could explain why coroners missed the real reason behind his death. Gyula may have been drunk before he died in Westminster, but the amount he drank (the equivalent of six pints of lager) wouldn't usually lead to heart failure unless the person had a pre-existing condition. The lethality of Spice when combined with alcohol lends credence to Gabor's claim that Gyula passed out after smoking a laced cigarette.

If Gabor was correct, it illustrates why the prohibition of synthetic cannabis, and the prohibition of drugs in general, is not only futile, but spectacularly ineffective. If drugs were legalised, they could be regulated and made safer for consumption. Suffering drug users wouldn't need to hide their habit; they could use in purpose-built facilities where trained health professionals could supervise them, and offer them advice and a way out. How many more lives need to be lost before we accept that the 'war on drugs' is an experiment that has never, and will never, produce the desired results? As a society, we must come to terms with the fact that people take drugs: they always have, always will. Let's get over it.

Our conversation with the professors turned to press coverage. Rob explained that he thinks the fuss around Spice in Manchester has been disproportionate to the reality, arguing that the proximity of the city's transport hub to the shopping district has caused homelessness to concentrate in one place, making the problem seem worse than it is.

'What is the media consistently getting wrong, in your view?' I asked.

'They're not zombies; they're people,' Oliver said, referring to the slew of zombie analogies littered throughout articles and programmes on the topic. He also mentioned *60 Days on the Street*, which seemed to have pissed off the whole city.

'That's just a political perspective thing. It's cheap and it is tabloid, but they are taking an image of people literally petrified and zombified, and using that. They're not saying these people are zombies,' Simon explained to Oliver. Simon added, 'I think it's a legitimate way of showing the horror of what it does to them. I would never see that as a way of dissing them.'

'I'm not having a go,' Oliver said. 'I'm just saying it's very common that people come to Manchester because they see this city as having an issue, but then they don't see the other side of it, and all the positive things the city has done to try and mitigate the situation. That gets diluted.'

As frustrating as some of these interactions in Manchester were, I do understand why charities and other organisations were so reluctant to talk. There's a genuine homeless crisis in Britain, and many front-line organisations feel aggrieved by the media's coverage, which predominantly focuses on the misery. This was especially the case in Manchester, where so much was made of the 'Spice zombies'. But, except for a few exploitative pieces, I think the coverage was fair. There's misery on our streets. The central government has shown nothing but callous disregard for it, local authorities haven't been much better, and charities aren't picking up the slack.

I also understand why it's so difficult for people to talk about people they cared for and lost so tragically. Friends, carers and family members often feel guilty about their roles in the lives of those they have lost. They blame themselves and worry that journalists will blame them, too. That's why I'm grateful to every relative and friend who found the courage to speak to us about their lost loved ones.

Throughout our frustrating travails in Manchester, Simon and I were looking to tell the stories of homeless people who had died in other major cities outside of England. In Wales and Northern Ireland, the names of the dead were reported in the local press, making finding their relatives and friends relatively simple. We knew there were stories to tell from Scotland, as the country had the highest rate of homeless deaths in Britain in 2018, with a death rate of 35.9 people per million of the population – twice the rate of England.[18] Still, I couldn't find a single name in the reports. Moreover, outreach groups and procurator fiscals (Scotland's coroners) were even less helpful than the English ones had been.

Then, on 8 July 2019, Police Scotland issued a statement: 'Police are appealing for the assistance of the public in tracing relatives of 53-year-old Mark David James Starr, who was found dead within the Glasgow Green area of Glasgow on 28 June 2019.'[19] Mark had been sleeping rough in Glasgow Green, the oldest park in the city. What caused his death was unknown at the time, but Police Scotland said there were no suspicious circumstances. Another appeal was posted three weeks later: 'Officers believe Mr Starr may have relatives in the Kent area, but have been unable to track down any family members despite a previous appeal on 8 July.'[20] Mark didn't have a presence on social media, but his nephew, Jude Starr, had responded to a post shared by Glasgow Live on Facebook. I contacted Jude, and he put me in touch with Mark's mother, Sue, and sister, Karen. According to Sue, Police Scotland had told Kent police about Mark's death, but Kent police had still not been in touch with the family when Simon and I met them at a café in Ashford town centre that September.

'I still can't believe it,' Sue said. 'Well, you don't ever imagine one of your children is going to end up in that situation, do you?' She noted that Mark had always told her he was fine in Glasgow.

Sue and Karen were huddled together on a sofa, with Simon and I seated opposite. They looked numb and despondent. Understandable. It had only been a month since they got the news, and a week since Mark's funeral. Sue was chatty, while Karen was taciturn, offering only monosyllables and shy nods. Sue passed us a slim order of service from Mark's funeral, complete with photographs from his childhood. There was one of Mark, Karen and their brother, Tony, on Hastings Pier, posing for their mum's camera, a capuchin monkey clinging to Mark's hands. The school bus driver used to call the trio 'the three musketeers' because they always looked out for each other. Tony didn't come along to the café; it was still too painful for him.

'[Mark] was a good boy. You had a happy childhood. Didn't ya?' Sue said to Karen.

'Yeah,' Karen said, softly.

Mark was born in June 1965, two months prematurely, and Sue didn't think he would survive. 'I was going to call him Jason. I just liked the name. But the priest came to see me and said:

"I think we better get the baby christened straight away," and I couldn't think straight. He suggested Mark, 'cause he was a saint.' Mark did survive, and after a month, the hospital allowed Sue to leave.

'Who did Mark gravitate towards; you or his dad?' I asked.

'I think it was you really,' Karen said to Sue.

'They knew what they couldn't get off their dad . . .' Sue trailed off, and seemed to be suppressing tears.

'Were you protective of him because you almost lost him?' I asked, although I probably should have given her a moment. She nodded, while wiping her eyes with a tissue.

Sue passed us another photo: a shirtless Tony with his arm around Mark's shoulder. They looked happy. Tony had several tattoos on his arms and chest, and I wondered if Mark had got any ink. One thing I've learned from Simon is that you always ask people about their jewellery and tattoos.

'All he had was "Humpy" on his arm,' Sue said.

'Humpy? What's that?' I asked.

'That was his nickname – Humpy! If he couldn't get his own way sometimes, he'd get the hump, so that's why they called him Humpy,' Sue explained.

Sue said Humpy was never going to be a scholar. He took a job as a gamekeeper's assistant, but he didn't bother to show up for work. He'd had a temporary gig in a bakery once, but that didn't last very long, either.

'Why couldn't he hold down a job?' I asked.

'Well, he started dabbling in, erm . . .' Sue paused, looking slightly embarrassed.

'How old was he when he started dabbling?' I asked.

'He was about twenty-six, I think,' Sue said.

At least, that's when the family found out. One day, Mark's father found a syringe in his son's bedroom. He was livid. Mark insisted to his dad, a skilled concrete finisher on building sites, that the syringe wasn't his, but his dad wasn't having any of it.

Around this time, Mark would disappear from Ashford for months at a time without mentioning where he was going, or what he was doing. This was a pattern he repeated until his death, over twenty-five years later.

'You'd be exasperated sometimes. You'd feel like giving him a good shake and saying, "Listen to me. You know where you're gonna end up if you carry on like this,"' Sue said.

No one else in Mark's family took drugs, so I wondered who could have got him involved.

'I don't know,' Sue said. 'But you can't blame it on anyone else; it's his own choice. There's nothing you can do. I used to sit and talk to him for hours: "You're throwing your life away. You only get one chance at it, so why waste it?"'

It was striking that neither Sue nor Karen seemed to know much about Mark's life. They didn't know how he got into hard drugs, or what he got up to when he absconded. Mark's frequent disappearing acts meant the Starrs only knew what Mark told them about his life, which wasn't much. Four years before our meeting in the café, Mark had upped and left Ashford. He didn't give his family any warning.

'Eventually, he phoned me up and I said, "Where are you, Mark?" And he said, "I'm in Scotland,"' Sue recalled. They all thought he was happy in Glasgow. 'He phoned me up [in January 2019] and he said, "It is really good up here." I was looking after my mum, who had dementia and couldn't be left, and he said, "You and nan will have to come up for a holiday when I've got my own place. It's really good up here. I'm happy."'

'It seems you know about as much as we do about his life up there,' I said. 'When we visit, is there anything you'd like us to ask people about Mark?'

'Was he happy?' Sue said. 'It's a strange thing to say, isn't it? Happy on the street. But I know he was happy there, sometimes.'

Five days later Tony Starr decided he was ready to talk, so I travelled back to Ashford to meet him at his local pub. 'Go Your Own Way' by Fleetwood Mac played on the jukebox as we shook hands on a dreary September afternoon. Tony was dressed in worn jeans and a black leather jacket, and had long red locks licking around his elbows. He looked like he was auditioning for a Led Zeppelin tribute band.

I liked him straight away. He's gentle, and there's a familiarity about him. He has the same wheezy laugh as his mum, and sounds just as Cockney, even though he's lived in Ashford all his life. Tony echoed Sue and Karen's account of an idyllic childhood filled with outdoor adventures and family holidays. His favourite memories of Mark were of them fishing with their father every Sunday, floating serenely down rivers on makeshift rafts with friends, crabbing on southern beaches, listening to nightingales in the woods and hanging off cliffs to collect birds' eggs.

'You made your own entertainment in them days. We weren't stuck in front of a screen eight hours a day, Danny,' Tony said as he swigged from his pint of lager.

Tony also talked about a side of Mark that his mother and sister weren't aware of, or perhaps were reluctant to talk about.

As a young boy, Mark suffered from night terrors that caused him to wake up in the middle of the night screaming. 'We never understood why,' Tony explained. The pair were camping out in their back garden one night when Mark began wailing in his sleep. He was so loud that a neighbour thought they were being assaulted, and leapt over the fence to intervene.

As an adult, Mark could be reckless. He drove cars without a licence, rode trains without purchasing a ticket, and didn't feel the need for a job nor money. Tony told me that on one of the last occasions he saw his brother, Mark went shoplifting.

'He said, "I'm just going to the shop, Tone." I said, "Hump, you've got no money." He said, "I don't need no money." I'm watching the door. I've seen Humpy come out with loads of food and the woman [the shopkeeper] chasing him. He just didn't care,' Tony said.

'Where do you think that came from?' I asked.

'I don't know, but he definitely had mental problems,' Tony said.

'When did that start?'

'I'd say when Rebecca died.'

Rebecca was Mark's sweetheart. They'd played together in the alleyways near their childhood homes, and had moved in together in their twenties. 'She was stunning,' Tony said. 'Honest to God, she'd make Page Three girls look ordinary. I thought, you're punching above your weight there, Hump. But Rebecca only had eyes for him. They'd been friends as kids – she was a bit of a wild child.'

Mark and Rebecca smoked cannabis together, then progressed to harder drugs. Before long, they were injecting heroin. One morning, Mark found Rebecca dead in bed next to him, having suffered an overdose in the night. She was twenty-four.

'He never recovered from that, Danny,' Tony said. 'A part of him never came back.' Tony claimed that local services in Ashford didn't do much to help Mark, even after the death of his girlfriend.

Mark's life had many of the typical ingredients found in the homeless recipe: emotional trauma, bereavement, mental illness, and dependency. The only inconsistency was a stable and loving family. Tony tells me that Mark lost three more loved ones after Rebecca's death: his aunt Elsie, who used to take them on holiday every summer, and who 'made the best chips in Kent'; his best friend Martin; and his father, who'd died suddenly twenty years ago while still working on building sites.

'Humpy took it badly. Dad adored all of us, but Humpy was his favourite. And Humpy loved Dad,' Tony said.

Over the next two decades, Mark's life spiralled into chaos. Tony visited his flat one day nine years ago and said it was like 'needle city'.

'I went mad. I said, "You silly bugger. Leave that stuff alone, it's a one-way ticket to misery,"' Tony told me.

'What did he say?' I asked.

'It was just like talking to a brick wall.'

Tony's frustration with Mark resonated with me; I used to waste hours trying to drill some sense into my brother's head, but he never listened to me, either.

Mark was evicted from his flat. After that, he did a few stints in prison for drug-related offences and would disappear for long periods without telling the family. Where he went, why he went, they don't know. He'd occasionally return to Ashford to live on the street, where kids would throw water over him and the rest of the local community would treat him with general contempt. When the family saw Mark, they would bring him back home for a while, until he got claustrophobic and scarpered again. Over the years, Mark's mental health deteriorated further and he became delusional.

'One time he said, "I've got to go; I'm meeting Jay-Z and Beyoncé tonight,"' Tony told me.

We laughed at this.

'That isn't the worst delusion to have, I suppose. What did you say?' I asked.

'I said: "Have a nice time, Hump." Then he'd tell us that Roman Abramovich had lent him his yacht.'

Tony said he was heartbroken when he learned that Mark was living on the streets. He took him into his home, but his brother always got itchy feet. 'That's just the way he was. You knew you'd see him again; you just didn't know when.'

We met up again a fortnight later, along with Simon, Maeve Shearlaw, video producer with the *Guardian* and Kyri Evangelou, a freelance filmmaker. Tony had decided to come with us to Glasgow, and they had come to shoot a short video of his trip. It was 9am as our train pulled out of King's Cross station, and Tony, sitting with Simon and I at an unreserved table, brazenly pulled a can of lager from his backpack and began supping. I was concerned by this. Throughout my reporting on homeless deaths, Simon and I would often call each other for midnight cry-athons, which we always felt guilty about – it wasn't *our* grief, our loss. We had no right to be upset, we thought, and yet we still were. Even though I was confident that Tony was tough and knew his brother better than anyone, this wasn't going to be an easy trip, and I was sure that he wouldn't be aware of the full extent of Mark's problems. With the second and third cans, I became worried that we were setting him up for a breakdown for the benefit of a newspaper article – but Tony was fine. You'd never know he'd been drinking steadily all day unless you saw him supping. Sometimes, he said, he would only drink a couple of cans in a day. He liked a spliff, too, but insisted he'd never used Class-A drugs; he saw what they did to Mark.

Tony explained that he felt he had to make the trip because Mark would have done the same for him. He took out the same photograph that Sue had shown us in the coffee shop a few weeks earlier.

'He was a bit bony by then,' he said. Tony told us the last thing he'd said to his brother was 'I love you': 'I had a sixth sense something was going to happen. I told a few friends, "I'm going to get a phone call soon."'

We had no grand plans of retracing Mark's footsteps when we arrived, save for turning up at charities with the hope that a grieving brother and a camera crew would induce enough guilt to convince people to speak up. Luckily, an hour after we arrived, Shelter Scotland invited us to their community hub to discuss Mark. We checked into our grim hotel, with no hot water or towels, and rushed to their office, where we met community hub manager Davy MacIver and the senior development worker Stephen Wishart. The pair told us that they're currently suing the city council for illegally denying temporary accommodation to homeless applicants.

When someone has a homeless application considered in Scotland, the local authority is obliged to provide temporary accommodation. The all-too-common practice of denying people this fundamental right is known in Scotland as 'gate-keeping'.[21] Glasgow City Council's figures show that 3,365 applications for temporary housing were not fulfilled in the year leading up to March 2019, up from 3,055 the year before – a rise of 10 per cent.[22] In January 2020, Shelter paused its legal case when the Scottish Housing Regulator intervened to investigate the council's ability to provide temporary housing, but the council claimed this decision had nothing to do with Shelter's case.[23]

We discovered that Mark was gatekept by the council at least twice before his death in 2019. The reasons were Kafkaesque. In the case notes Shelter kept on Mark, it was mentioned that 'Client [was] accommodated until last week (30/4) in the Copland Road Hotel. He travelled to England for a day trip for family bereavement and on his return [was] notified that his accommodation was closed and has not been accommodated since.' He was gatekept again after giving up a temporary furnished flat when he had started hearing voices. On 28 June, the day he died, Mark was due to meet Shelter for help with his Personal Independence Payment (PIP) claim.

For someone like Mark to have a prayer of securing stable and permanent accommodation, they have to jump through a series of hoops to prove they are 'housing ready.' This is known as the Staircase Model – or sometimes the 'Elevator Model' in the UK – and it's an appallingly illogical approach.[24] It demands that people do things like abstain from drugs and alcohol, and prove they're getting treatment and receiving training to run their own home. How can you expect someone like Mark, who had abused drugs for half of his life and suffered with severe mental illness, to get 'housing ready' when they're sleeping in a doorway and shooting up in alleyways? I never suffered some of the indignities that Mark would have experienced on the streets, but I do know what it's like to have your whole life centred exclusively around survival. When you're in that position, when you're preoccupied about things like where you're going to use the toilet from day to day, the furthest thing from your mind is self-improvement.

Before we left Shelter's office, Tony honoured his mum's request and asked if his brother had been happy in Glasgow.

'I wouldn't say he seemed unhappy, if that makes sense,' Wishart said. He added that a lot of angry people visit Shelter's offices, but Mark wasn't one of them. 'He was never up, never down, always even. Mark was a nice guy.'

In the evening, we approached rough sleepers with a photograph of Mark and asked if they knew him. It was only mid-October, but it was deadly cold that night – too cold to be out, let alone sleep rough.

'Excuse me, love,' Tony said to a woman propped up against a bin in a ragged sleeping bag outside Glasgow Central station. 'My brother died, and I'm trying to find out about his life up here.'

Tony had a good bedside manner. *He would be a good reporter,* I thought as I listened to him approach people, but his picks were too strung out to have a conversation. They weren't too happy about our camera crew, either.

'I'm not going on fuckin' telly, all right,' one man bellowed with his eyes half-shut.

'Ach, fuck off, man!' said another.

We walked to the other side of the station, where we had similar luck. But we all carried on approaching people until we found Barry, a rake-thin man who looked like he'd been dragged backwards through a bramble bush. Barry was in his late thirties but looked fifty due to roughing it for the best part of twenty years.

'That's a face I don't know,' Barry said when Tony showed him Mark's photo.

'How d'you cope every day on the street, mate?' Tony asked. 'Blimey, you must be battle hardened by now, Barry.'

'Aye, I'm used to it. There have been a lot of deaths when it's been cold, but cold doesnae bother me. They've knocked a lot of the hostels down and built student accommodation. The only one that's left is the Bellgrove. If he [Mark] went in there, he would've turned round and walked out.'

'It's that bad, is it, Barry?' Tony asked.

'They've offered me that God knows how many times, and I give them the same answer: "I'd rather sleep on the street." Some of the public can be all right, but you've also got the ones that walk past and spit on you. You need to find somewhere safe at night, in case a crowd come and set on you.'

We weren't getting anywhere, so we decided to call it a night. Before we arrived back at our hotel, a woman hobbling along with a sleeping bag asked me for a cigarette. I handed her one.

'Thanks, love,' she said.

'What's your name?' I asked as I lit her fag.

'Semra,' she said.

'Semra, do you know this man?' I asked, handing over Mark's picture. 'He was called Mark Starr. He died up here a couple of months ago.'

'Aye, I knew him!' she said.

I beckoned the crew and Tony over.

'That's a nice photo of you and your brother,' she said to Tony. 'He kept himself to himself. He wasnae a troublemaker. He was quite funny. There were scumbags who, if you injected and OD'd, the bastards would run away and take you for everything. He wasnae like that.' She added that Mark stuck to people who were 'civilised'.

'I've just been given a sleeping bag because there's no accommodation for me,' she told us.

Tony asked her if Mark had still been on drugs, and if he drank.

'He was still using. He was doing rock. But he was never a drinker. Just the odd can.'

Semra must have known Mark from hostels or hung around in similar circles, as she told us that this was to be her first night sleeping rough, and she was terrified. 'They told me to sleep under a camera so I can't be murdered. What fucking chance have I got?' She paused and considered Tony. 'You can see the sadness in your eyes. You can see the hurt. I'm so sorry for your loss,' she said, taking Tony's hand.

'Lovely to meet you, love,' Tony said.

'May God be with you,' Semra said and disappeared into the night.

The next day, we visited a few more homeless charities in the city and learned a little more about Mark's deteriorating mental health, his addiction and his unreadiness for support. What I've found through my experiences of homelessness and reporting on it is that you're either not fucked up enough or too fucked up to get help. I'm constantly reminded of the spiel I got at the Housing Options centre: 'You have to prove that you would be worse off than me if I were homeless.'

We headed to Glasgow Green, where Mark had spent his last night. The air was crisp, and the park was bathed in golden autumn sunlight as we ambled to the Nelson Monument in the centre of the Green. Tony brought Mark's ashes along, and before we entered the park, he'd sprinkled some of them on a joint. He took a few puffs, before taking the rest of the ashes to spread on the monument. Somehow, Tony had kept it together for the duration of our visit, but here the grief poured out of him.

'There you go, Hump. There you go, bruv.' He knelt and kissed the monument and crossed himself. 'I love you, Hump. God bless you, brother. Will you keep a space for me up there, Humpy? Take care, bruv. I love you.'

After gathering himself, Tony phoned Sue to tell her he had scattered Mark's ashes, and that the people he'd met had had good things to say about Mark. He couldn't tell her that Mark had been happy. When he hung up, he told us he was shocked by the life Mark had led up here, but he felt comforted by the fact that Mark's ordeal could be cited as evidence of the council not performing its statutory duty to homeless people in Glasgow. 'If Humpy stops more people dying on the streets by holding the council to account, then his death won't have been in vain.'

A year later, I gave Tony a ring. He told me that his family finally knew the cause of Mark's death. It was what we had all feared: Mark died of a drugs overdose. Opiates and painkillers were found in his system. If Mark, with his addiction and mental illness, was trying to find a better life outside Ashford, he couldn't have picked a worse place to go than Scotland. The country is in the grips of one of the worst drug crises in the world. Statistics show that 1,187 people died of drug misuse there in 2018, a 27 per cent increase from 2017.[25] The record numbers of deaths led to the crisis being called a public health emergency in December 2019.[26] Moreover, the rate of drug-related deaths in Scotland is the highest in Europe, and three times that of England and Wales.[27]

In September 2020, I returned to Glasgow. The city was just emerging from one of the strictest lockdowns in the world. Tony's hope that his brother's death wouldn't be in vain has been far from realised. The Everyone In policy passed by the government to protect the homeless during the pandemic had done little to prevent the number of homeless deaths in the city. Between 25 April and 28 August, eight homeless people had been found dead in the Alexander Thomson Hotel in the city centre, which was being used to temporarily house rough sleepers during the lockdown. All but one of the deaths was drug-related.[28]

I had returned to the city to meet Peter Krykant, another vigilante activist like Pottsy, who's trying to address the city's drug crisis with civil disobedience. Krykant, a former drug worker and addict, transformed his white Ford Transit van into a mobile supervised injection site (SIS) to allow people to take drugs in a safe, sanitary space under medical supervision. Krykant was in conversation with a police officer when I arrived on a cold and clear morning on a quiet backstreet, less than a mile from where Mark had passed away a year earlier. A couple of Krykant's helpers and some newspaper photographers were milling around the van, looking bored and cold. While I waited to speak to Krykant, I had a gander inside his van. There were a couple of seats and tables covered with plastic sheets; a biohazard bin sitting next to a large cabinet with several drug advice leaflets stacked in neat piles; life-saving naloxone was on board, along with a defibrillator. The pandemic had been catered to with all the accoutrements of the time: face masks, hand sanitisers and soap.

The van was parked strategically near a secluded alley frequented by the city's users.

'My van has been about challenging the framework, challenging the establishment, and hopefully we'll get an official facility soon,' Krykant told me after he'd finished with the police. Krykant was owlish, and with his specs and outdoorsy clothes, looked like a geography teacher on a field trip. He wouldn't divulge what the conversation with the coppers was about, but said that, so far, they hadn't obstructed his work. 'I think they would tell anyone with a camera, or a recorder, or anyone with a piece of paper, "no comment",' he said. 'Secretly, I know – having spoken to a lot of police officers – they know that we have to do something differently because what we have been doing for the last fifty years has not been working.'

Krykant began using drugs in Falkirk when he was eleven. He started with weed and progressed to alcohol, LSD, amphetamines, ecstasy and then heroin. 'Heroin came along when I was seventeen. I didn't smoke. I just went straight to injecting it.'

'That was a big leap; straight to injecting,' I said. 'Were you not scared?'

'It was just the circles I was in, and that's what the people I took it with were doing. I never had any fear of drugs, because I had been taking them every day for six years prior to that in one form or another.'

'Where did you get the idea for the van?' I asked.

'Copenhagen. That's how they started it,' he said.

Krykant was referring to Fixerum (fix room), a mobile injection room started by social entrepreneur Michael Lodberg Olsen in collaboration with Danish journalists, doctors, lawyers and other activists. In 2011, Olsen began by offering addicts in Copenhagen an alternative place to use their drugs in his converted van.[29] Olsen has since created Sexelance, an old ambulance converted to protect street sex workers.[30] Krykant said that six months after Olsen began his work in Copenhagen, the city established its first drug consumption facility.

Supervised injection sites have been operating in Europe for over thirty years. They began as informal meeting rooms in the 1970s – known as shooting galleries in some countries – where users could meet, exchange needles, take their drugs and receive counselling.[31] The first legal drug consumption facility was opened in 1986 in Berne, Switzerland;[32] there are now hundreds of them around Europe, and they have spread as far as Australia and Canada. Glasgow City Council first proposed introducing

Supervised Injecting Sites in 2016.[33] They received backing from Holyrood, but were blocked by Westminster, as drug legislation is not devolved.[34]

'I used in Glasgow. I've used [in] abandoned buildings, under bridges just over there at the Clyde,' Krykant said. 'I've got that experience of publicly injecting myself, and it's absolutely disgraceful that, fast forward twenty years from when I was publicly injecting and homeless, we're treating people exactly the same, when the evidence is absolutely overwhelming that these places work to keep people alive.' He pointed at the van.

I was hoping to speak to the people using the van, but Krykant politely suggested that I left and returned later; he was worried that seeing people hanging around would put service users off approaching. I saw his point and went for a stroll. Before I left, Krykant suggested I visited the alley near the van to see how much drug paraphernalia was there. I took his suggestion, and he wasn't fibbing. Along with the ubiquitous canisters of nitrous oxide that you find anywhere, the alley was littered with twisted and singed metal spoons, syringe tops and human shit. Whatever you think of consumption rooms and Krykant's van, it has to be better than that hellscape.

It turned out I was the only mug to heed Krykant's wishes, and when I returned in the early afternoon, the other hacks were still on-site, rubbernecking. One of the photographers looked like the cat who got the cream when he told me that a user had puked on himself. I stood around for a while, hoping to have more of a conversation with Krykant, but a horde of medical students turned up to ogle the van. An hour or so later, two homeless men and a homeless woman, all of whom looked like the walking dead, arrived. They may have been there to use if it wasn't for the growing poverty safari that had gathered around the van – which I was undoubtedly a part of. Using drugs isn't a performance art. A month after our meeting, I learned that Krykant had been charged under the Misuse of Drugs Act for obstructing police who were monitoring his van. The charges were dropped,[35] but it's unlikely that he'll get his SIS facility any time soon.

I thought a lot about Mark during my second visit to Glasgow. Would he have survived if there was a SIS facility he could have visited? If Mark had suffered his overdose in a consumption room, naloxone and a 999 call could have saved his life – or, at the very least, prolonged it. However, even Krykant acknowledges that consumption facilities aren't a silver bullet, and that such initiatives must be one arm of an integrated system that includes residential treatment and rehabilitation. Provision for dependency and mental health is much like the provision for everything in Britain: fragmented, privatised, and inconsistent, with bonkers rules that trap people in cyclical nightmares. What's most frustrating about the homelessness crisis is that we know how to solve it, yet we continue to throw money at things that don't work. It's like having the algorithm to solve a Rubik's Cube and continuing to turn the layers at random with the blind hope that they'll miraculously fall into place.

That algorithm is Housing First. Dr Sam Tsemberis developed the Housing First model in New York in the early 1990s, and it has virtually ended rough sleeping in some countries.[36] The driving principle behind Housing First is that housing should be a basic human right. Unlike the Staircase approach, Housing

First provides homeless people with a home without pre-conditions. Then, and only then, are their other various support needs addressed.[37] It's that simple. So simple that it's patently absurd to refer to it as radical, yet given our calamitous history with this topic, it probably merits that description.

I spoke to Tsemberis in December 2020, just after Joe Biden had booted Donald Trump out of the White House. Tsemberis, CEO of Housing First Pathways, talked to me on the phone from his office in Los Angeles, California, where the challenges faced by the new administration have never been more desperate. The state is at the epicentre of the homelessness crisis in the United States – if not the entire West. According to the latest data, 108,432 (or 53 per cent) of the nation's unsheltered homeless population live in the state.[38] Tsemberis explained that there's just as many homeless people in New York City, but California's tropical climate has made the problem more visible in LA.

Homelessness in America, much like homelessness in Europe, became a significant issue after the rebirth of neoliberal economics in the 1980s. Tsemberis was working in Bellevue, a psychiatric hospital famous for housing John Lennon's assassin.[39] 'During that time – when I was working at Bellevue – I found myself walking to work and back, and meeting people on the streets; people I had provided treatment for, who were in the hospital. It was like, "Oh my God, what are you doing here?" It was quite personal.'

Part of Tsemberis's job was driving around New York City looking for homeless people with mental illnesses and trying to get them into treatment. He was impeded by Staircase thinking, and struggled to get people into programmes – the proprietors felt that people with severe illnesses wouldn't be able to cope in an apartment. That's when Tsemberis started Pathways.

He told me that Housing First isn't about the housing at all – it's really about the treatment – but 'you can't really talk about the treatment unless the person is housed, otherwise the whole conversation is only about survival. Y'know, where are you going to eat, where are you going to sleep, where are you going to keep your stuff without having it stolen? So, if you're having survival conversations, you're not going to be talking about how you take care of yourself and your wellness – that's not in people's range at that time. Once they're housed, it becomes very, very different.'

Inspired by Tsemberis's research, the Housing First model has proven to be highly effective in states like Utah, which has reduced chronic homelessness by 91 per cent.[40] Finland eliminated rough sleeping after they introduced Housing First in 2007. In 1987, there were more than 18,000 homeless people in the country; thirty years later, there's little over a third of that number.[41]

Housing First could have really helped someone like Mark Starr, and the model is being gradually rolled out in several British cities, including Glasgow. But the crippling of services and the lack of social housing has severely diminished the city's ability to follow Tsemberis's model. A year earlier, in Shelter's office, Stephen Wishart had said that Housing First was designed for someone like Mark.

'Yet I sit in meetings and hear about people being "too complex" for Housing First. So, what are they not too complex for? Or are they just never to have a house? Is that it? OK, well, let's just throw the towel in, because we're in the wrong game!'

Housing First isn't radical, but the impetus needed to make it work requires the kind of economic transformation not seen since the Attlee government. I'm not arguing for the destruction of capitalism. Nevertheless, the profit motive should be removed from our social infrastructure, as it has achieved nothing but a market for misery. We must build enough social housing and invest in an integrated social-care system. Only then can Housing First work.

Most of the hundreds of thousands of homeless people in the UK aren't suffering at the sharp end of this crisis. They don't have addictions or mental illnesses; most just need a secure and stable roof over their heads. This should convince pull-up-your-socks Conservatives that poverty isn't just a consequence of moral vice; something that only happens to shirkers and junkies who refuse to take responsibility. The fact is, homelessness can happen to anyone, and even if you're not Mark Starr now, all it takes is a job loss, a benefits sanction, a relationship breakdown, illness or bereavement, and you could be leaving behind an empty doorway.

Chapter Eight

Precarity

It was ten to midnight on New Year's Eve 2017 and fireworks were already searing the sky above Alexandra Palace.

'See, I bet you're glad we came now, lazy arse,' I said to Dom, as we stood on a steep hill at the base of Ally Pally, the whole of London in our sights.

'Not really. We've been evicted, mate,' Dom said.

'Yeah, but fireworks, Dom. Fireworks! We'll be able to see every single one in the city without paying a penny,' I said, with as much faux enthusiasm as I could muster.

'Brilliant,' said Dom.

Ninety minutes earlier, Jack, our live-in landlord, had sent us an eviction text from his holiday home in China as we were about to head out from our Islington high-rise.

Dear all,

I have an important and bad news for everyone [sic]. I have been informed by the property owner yesterday, our flat is going to have an entirely refurbishment [sic] in the next 6 months before place on the housing market for sale. Thus, our tenancy is interrupted and terminated. The notice is formally giving to everyone [sic] from today and the last day to vacate the property is confirmed as on the 30th of January 2018. Please take advantage of this notice period time to make your own arrangement and look for your alternative place to stay.

As midnight ushered in 2018, groups of friends drank and hugged and cheered; lovers kissed and cuddled. Dom and I stared blankly into the exploding night sky.

'*Hootenanny*?' I said, looking glumly at Dom's glum face.

'*Hootenanny*,' said Dom. We left the hill. Heads down, pissed off, on our way home.

On the five-mile trundle back to Arsenal, I began to deconstruct Jack's completely-and-utterly-illegitimate-eviction text: 'Can you believe he decided to send it on New Year's Eve?!' I shouted into the night. 'What a prick. And what does he mean: "I have been informed by the property owner"? I thought *he* was the property owner?!'

All Dom could manage was a few grunts.

We were several beers deep, about to reach the apex of our New Year bender, and we promised ourselves that Jools Holland and harder spirits would expunge the pain and uncertainty of it all. But when we got through our front door, the lights wouldn't come on. The whole building's power had been cut – so no *Hootenanny*. Dom and I sat on my mattress in the darkness, laughing at the grim absurdity of it all. I've had better starts to the New Year.

I'd thought I'd put all my housing turmoil behind me when I'd made it to London eighteen months earlier. After nearly two years of homelessness, I'd felt my life was circling a drain until I got accepted at Goldsmiths to do an MA in journalism. I didn't have the grades for Goldsmiths, but the course convenors Becky Gardiner and Terry Kirby saw something in me, and decided to make an exception.

When I arrived for my induction session on a bright and sticky day in late September 2016, I listened to my soon-to-be classmates give thoughtful, considered and noble reasons for why they were pursuing journalism as a career. Some of them knew Westminster politics inside out; others had a finely tuned ear to every passing fad or had a wealth of knowledge about sport, music, culture and a host of other topics. I didn't know why – or even if – I wanted to become a journalist; I just knew I had stories to tell. I was twenty-nine when the course began and was just starting to notice my life in my rear-view. Time had extinguished the emotional heat from past traumas, allowing me to see them with cold eyes. Even though I didn't have my classmates' grades, I had experiences that provided me with unique insights into specific social issues, and I realised this could enhance my reporting.

My time at Goldsmiths was one of the most stable periods of my adult life. All of us were fortunate to have Becky and Terry as our teachers. Before taking her post at Goldsmiths, Becky had been an editor at the *Guardian* for fourteen years, and could transform the blurriest of ideas into something crisp and coherent. Terry had been a founding member of the *Independent* and became the paper's chief reporter; what he doesn't know about reporting isn't worth knowing. As part of our course work, we were required to write a political opinion piece for entry to the *Guardian*'s inaugural Hugo Young award. It was Becky's idea that I write about Emmaus. I did. I won.

In March 2017, I stood on the small stage in the middle of *Guardian* towers in a plush corner of King's Cross, smiling awkwardly, sweating profusely, as the *Guardian*'s editor-in-chief, Katherine Viner, handed me a razor-sharp glass brick. I thought about where I'd been a year before: in Emmaus, homeless, unsure of my future and fearing the worst for it. I was elated and beyond grateful to have won; I was also pissed off. *How can one's life just turn around so randomly?* I thought as I watched columnists like Owen Jones and Gary Young pluck delicate hors d'oeuvres from the trays of smartly dressed waiters. I didn't understand why I had deteriorated so rapidly while living in Mossley; I didn't understand why I had managed to keep it together while at Goldsmiths, and I certainly didn't know how I'd made it to that room. It just felt so random. Like my will made no impression on my life.

I made up for my poor showing at MMU and graduated Goldsmiths with a distinction. Afterwards, I secured a twelve-week internship with the *Londonist*, an online encyclopaedia of all things London. The gig mainly involved organising the site's social media output, compiling daily event listings, editing short videos and editing copy. I also got to write about Smithfield's Market, the pleasure to be had on an unexpected journey on a red double-decker bus, and the capital's unfortunate history with acid attacks. The Hugo Young award provided me with work experience with *G2*, the *Guardian*'s feature section, and this lent me the ear of Kira Cochrane, the *Guardian*'s brilliant head of features, who gave me regular commissions. Things were looking up – but normal service was about to resume.

A fortnight after I was evicted from Emmaus, the community gave Dom his marching orders after a staff member discovered a bag of skunk in his room. We stayed in touch and promised that we'd reunite in the capital. When my lease was up at Goldsmith's residence halls, I moved in with Dom in Islington in summer 2017. We lasted six months until Jack's eviction text.

When Jack returned from China, he asked for the next month's rent as usual, and explained that he would reimburse our deposits once we'd left. I didn't trust him. He'd assured me he was the landlord when I had moved in, but now claimed he had to terminate our tenancies because the real landlord wanted to refurbish the place. I told him he wouldn't be getting the rent.

'You must pay the last month's rent. If the room's OK, I'll give you your deposit!' Jack shouted at Dom and me as we huddled in the narrow corridor of our cramped flat on one freezing January evening.

'Yeah, I'm not paying you the rent, Jack. You lied about being the landlord, and I don't trust that you'll give us our deposits back,' I said.

'I'm not a thief. Of course I will give you the deposit back. Ask the others who have lived here in the past; I gave them their deposits,' Jack said.

'Good for them,' I replied. 'But what's the difference? You have my deposit, which is the equivalent of one month's rent, so pocket that and I'll be out at the end of the month.'

'OK, OK, that's enough. We're clearly at an impasse, so let's call it a night,' Dom said, ushering me into his room.

Jack's face curled into an angry sneer as he marched back to his own room and slammed the door behind him. I sank into a chair at Dom's cluttered desk and began shuffling through one of the many decks of playing cards he'd collected. Dom perched at the end of his double bed, wearing the same defeated expression as me.

'I'm not paying him, Dom. And you shouldn't either,' I said.

'I've got no choice,' Dom said, gesturing to a bedroll covered by a mess of yellow blankets strewn on the floor at the opposite side of the room. The bedding belonged to Joe, Dom's childhood friend and erstwhile roommate, who was holidaying with his family when Jack broke the news on New Year's Eve. It turned out that Joe had used his student loans to pay their rent three months in advance – including January. Dom and Joe had been sharing the same room to save money for the last year.

When walking into Dom and Joe's bedroom, you might think it belonged to a health-conscious burglar with a split personality. On Dom's side, clusters of fake thumbs were strewn in mountainous piles on his desk, alongside stacks of exhausted playing cards which fanned haphazardly around a tangled web of bulky padlocks interspersed with lockpicks. They were all innocent aids to Dom's repertoire as a magician. Joe's side was more orderly: a neat row of health supplements in colourful plastic containers with all their labels facing out stood atop his wardrobe, next to packets of wholegrain cereals and tubs of nutritionally enriched peanut butter. I don't know how they decided who would get the double bed, but it was Dom's. I didn't have many conversations with Joe, a reserved man. Still, I'd learned that he was a survivalist enthusiast, a fan of famous psychologist Jordan Peterson, and seemed to enjoy walking around the communal areas with his shirt off. Maybe sleeping on the floor, partial nudity and unnecessary dietary supplements are some of the *12 Rules for Life*.

We could have dug our heels in and stayed in the flat. Even though landlords can issue no-fault evictions on a whim, you can't just evict someone via text message. An eviction notice must be issued on a document called a Form 6a or on a letter with the information contained in Form 6a. The letter needs to include the tenant's name and address – misspelling any of that can void the notice. Moreover, at that time, landlords were required to give their tenants two months' notice.[1]

We should have waited until the end of January – when we were expected to do one – to explain to Jack that his eviction text was bollocks and inform him we would be staying until he issued legitimate eviction notices. We decided that it would be easier just to leave. We had rights, but there was no guarantee that Jack would honour them, and I'd heard many horror stories involving unscrupulous landlords who will change locks and hurl tenants' belongings on to the streets after they've tried to exercise their rights.

January was an anxious malaise. I was just about managing to get one feature a month in the *Guardian*, but it still didn't cover my rent and living expenses, so over the festive period, I applied for gigs in the retail sector. The application process for these jobs had changed dramatically from when I'd worked in shops a decade earlier. Back then, a natter with the hiring manager was all it took to get an opportunity. Now, applying for some retail gigs can take hours online. I slogged through loads of applications until I managed to secure an interview with Asda in Stratford, east London. When I'd rocked up to the supermarket on a bright, crisp day in November, I'd expected that the discussion would unfold in much the same way it had at Sainsbury's ten years before, with generic questions about experience, skills and aspirations.

But I'd turned up for a group assessment session – what they call 'Asda magic'. As I sat in the waiting room among several other candidates, I eavesdropped on their conversations. Some talked about what they had learned about the interview process through Glassdoor, a website that provides anonymous reviews from employees who provide information on everything from salary, working environment and the interview process. One candidate warned me that we could expect to have to devise a poem or play, or sing a song to sell a product back to our assessors. I felt the panic running cold in my chest as I heard this, and I bolted.

After the 'magic' at Asda, I resolved to better prepare for any wacky hoops I might have to jump through at future job interviews. Eventually, I got a temporary job with HMV at their flagship store (which has since closed) on Oxford Street. The interview process wasn't as elaborate as some on the high street, but it was still in a group, took over an hour and involved public speaking and mock-selling the store's rewards card. I had two degrees, had won an award for my writing and had semi-regular commissions with a national newspaper when I pulled on the store's purple T-shirt for the first time; getting a gig with HMV on Oxford Street felt more exciting and more rewarding than any of that.

When I was on the dole in my late teens and applying for menial, dead-end jobs that I was still underqualified for, I dreamed of manning the counter at the local HMV. I don't know why I thought working among film and album covers was preferable to working among groceries. It was almost like I thought the creativity contained in those rows of rectangles would somehow imbue me with inspiration. The staff in there looked different to regular shop workers, too. They seemed liberated, with their prominent piercings, colourful tats, dyed hair and stonking Dr Martens. They always seemed jolly at the tills, cracking jokes or sharing knowing grins when a record they disapproved of passed through their scanners. It looked fun.

It turns out that inanimate objects are inanimate objects. I spent most of my time at HMV walking around in endless circles, occasionally directing a customer towards products they could have discovered themselves if only they had a basic grasp of the alphabet.

I would have struggled to pay January's rent anyway. When the HMV contract expired in early January, I had no money coming in, and less than three weeks to cobble together enough pennies to fund a move. Luckily, I was able to con my way into a job with Squawka, a football news and statistics website. The site paid just over the London living wage, and with the final pay packet from HMV I was just able to save enough money to move.

On our final day in the flat, as we were scrambling to move

to east London, Jack was having an absolute fit about the state of my room.

'Here, use this to scrub the mould from the walls,' he said as he attempted to hand me a bottle of bleach and a brush.

'But it's mould. It's a structural problem, which has been here since I arrived. If anyone should be cleaning that, it's you – the fuckin' landlord! Oh yeah, you're not the landlord, innit,' I said.

I started laughing in his face. I was quite proud of myself. Not only was it nice to get one over on a piss-taker like him, but in the past, I would have matched his abuse with my own. But this time, I remained calm. I was in the right, and I knew he was angry because he couldn't bully me into doing what he wanted. Dom and Joe weren't so lucky. Jack still had their deposits, and refused to give them back until they'd scrubbed all the mould from their walls. The fact that the mould was all over the house didn't deter Jack. After hours of scrubbing and sweating, Dom and Joe had succeeded in doing a cosmetic job of reducing the appearance of mould on the surface of their bedroom walls.

I probably should have pre-empted this hassle. The ad hoc rental agreement Jack thrust under my nose six months earlier was threadbare, and about as legitimate as his New Year's Eve eviction text. Moreover, all security deposits are supposed to be placed into a government-approved tenancy deposit scheme, but he'd pocketed ours. So, legally, I was entitled to withhold the last month's rent, because I'd already paid it when I moved in.

At least we had a contract. Many rely on a verbal agreement when renting at the bottom end of the market. The deepening housing crisis, wage stagnation, insecure employment and our oppressive benefits system allow landlords to exploit their tenants like never before. The government have estimated that there are 10,500 rogue landlords like Jack renting out properties in England. Stories of tenants cramming together in their dozens in disintegrating, damp and cold homes designed for four or five has become the norm. Dodgy landlords who are aware of the precarious predicaments of their low-income tenants will often fail to address repairs or update utilities. They're also confident you won't complain. The law allows landlords to kick their tenants to the curb on a whim, and most will assume their tenants are not even aware of the few rights they have to delay evictions.

Over the last three years, efforts have been made to hold rogue landlords to account. In April 2018, the government started the rogue landlord database. The database was originally intended only as an enforcement tool available to local authorities, and at the time of writing lists only serious criminals convicted of banning order offences. The policy is currently under review, and the database may become open to the public, like the Mayor of London Sadiq Khan's Rogue Landlord and Agent Checker, which allows Londoners to check on prospective landlords and agencies and report rogue practices. Before the government launched their database in 2018, they predicted that more than 600 of the worst offenders would make it on to the database. However, according to data I obtained in March 2021, only thirty-nine entries from twenty-five local authorities had been made.[2]

Dom, Joe and I didn't have a lot of time to find new digs, so we had to settle on the first place that we could afford, in what might as well have been the house that George Orwell built. The beige box I moved into in Plaistow, east London, at the end of January 2018 only cost me £450 a month – a steal in the capital – but when I stood in the middle of my glorified closet, I could touch the walls on both sides with my fingertips. Big Brother awaited beyond my threshold, with live surveillance cameras feeding into the landlord's office adjacent to the property. When we signed up, our landlord assured us that the cameras were there to resolve cleaning disputes. I found this more than a little unsettling but thought there was no way the staff could monitor these cameras around the clock.

How wrong I was.

The slats on my plywood single weren't long enough to reach each side of the bed frame. I didn't think to check this when I moved in, and I discovered the issue the hard way when the bed collapsed underneath me in the middle of my first night in the box. The following day, I dismantled the frame and carted the timber to the bins outside the front door. I was about to ring Newham Council to arrange a collection when one of the landlord's staff knocked on my bedroom door. An interrogation of sorts ensued. The staff member instructed me to leave the bedframe outside their office, which I dutifully did moments later. I didn't bill the landlord for the new bed I bought – he was outwardly reasonable, but I feared that he would rather evict me than pay for a replacement bed.

Plaistow was one of the strangest living arrangements I'd ever experienced. Along with Dom and Joe, I shared the flat with eleven other housemates. On my floor, there was a Romanian couple living next door to me. They were quiet and kept to themselves. The occupants of the room next to them changed so often that I lost track of who was living there; the same goes for whichever loud couples occupied the converted attic, accessed via a spiral staircase just outside my door.

Dom and Joe piled into a double room on the ground floor, where their belongings left even less room for feng shui. The landlord had converted half of the kitchen to make room for two more bedrooms, which faced each other on either side of a narrow corridor that led to the back garden, where another resident lived in a converted shed. On one side of the corridor, four jolly Romanian builders crammed together in a small double. They barely spoke English, and I'm ashamed to admit that I never learned their names, even after living there for two years. They'd occasionally offer me a glass of wine, a can of lager or a cigarette; we'd exchange approving noises and go our separate ways.

Opposite them was a man in his mid-twenties called Dave. Dave was around six foot three, as wide as a house, and lived in a room that would've made Harry Potter claustrophobic. Dave was a recluse and would go out of his way to avoid human contact. I was on the way out of the house one evening when I saw Dave about to turn his key on the other side of the front door. When he noticed me approaching, instead of waiting for me to let him in, he turned around and darted up the street. Neither I nor anyone else in the property ever spoke a word to him; the only time I heard his voice was indirectly, via his smartphone. Dom and I were in the back garden one evening, poisoning our lungs with ghastly menthol cigarettes, when we heard Dave open his bedroom door.

'All right, Dave,' Dom said.

'Hi, mate,' I said.

Dave, like a deer startled by a careening truck's headlights, scrambled back into his room and slammed the door behind him.

'What the fuck?' Dom and I whispered to each other in unison.

Then came the soft creak of Dave's bedroom door, which opened about a centimetre. You could have cut the tension with a knife. After a few moments, a computerised voice emanated from his room and said: 'Now that you know my name, please keep the bathroom tidy at all times.'

I thought this was a bit rich coming from computer Dave. Dave and I were the only people in the flat who didn't have en-suite bedrooms, and we had to share the same bathroom. Dave didn't appear to understand the efficacy of shower curtains or how to use a mop; every time I used the bathroom after him, it was like I'd visited the most depressing paddling pool in London. Dave's swamp could be left unattended for days if I was away from home, and because the bathroom – a converted broom closet next to the staircase – wasn't ventilated, mould and limescale had a field day. It's the only bathroom in the world where you'd emerge dirtier than when you entered. It got so bad that I started taking showers at the leisure centre over the road. I did feel sorry for Dave, though. He had severe learning difficulties and wasn't getting proper support.

Overall, the next two years in Newham were stable. I knuckled down with Squawka, even though I was entirely out of my depth in that job. I'm a red-hot Manchester United fan. How could a Mancunian child of the nineties be anything else? I suppose I could've been a City fan, but I had enough misery in my personal life without needing any more from the Kippax. In the nineties, United were finally knocking the Kopites from their perch after twenty-six years of title wilderness. Their success was mixed up with the Madchester scene and all its rocking, arrogant swagger. Rock 'n' roll football. Manchester was cool. But I'm not an actual *football* fan. I find the game boring and almost impossible to watch when United aren't playing. This presented a problem for me at Squawka, as the website caters to pedantic soccer anoraks whose lifeforce seems to be centred around reducing the beautiful game to cold numbers and trivial factoids concerning things like ball-recoveries, won and lost aerial duels, completed passes and so on. I was desperate for work, so when I applied for the gig, I made out that my anorak was big enough to impress all the other anoraks. I was about to get saturated (I think I've beaten this metaphor to death).

One was expected to perform several roles at Squawka, ranging from news reporting to feature writing and match reports. For news, the site's editors would ping over a list of news headlines from mainstream outlets; they expected you to find a new angle to the story and augment it with relevant data collated from their comparison matrix and other stats farmed from the Web. We had forty-five minutes to write each news piece, and my poor football knowledge put me at least ten minutes behind everyone else. It was like diffusing a time bomb armed only with *Electronics for Dummies*. The features weren't as strictly timed, but they required more numbers and more knowledge – knowledge that I didn't have. Even though match reports were the most stressful tasks, I was a lot more competent with them (in my opinion; the editors may not have agreed). It was a simple matter of awarding ratings out of ten for players, accompanied by a pithy blurb on their performances. Centre-backs, unless they did something fantastically daft or brilliant, would typically earn six marks out of ten and receive adjectives like 'solid', 'watertight' and 'efficient', so you didn't have to worry too much about them – the same went for full-backs. You had to pay more attention to midfielders, who act as conduits to the defence and attack, and you really had to wax lyrical for goal-scorers and assisters.

I managed to fake it for over a year until my other journalistic commitments began hogging my attention, making it blatantly obvious that I didn't know what I was doing. The site's editor became increasingly exasperated with my plodding work rate, and offered me fewer and fewer shifts.

The whole time I was at Squawka, I was juggling commissions with the *Guardian*. I was writing 'Shortcuts', 350–450-word quick takes on popular news stories. Shorties were fun to write. I covered everything from the dinosaur bone market and scallop wars in the English Channel to animal-themed yoga retreats and cockroach milk. I also got more long-form features to write, which focused on culture, social justice and mental health issues. I still have to pinch myself when I see a piece of mine in the *Guardian*. I only wish my grandma had been alive to see my first byline; I know she would have been proud.

My situation was becoming precarious again in May 2019. Squawka had made up most of my income over the last year, but shifts were dwindling, and I could hear the Job Centre beckoning. Then, out of the blue, Simon Hattenstone recruited me for the *Empty Doorway* series.

Simon is a happy-go-lucky pessimist. When he rang to ask me if I would join him on the series, he ended the conversation by dampening my expectations. 'It almost certainly won't happen, and when it doesn't, we'll have a drink and a Chinese,' he said.

'Fine,' I said.

I got the gig a few days later.

When we began research for the series. Simon continued to manage my expectations. He said it would be amazing if we managed to get a single piece written, as we were mostly relying on talking to bereaved friends and relatives, and would face a hideous obstacle course made up of privacy and defamation laws.

'This could go tits up,' Simon warned as he danced around me in his white vest and shiny Dr Martens on *G2*'s desk one sunny May afternoon. 'But fuck it, if it does, we'll have a massive piss-up and a massive Chinese.'

We ended the series with nine long-form pieces totalling around 6,000 words each.

In December 2019, the series got nominated for a Press Gazette British Journalism award in feature writing. We were both over the moon. The series had completely eclipsed the rosiest hopes we'd had for it.

'It's great,' Simon said as he spun me around. 'But we're not going to win, and when we don't: fuck it, we'll have the biggest piss-up of all time and the tackiest Chinese buffet ever!'

We won!

Later that December, I stood nervously alongside Simon on a dimly lit stage in the ballroom basement of the Bankside Hilton. Simon gave a moving impromptu speech, thanking those who had contributed and highlighting the importance of the issue. When he handed over to me, all I could manage was 'Cheers' and a quick nod of the head. The ballroom roared with laughter. I was quite pleased with myself at the time; I thought I was the Wise to his Morecambe, but it turns out it was a sympathy laugh. After accepting the sharp glass brick (the best paperweight ever), we went our separate ways to schmooze and socialise.

A hack from a rival paper approached Simon to congratulate him and remarked: 'Hey, it was really nice of you to bring that homeless fella along with you.'

'Who, Danny?' Simon replied incredulously. 'He wrote it with me.'

I was the only one in attendance without a fancy suit, opting for jeans and a T-shirt – imposter syndrome in full effect, but there was a touch of vagrancy about me. The guy excused his blushes and moved along.

A week after receiving our brick, I headed back to Manchester to spend Christmas with some friends. Jack Frost had already visited the platform at Piccadilly station when Dom rang me with some festive cheer:

'We're being evicted, mate,' Dom said, giggling.

'Oh, stop it, Dom. Don't take the piss,' I said. 'What do you really want?'

'No, no, really,' Dom said, and his voice became more measured. 'We have to leave. We got an eviction notice in the post today, so . . . yeah.'

Dom photographed the letter and sent it over. He wasn't lying. We had two months to skedaddle. We'd lasted two years this time, good going for renting in the capital. We hadn't done anything wrong, and no secret landlord was lurking behind the scenes this time. Effectively, we were given our marching orders by Newham Council. According to Newham, our landlord – like so many London landlords – had got greedy and transformed a house intended for families into a House in Multiple Occupancy (HMO) without the necessary planning permission. London's landlords slice their properties into the smallest possible segments so they can squeeze as much money out of as many people as possible, forcing people, especially those on low incomes, to accept poor living conditions in order to secure affordable rents. It was difficult to argue with the council's reasoning: Newham claimed that the conversion contributed to an increase in noise pollution and did not provide 'an adequate or healthy living environment' for current and future residents. They also said that the loss of a family dwelling in the borough 'prejudices the ability to stabilise the community'.

Greedy bastard or not, I took the view that the council, not my landlord, was making me homeless, so I contacted Newham Council's press office to see if they were planning on rehousing us. They didn't see it that way. A council spokeswoman said:

The council has not made these residents homeless. The landlord is threatening to do so by issuing a notice to quit. The landlord has changed a family residence into a House in Multiple Occupation (HMO), without the necessary planning permission and in contravention of the Local Plan. The council's planning decision was upheld at appeal. Any resident who finds themselves threatened with homelessness as a result of being asked to leave by a landlord, is entitled to advice and support from the council's Homelessness Prevention Advisory Service (HPAS).

I found the council's logic breathtaking. It would be like setting fire to a building and then blaming the fire for burning it down. I contacted HPAS, but they didn't reply until the end of January 2020, by which time I'd already left Newham.

I didn't want to stay in that box forever. I was contemplating leaving the capital altogether at the time. Even though I was poor when I lived in Greater Manchester in my late teens and twenties, I'd had whole houses to myself. I'd had space. Privacy. In London, I ricocheted from one stifling, overpriced box to the next, living with complete strangers and queueing for washing machines, oven hobs and bathrooms while every move I made was closely monitored.

I didn't have the funds to move. As a freelancer, you never know how your paycheque will tot out from one month to the next, making it difficult to plan for anything. The notion that lots of people are a missed payslip away from poverty has been a well-worn trope over the last decade, and one that often has sceptics rolling their eyes. But during the first months of the coronavirus pandemic, the reality of this notion was laid bare for all to see. When Boris Johnson – after weeks of deadly dithering – finally sent us into lockdown, almost a million people flocked to the dole queue for Universal Credit (UC),[3] exposing the government's brag that the UK is the 'jobs factory of Europe'[4] for the thinly veiled lie that it is. OK, in 2019 unemployment did fall to its lowest level since 1975, and the Office for National

Statistics did find that the UK employment rate was at a joint record high of 76.3 per cent.[5] But this picture is less rosy when you look at it a little more closely. Almost one million UK workers are on precarious zero-hours contracts,[6] which means there's no guarantee that the individuals who comprise those figures are the same from one day to the next.

The thing about having a zero-hours job is this: you don't *have* a job. You're certainly not considered an employee. You can be hired, then fired five minutes later with impunity. Employees with employment contracts don't fare much better. To secure full employment rights, which protect workers from things like unfair dismissal, one would need to be working in their job for two years.[7] Millions of Britons have been subsisting on a cliff edge for years. Any false move or lose rock will cause you to plummet to the ground, with your only hope of survival a wafer-thin safety net riven with holes.

Austerity and George Osborne's callous welfare reforms have laid waste to the UK's social security system. Universal Credit was the most significant of these reforms. UC combined unemployment benefits, like Job Seeker's Allowance and Income Support, with tax credits and housing benefits, bundling them into one monthly payment.[8] A sound idea in the right hands, but under the coalition government and subsequent Tory governments, it has been a disaster. Long waiting times – lasting up to eleven weeks in some cases – between initial claims and first payments have driven many people into debt, causing them to prioritise food and bills over their rent.[9] Compounding this is the draconian sanctioning system that has left many claimants penniless over trivial things like arriving late for a Job Centre appointment or, in the case of former Department of Work and Pensions worker Garreth Forrest, missing an appointment to attend a funeral.[10] Eviction then deprivation is often the consequence, with 65 per cent of local authorities saying that UC has increased homelessness.[11]

Even if you avoid debt and everything goes smoothly at the Job Centre, the ground can still erode underneath you. In some areas, rent hikes are coupled with freezes to the Local Housing Allowance, which has created shortfalls between people's rents and the amount of housing benefit they receive.[12] The government will penalise you further for having a spare room. In 2012, the coalition arguably created their most insidious policy. The Bedroom Tax (removal of the spare room subsidy) took 14 per cent of someone's benefit for having a spare room, and 25 per cent if they had two or more.[13] This policy continues to plunge people into poverty and despair.[14] If losing work, delayed benefits and spare rooms can see you on the streets, you won't be surprised to learn that illness can see you there as well.

'I don't want people to do the five stretch and have the mental torment that I've had for five years,' Colin said, as he offered me a cigarette outside a greasy spoon in Redbridge town centre on a sticky day in June 2020. 'It broke me. I done a lump of bird. Durham, Whitemoor. All proper top nicks, you with me, Danny? That didn't break me. This has broke me.'

Colin is middle-aged and sounds exactly as one would expect an old Cockney villain to sound. Add a sheepskin coat and some sovereign rings, and you'd have the typical Guy Ritchie East End gangster. Colin had been living in Cambridge Park, a run-down homeless hostel, since 2015. He moved there after breaking up with his partner, who moved out of the flat they were sharing. Redbridge Council told Colin that he was under-occupying his home and would have to move. Redbridge also told him that hostel placement would be temporary – no more than six weeks.

We were joined by Brian and Harry, who lived with him at the hostel. Brian was also Cockney and middle-aged, and the more laid back of the trio. He became homeless when a diagnosis of multiple sclerosis prevented him from continuing his job as a lorry driver. Harry was just as Cockney, but had West Indian roots. He also became homeless due to illness and precarity.

It was Harry, a former housing officer, who had reached out to me over email a week earlier with a laundry list of complaints about the living conditions in the hostel. Harry had told me that young single mothers, elderly people with severe physical disabilities, people with mental illnesses and addicts lived in the hostel, along with former high-risk offenders. He said that residents were allocated places at Cambridge Park without having their needs evaluated and without risk assessments in place. There was no support for residents with benefit claims, housing and employment applications and other needs. Harry explained that even though several residents fell into the Covid-19 high-risk group – either due to age or illness – new residents were accepted at the hostel throughout lockdown without being tested for the virus. Moreover, the hostel provided no dustbins, cleaning materials, sanitisers or wipes in the communal areas.

After Colin had plied me with a few more cigarettes and strong coffee (he wouldn't let me pay), they all spoke over each other at a mile a minute about the many injustices they'd witnessed and experienced over the last eighteen months.

'What's the worst thing you've seen there?' I asked.

They practically fell over themselves to get their stories out – there were so many of them.

'Well, the worst one for me was old Charlie lying in the hallway after he died,' Brian said. Harry and Colin nodded solemnly. They told me Charlie was a kindly middle-aged academic who had been living on kidney dialysis before he collapsed and died near the front door.

'When did Charlie die?' I asked.

'It was the day after Liverpool won the Champions League, because he watched it the night before. He had his shirt on that night, his mate come round, and the next day he died,' Brian explained. They told me he lay dead at the front door for two hours before his body was collected.

Throughout our chat, they reel off more harrowing stories. They said that the armed police had visited the premises on several occasions looking for wanted men. They told me how a blind man was placed on the second floor of their building and expected to 'feel his way around'. A young woman with a newborn was not provided with an en-suite bedroom and had to leave her baby alone when she showered; no action was taken when a mentally ill woman battered another female resident. I put all of their claims to Redbridge Council when we parted ways that afternoon. A Redbridge Council spokesperson said:

Following the start of the Covid-19 outbreak, approximately 180 rough sleepers were helped off the streets and given a place in temporary accommodation to help keep them safe. While we're pleased all Redbridge rough sleepers were provided with accommodation, this, unfortunately, did have a destabilising impact on the other tenants at this particular property. We're aware there were a number of issues experienced by the original tenants. We accept the situation was far from ideal, but the council was under extreme pressure to ensure rough sleepers were not left at risk during the height of the Covid-19 pandemic.

The individuals placed at Cambridge Park through the rough sleepers' programme are no longer situated there. We're also pleased to confirm that most of the problems have now been resolved, and we've arranged for cleaning and sanitary materials to be provided at this property. We're in contact with the warden of this property and have asked to be updated on any future issues.

Over the next six months, I stayed in touch with Harry. The story of how he became homeless is one that should alarm us all. Two years before our meeting, he was thriving. He'd been working full-time for eighteen months as a manager with a housing organisation in Haringey, where he oversaw a team of twenty-one staff. He was renting a comfortable flat in Redbridge and had a full social life. He then fell violently ill in March 2019.

Harry was scared that he might have contracted the auto-immune disease lupus, as his two older sisters had died of the condition, and he had similar symptoms. After several hospital visits, he was diagnosed with five debilitating conditions at once:

fibromyalgia, rheumatoid arthritis, acute asthma, type two diabetes, and a blood clot in his right leg. 'They all hit me in one moment. So, all of a sudden: boom! I couldn't walk.'

Sometimes he couldn't even get out of bed: 'When that happened, I couldn't do anything. I was in constant pain. It was to the point where I should have had a permanent carer,' Harry said. He wasn't well enough to carry on working, so he stayed at home, collected sick pay and lived off his savings, but that only sustained him for nine months. He lost everything.

After leaving his flat, he stayed on his brother's sofa for a few months, but he couldn't survive there. He couldn't claim Universal Credit from his brother's address, because it would've reduced the amount of housing benefit his brother was entitled to. And because Harry had no money coming in, he felt like he was always 'treading on eggshells'. Ultimately, he decided to make a homelessness application, and was placed in Cambridge Park with Colin and Brian.

From being a housing worker who worked with vulnerable homeless people to becoming a vulnerable homeless person himself in less than a year was a humiliating experience for Harry. 'It broke down my self-esteem. I lost three and a half stone; people around me could see the deterioration. I was hiding myself away. I got depressed, because I was thinking: "Is this it?"'

Harry has a large and supportive family, including three children and six grandchildren who are more than willing to go out of their way to help him. He said they would have let him live with them, but he didn't want to be a burden. He even hid the full extent of his illnesses from them, carefully timing visits for when he felt healthy enough to keep up appearances.

'Somebody said to me: "Harry, you shouldn't have hidden the full extent," but if they saw where I was really at, I think it would have hurt them,' he said.

At the time of writing, Harry has been trying to secure permanent housing for the last two years. Due to his mobility needs, he requires a ground-floor property, but, so far, has been unsuccessful in finding one. After someone makes a successful housing application, they're placed on a housing waiting list by their local authority and invited to make bids on available properties that meet their requirements.[15] Harry has been bidding for properties on Redbridge's housing register since 2019, but the council has still not offered him a permanent home.

After six months in Cambridge House, Redbridge offered Harry a temporary flat in a converted office block. The flat offered to him was on the third floor. The council argued that the office block was suitable because there was lift access; Harry argued that if there was a fire on one of his bad days, he wouldn't be able to use the lift. Because he rejected their offer, Harry believes the council are no longer considering his bids: 'I bid every week, so if you imagine that's more than a hundred and thirty times, because of the length of time I've been there,' Harry told me. The council has not confirmed or denied Harry's suspicions, so he remains in limbo.

During the UK's second nationwide lockdown, Redbridge moved Harry and the rest of Cambridge House's residents out and into hotels. 'All of us were given short notice of about a week to move out. So, we're treated as shit. It's like we're fodder,' Harry said.

I was astonished by his composure. Throughout our

conversations, Harry talked about his serious problems in a detached, almost matter-of-fact way. It was almost like he was talking about someone else – a troubled client from his old job. And he still does his old job. Despite his many issues, Harry still finds time to help other residents – both at Cambridge House and in the hotel he's in – with their benefits and housing applications. Many of the people Harry lives with don't have English as a first language, are poorly educated, and seldom clued up about their rights and entitlements.

'You just can't ignore it. Nobody knows about the support. There are people who haven't even made their Universal Credit claim; there's people who don't know about bidding. It hurts me to know that the housing isn't even contacting the people,' Harry said.

'How do you remain so composed?' I asked.

'I'm always like, "the cup is half full". Because there are times when you lay out your situation: "I'm fifty-seven years old, not got a pot to piss in, haven't got my own place." While this is going on, there's a lot of heaviness. I want to be like everybody else. I want to be able to turn round and say to my friends and family: "Come round and see me." Just getting a hug from them – you walk tall for about a month.'

Harry's illnesses are debilitating and life-threatening; he worries that he won't make it to the end of some days, and lingering over this is relentless uncertainty.

'I think I'd have lost my sanity if I was in your situation,' I said.

'My thing is: If I can do something about it, I'll do it; if I can't, I'll resign. OK, if there's nothing I can do, I just cut it out of my mind. How much control do I have in my own life because of all these different things: the housing, the Covid – the only thing I have left is the ability to think.'

Harry's Christian faith keeps him going. 'There were times when I was literally not moving other than to go to the toilet. That was a time when I was thinking: "Am I gonna be popping off here? Things are deteriorating. Am I gonna be seeing my next birthday?" And even then, is when the faith comes in: "Yes, I am!"'

I wish I shared Harry's faith, but I fear that he will have to struggle for the foreseeable future, like so many other people languishing in temporary accommodation. It is far too easy to become homeless in this country. A missed paycheque, a delayed benefit payment, an unscrupulous landlord or illness is all it takes to lose everything. The changes needed to put this right are wide-ranging and demand comprehensive government reforms, yet as the government continues to be parsimonious, the help available amounts to treating a shotgun wound with gaffer tape.

The government banned evictions to protect tenants during the pandemic, but over 45,000 renters lost their homes in 2020.[16] Renters in south-east England and on the outskirts of London are most at risk of receiving no-fault evictions.[17] I received two of these in the space of two years. So far, I've been fortunate enough to scrape enough cash together to finance a move each time, but if those evictions came along during a bad month, I could've easily ended up homeless again. I worry about Dom, not only because he's my best mate, but because when we were evicted the first time, he was between jobs and had to lean on others for financial help (which he paid back). The second time, he was fortunate enough to have enough savings to arrange a move. Dom mostly works in retail on precarious zero-hour contracts, and his working hours fluctuate from one month to the next, depending on demand in the market. Shortly after the first lockdown, his employer refused to furlough him. When I asked them why, they responded by sacking him. The reason? For speaking to a journalist. Dom subsequently sued and the matter was settled out of court, but if it wasn't for the eviction ban and emergency measures to expedite the application process for Universal Credit, who knows where he would be now.

When it comes to protecting tenants, transparency is welcome, and things like rogue landlord databases are a good idea. But the simple fact is the private sector cannot cater to our most vulnerable tenants. In the absence of a comprehensive, nationwide social-housing-building project, the welfare system needs to be redesigned to support people in their homes, not to catch them out at every opportunity. Ending the long delay between application and first Universal Credit payment should be a priority; so should reviewing the sanctioning system and eliminating the harshest punishments. The spare room subsidy should be restored, employment rights strengthened, and sickness should never lead to homelessness. But if we're ever going to truly end homelessness, nothing short of a complete overhaul of the economy will do.

Conclusion

Ending Homelessness

It was bitingly cold on a dreary morning in mid-December 2020 when I walked through a grubby underpass on my way to the Jubilee line at Westminster tube station. Two years earlier, Gyula Remes had collapsed here after taking a drag on a laced cigarette. He was rushed a few hundred yards across Westminster Bridge to St Thomas' Hospital, where he died, aged forty-three. Remes was the second person to die in that underpass in under a year. His death sparked outrage in Parliament. The Labour MP David Lammy tweeted: 'There is something rotten in Westminster when MPs walk past dying homeless people on the way into work.'[1]

Later that day, Remes' death was debated in the Commons. The Liberal Democrat MP and former health minister Norman Lamb said: 'It is grotesque and obscene that we have a homeless-ness crisis visible just outside the building.' The next day, James Brokenshire, then secretary of state for Housing, Communities and Local Government, told Parliament: 'Every death of someone sleeping rough on our streets is one too many. Each is a tragedy, each a life cut short. We have a moral duty to act.'[2] Since then, we've heard platitudes like these from the government and the opposition every time a tragedy like Remes' hits the front pages, and yet, year on year, we find ourselves in a worse position.

The Office for National Statistics reported that the number of people dying while homeless in England and Wales had risen for the fifth consecutive year to its highest level in 2019. The year after Remes' death, 778 homeless people died, an increase of 7.2 per cent on the 726 deaths in 2018.[3] Two months later, research published by the Museum of Homelessness revealed that 976 homeless people had died in the UK in 2020 – a 37 per cent increase from their previous study published the year before.[4] This increase occurred despite the government's Everyone In strategy and efforts to curb rough sleeping during the coronavirus pandemic.

As I walked through Westminster station two years on from Remes' death, it occurred to me that only one thing had changed during that time: MPs had been spared the indignity of walking 'past dying homeless people' on their way to work, as the tunnel leading to the Houses of Parliament has been closed off to rough sleepers.

The causes of homelessness are complicated and have many variables: childhood traumas, bereavement, relationship breakdowns, dependency, social precarity, irresponsibility and a raft of other causes specific to individuals.

After looking back at my life, I've tried to identify when I started on my path to the streets. There's no specific moment I can point to and say, 'That's when I was doomed,' but I experienced many of the things that have a causal link with homelessness. My disruptive and incomplete education is highly correlated with poor outcomes in adulthood, as are early childhood traumas, abuse, neurological disorders and separation from family. Lucy, my friend from Nelson Avenue, had different beginnings to my own, but they were just as disruptive, and she ended up on the street and in hostels. Sunita, who was in the system at the same time as me, followed a similar pathway to the street.

Even if you make it through childhood relatively unscathed and have a supportive and loving family, dependency can see your life unravel. Noel's opiate dependency saw him go from a top job in engineering to living in an Emmaus community. Mark Starr had an idyllic childhood and the best parents, grandparents and siblings one could ask for, but life-long addiction, mental illness and broken support services contributed to his death on Glasgow Green.

If you've done everything right in life, you can still end up destitute. There's no room for mistakes or misfortune in modern Britain, as Harry learned the hard way during the pandemic. He was a housing worker who worked with the homeless before he became ill. Then he lost everything – except his dignity.

The enraging thing about all of this is that solving these problems is relatively simple. That's not to say it will be easy. Running a marathon is simple: one runs from point A to point B – but the stuff in the middle is hard. Solving homelessness is going to be hard. That's because homelessness is not a social ill that has risen in a vacuum; it's a symptom of an economy with poverty and suffering built into its design. Solving homelessness will require a government that's intent on radically reforming our political and economic system. This begins with ending austerity; inaugurating a tax system that forces multinational corporations and the super-rich to make a fair contribution to our society; returning our fragmented and disjointed social infrastructure into public hands; and investing in that new infrastructure. When that apparatus is in place, we will have the resources to engender change. And many things need change, but a good place to start would be prevention.

'The kids have said they walk on to this site, and they feel safe. A farm is the most dangerous place you could ever be, and they feel safe; they feel safe that nobody's gonna trap them. Because if they want to walk away, they've got thirty acres,' Julie Plumley told me as we trundled through the morass at the edge of a small pond, where a paddling of ducks had emerged from clusters of reeds for their morning feed. It was early August 2020, and I was visiting Plumley's Dorset farm because I'd heard they do education a little differently there.

Plumley, who has a friendly demeanour to match her friendly face, has been running Future Roots, a care farming programme that offers education courses for people with learning difficulties, mental health issues and physical disabilities, since 2008. There are 250 care farms currently operating in the UK. They typically offer agricultural activities to their clients, including animal and plant husbandry, horticulture and land management. Future Roots managed to stay open throughout the pandemic and were hosting two groups during my visit: the Countryman's Club, a programme that assists men in their fifties with degenerative diseases such as Parkinson's disease, and the Future Farmers course, which caters to students aged between fourteen and eighteen. The Future Farmers course includes a City & Guilds Award in Land-based Operations, and covers basic literacy and numeracy.

Two of the farm's dogs, Alfie, a dainty, ageing terrier, and Mutty, a big fluffy Alsatian-Malamute cross, weave our legs as Plumley tells me how she had the idea for Future Roots. She had worked with troubled kids as a social worker and visited them in schools. After observing the kids, she thought that some who misbehaved could have benefited from the environment on the farm she grew up on.

'Dad was my hero. So, he was never the best at anything. He was a dairyman, he fixed tractors, he was a builder, he was a plumber; whatever went wrong on the farm, Dad would just fix it,' she said. 'And I was like: "God, the farm can teach you something that you might enjoy." That's not hard to recreate. It's not about money. It's feeling you belong somewhere, you're a part of something, you're useful and you've got hope for the future.'

Future Roots accepts young people from up to twenty schools across Dorset and neighbouring Somerset. They receive 70 per cent of their income from local councils and schools who send their pupils to the farm; the remaining 30 per cent is made up of donations. Plumley said that the kids who come to her are bright, just not academic. Despite their reputation for disruptive behaviour, Plumley has never excluded anyone from the farm.

The young people who attend the farm come from a variety of backgrounds. Some are care experienced; some have struggled with addiction and some have been excluded from mainstream education. A study conducted by Bournemouth University found that young people attending care farms improved their mental health and gained more control of their behaviour; they socialised more and re-engaged with education.[5]

The students arrived, and Plumley and I walked from the pond to meet them at the cow barns. On our way, we passed by Marshmallow and Favourite, a pair of elderly ewes who were on their last legs. The farm also has around thirty cows, a couple of donkeys, a pair of pigs, a brace of goats, rabbits, ducks, geese and chickens. I talked to some of the students as they attended to the stars of the farm, a herd of Simmentals – posh cows from Switzerland. The Simmentals provide bovine therapy and education to the kids and adults who look after them, although their primary purpose is to make money. As well as refilling their troughs and replacing their bedding, the students have to look out for 'bulling' and other tell-tale signs that the cows are in season. All of the students I spoke to talked about their frustrations with mainstream education; how they felt stifled, bullied, not listened to and out of place. And all of them talked about how much they enjoy working on the farm.

As I wandered the farm with the group, I was reminded of the freedom and tranquillity I experienced at Grange House, and how the ethos here would've been anathema to the discipline and structure prescribed at Dippydale. I told Plumley about my time at Dippydale, and how it felt more like a Borstal than a school.

'Some of the special schools say, "Oh, you need to plan out your day, and you give them a routine – and you must do this,"' Plumley said. 'It doesn't actually teach you anything, because when you get in the real world, you can plan for tomorrow, then it pees with rain. And certainly, on a farm you can plan for tomorrow, and then a cow drops dead.'

At Dippydale – and I'm sure the same is true for many special schools like it – I wasn't there to be understood; I was there to be corrected. Walking off site would result in being chased down over the Moors by a team of staff in 4x4s, followed by a gratuitous restraint, further punishment and shame. Outbursts are handled differently at Future Roots, and kids have acres of space in which to blow off steam.

I don't know if the kids were on their best behaviour for me and my tape recorder, but all of them were glowing with enthusiasm for their work, for the animals. One would expect a group of socially excluded teenagers to be carrying the weight of the world around with them. Guards up. Heads down. Constricted. If they are burdened with such weight, they must have left it at the entrance. It must help that they have mentors who seem to encourage them, who champion them, who won't condemn them for having a tizz when it all gets too much. They're understood here, and it shows.

I'm not suggesting that all troubled kids should be sent to muck out pigs, but not everyone is suited to the classroom, and given that a good education is highly correlated with career success, wealth, health and life expectancy, shouldn't our education system cater to everyone?

Along with improving special education, we must do better at looking after looked-after children. We have to ensure that care home staff *want* to work with troubled kids and have the appropriate training. When I was in the system twenty years ago, there was a high turnover of staff. Many were low-paid agency workers who drifted across homes in Greater Manchester, and the full-timers were frequently absent and, when they were there, incompetent. Nelson Avenue occasionally asked the home's cleaner to fill in for absent care staff when no agency workers were available. Things haven't improved much over the years; they may have even got worse. In 2018, the Independent Inquiry into Child Sexual Abuse recommended that staff working in care roles in children's homes register with an independent body that regulates their training and standards.[6]

Their inexperience and lack of quality training leads staff to panic when confronted with poor behaviour, which leads to the unnecessary criminalisation of children over infractions that would earn nothing more than a minor reprimand from the average parent. According to the Howard League for Penal Reform's 2017 study into the criminalisation of children in residential care, poor children's home workers are policing rather than parenting the kids under their charge, and 'some homes were calling the police in order to punish and control children'.[7]

I can understand why children's home staff want to call the police rather than make an effort to resolve difficult situations themselves. Staff in children's homes are underpaid and overworked,[8] but involving the police only creates animus and a loss of trust, which, in my experience, leads to an escalation of bad behaviour – and, eventually, criminal behaviour. This is what happened to Carter at Nelson Avenue. His defiance had relatively innocuous beginnings: bingeing on confectionery and cereal, ignoring curfews and making a big song-and-dance around bedtime. Eventually, these song-and-dances would lead to handcuffs, because the staff were completely inert and incompetent. In the aftermath, Carter saw himself as a criminal, when he was actually a silly teenager with a bad attitude – a common and treatable condition. If we're going to avoid producing more Carters, care home staff should be trained to the same standards as social workers – and their pay should reflect the value of the work they do.

As well as improving the support for children in the system, we need to devise a better approach for young adults preparing to leave it. I began living on my own aged seventeen, and even though I had key workers and social workers paying me visits each week, I wasn't ready to look after myself. I was still a kid – a very immature kid with learning difficulties, a mental illness, no qualifications and few friends. I still needed to be in a supported environment. I believe social services failed me, but I shudder to think how I would fare if I was leaving the system today. Privatisation has smashed the care sector to bits, leaving young care-leavers abandoned to market forces. Looked-after kids aged sixteen and over are languishing in unregulated accommodation and then left to their own devices. We should remove the arbitrary age barrier for people leaving the system. Care-leavers should only become truly independent when they, and their social workers, feel they are ready – and if it all goes tits up when they're on their own, a door in supported accommodation should always be left open to them.

This lack of follow-up care contributed to the misery that Lucy and Sunita experienced in early adulthood. When Sunita fled from her first flat due to horrific domestic violence, she was made to choose between a chaotic refuge and the street – and she chose the street. And many other homeless people decide that a doorway is preferable to an emergency bed in a hostel like the Narrowgate in Manchester. This is a disgrace.

For the chronically homeless, the situation is dire. Austerity has vitiated local services to such an extent that those most desperately in need depend almost entirely on charity and the goodwill of strangers for respite. Austerity was always a maladroit solution to the global recession. As John Maynard Keynes' maxim expressed so clearly in 1937: 'The boom, not the slump, is the right time for austerity at the Treasury.'[9]

The United Nations concluded that cuts to public services since 2010 have resulted in 'tragic social consequences'. Philip Alston, the UN's special rapporteur for extreme poverty, said in 2019 that 'much of the glue that has held British society together since the Second World War has been deliberately removed and replaced with a harsh and uncaring ethos. A booming economy, high employment and a budget surplus have not reversed austerity, a policy fuelled entirely by ideology.'[10]

Austerity has pushed homeless provision into the hands of the third sector, charities and private companies. These organisations are innately compromised. If there's no homelessness, there are no homeless charities. Austerity has also fragmented our response to homelessness, preventing us from addressing it holistically – there's no joined-up thinking. Let's say a rough sleeper – Fred – gets arrested for a public order offence in central London. Fred is a mentally ill alcoholic and was drunk at the time, but he gave his opponent a bloody nose, and, as it's not his first offence, the Magistrates hand him a six-week custodial sentence. Problem solved! Except the prison service in the UK is a rotting Victorian corpse that successive governments have gutted to the bone. None of Fred's issues are addressed inside, as he spends twenty-three hours a day cooped up in a two-man cell. He doesn't get sober and develops a taste for Spice, which he takes with him to the outside. The prison has done its job and doesn't feel compelled to liaise with housing services before his release, so Fred goes straight back on to the streets to fend for himself.

On his first night, a friendly outreach worker approaches Fred and refers him to an emergency shelter, where he's given a bed for the night. He's off the streets. Problem solved! Except, because Fred is shit-faced half of the time, he gets refused entry to night shelters on many subsequent evenings, and he doesn't have a prayer when it comes to making it on to his local housing register. Fred is a mentally ill alcoholic Spice addict, and, because he doesn't know where he's going to get his head down from one night to the next, and because his whole existence has been dedicated to survival, he's not ready to get clean. The booze and drugs take away the pain. They kill time. Even if he was ready, there's no guarantee he'd get into rehab. So, Fred remains in a cyclical crisis, rebounding from prison to hostels, squats, tents and doorways – until it kills him.

Fred is a fictional character, but elements of his story apply to almost every homeless death I have reported on. For the *Empty Doorway* series, Simon Hattenstone and I wrote about the deaths of Aimee Teese and Catherine Kenny. Teese and Kenny were much-loved young mothers who suffered from drug addiction and had many other vulnerabilities; they both died shortly after being released from prison. In summer 2019, Simon and I travelled to Liverpool to tell Aimee's story. We interviewed the then-Mayor of Liverpool, Joe Anderson, at the Whitechapel Centre, a homeless day centre and hostel that provides meals and a bed to the city's rough sleepers. Anderson said he felt guilty about Aimee's death because he managed a city council that was not joined up:

'It hurts. I remember David Cameron coming in and talking about the "Big Society" – and it's the fucking broken society,' Anderson said. 'That's what we're dealing with. And you can't cut and cut and cut, and not accept consequences. Aimee's death [was the result of] a mixture of lack of joined-up thinking and cuts. If we'd had more public health workers connecting into probation, connecting into the prison service, we would have been told about her [Aimee].'

The most tragic thing about the thousands of homeless people who've died is that their deaths were wholly preventable. Countries such as Finland, and American States such as Utah, have proven that Housing First works. The fact is, no one should have to sleep rough or cram into a grim hostel, as housing is a basic human right under the United Nations.[11] Under Housing First, people like Aimee Teese, Mark Starr, Catherine Kenny, Michael Leadbetter, and the thousands of homeless people who have died over the years, would have been offered their own homes, with the wraparound support tailored specifically to their needs. I'm not arguing that Housing First is a panacea; I don't know if it would have solved all of their problems, or if they'd still be alive today, but at least they would have had the best chance. So far, the UK has piloted this model in a half-hearted way. The schemes often exclude rough sleepers because their needs are too complex, their lives too chaotic – which is confounding, as Housing First was developed with the express intention of supporting the most vulnerable in our society.

Homelessness can happen to almost anyone. You may have had a perfect paint-by-numbers existence: good schools, straight As, a glowing career, a flourishing social life and a supportive family. Then, one day, you are blindsided by illness, redundancy, a relationship breakdown, a rogue landlord or some other unforeseen circumstance, and find yourself without a pot to piss in nor a window to throw it out of, because you fell through a safety net that's holier than a block of evangelical Swiss cheese. Britain's benefits system is broken. Well, no – that's not strictly true. It's all a matter of perspective. And from the government's perspective, it's working perfectly. The last thing the Tories want is an empowered workforce or comfortable benefits claimants; power and comfort are commodities that the ruling classes would rather keep to themselves, thank you very much.

Moreover, the low-paid and jobless provide the Tories with useful political capital. They can argue to the hard-working squeezed middle that the low-paid didn't get on their bikes, and the Dole-ites are simply feckless shirkers too shy for graft; a taste of a doorway might convince them to pull up their socks. The Tories will never seek to end poverty or homelessness, as they have no interest in doing so.

If we ever succeed in electing a government that does want to meaningfully address homelessness, poverty and social exclusion, then strengthening workers' rights and conditions and repairing that safety net needs to be near the top of their list of priorities. Currently, many employees are treated as mere cogs in a machine. Cheap. Disposable. Any employee must have worked for an employer for two years before they can pursue unfair dismissal when they are sacked from their jobs. At the very least this should be brought back to twelve to twenty-four weeks. Most companies have probationary periods that last that long, because employers have determined it's an appropriate length of time in which to glean an employee's quality – and that should be good enough for lawmakers. Ideally the right to claim unfair dismissal should be afforded to employees from the very start. If a dismissal is unfair, then it's unfair; how long they've worked in a job is irrelevant.

At the bottom end of the jobs sector, a lot of workers aren't even considered employees. To avoid being held to account, employers have figured out how to hire people on a full-time basis while maintaining the facade that their workers are independent contractors hired on an ad hoc basis. These are zero-hours contracts; they are appalling, exploitative and must be banned.

It's worse for those out of work. Being unemployed is almost considered a crime in the UK. Our welfare system, which was devised to provide security to people in times of hardship, has become a cruel, unforgiving labyrinth designed to catch people out at every turn. The draconian sanctioning system needs to be abolished. If someone has all their income stopped, they won't be able to pay their rent and utilities; they won't be able to feed and clothe themselves. Where do you think these people end up after that?

Moreover, the time it takes to receive benefits like Universal

Credit (UC) needs to be significantly reduced. It can take up to eleven weeks to receive a first UC payment, which thrusts people into unmanageable debt and makes things like homelessness more likely. Also, before UC amalgamated benefits into one payment, local authorities usually paid housing benefit directly to landlords, removing any temptation to spend one's rent. Housing benefit is now a component of UC, and it is paid directly to claimants.[12] Is it really a surprise that poor tenants spend their housing benefit on other essentials when they're so hard up?

The qualification criteria for Personal Independent Payments (PIPs) and Employment and Support Allowance (ESA) are so exclusionary that people with terminal illnesses can have their applications rejected. Sixty-four-year-old Liverpudlian Stephen Smith suffered from debilitating illnesses that left him emaciated (he weighed six stone), in chronic pain, and barely able to walk. When interviewed by the *Liverpool Echo* in 2017, Smith said that his condition prevented him from standing up and he could only make it to his kitchen to make food once a day.[13] Nevertheless, Smith failed a DWP work-capability assessment. He was declared fit for work and instructed to sign on to receive Job Seeker's Allowance at the Job Centre, and was expected to actively look for work. In February 2019, after a lengthy legal battle, the government backtracked on their original decision and awarded Smith a backdated payment worth £4,000. Smith died shortly after; the money was spent on his funeral.[14]

Thousands of people like Smith have lost their livelihoods or died after being denied disability benefits, so welfare reforms could not be more urgent.[15] But even the changes I have suggested amount to nothing more than half measures. We live in extraordinary times. It remains to be seen what long-term effects the coronavirus pandemic will have on the global economy, but experts continue to make grim forecasts. Added to this is the slow march of automation, which will gobble up many industries and lead to mass unemployment – and the ever-worsening climate crisis hovers like a destructive spectre over all of this. In 1936, when Nazi Germany was preparing its war machine to conquer Europe, Winston Churchill, in a prescient speech to the Commons, argued that 'the era of procrastination, of half measures, of soothing and baffling expedients, of delays, is coming to its close. In its place, we are entering a period of consequences.'[16] Thirty years of profligacy followed by a decade of austerity has done irreparable damage to our society; far more damage than the Luftwaffe ever inflicted on our country. The UK safety net is a write-off; we must build something radically different in this new period of consequences.

A Universal Basic Income (UBI) is a modest, non-means-tested sum of money paid unconditionally to all individuals, regardless of personal wealth and employment status.[17] Arguments for some kind of UBI have been around for centuries; they entered the popular mainstream in 2020, when former Democratic presidential candidate Andrew Yang made it the centrepiece of his election campaign. Yang made some lofty claims for UBI, arguing that it would permanently grow the US economy by $2.5 trillion by 2025, and would add up to 4.7 million more people to the workforce. 'Putting money into people's hands and keeping it there would be a perpetual boost and support to job growth and the economy,' Yang wrote on his campaign website.[18]

Yang's detractors argue that UBI is unaffordable, removes incentives to work and will line the pockets of drug dealers, bookies and pub landlords. Shaun Bailey, who stood for the Tories in the 2021 London Mayoral election, claimed that the 'human condition' would cause some to buy 'lots of drugs' if handed a basic income.[19] Former Liberal Democrat leader Vince Cable said UBI would be too expensive, and claimed that it would 'destroy the incentive to work'.[20] I never cease to be amazed by how politicians view other human beings. If Bailey and Cable were asked if they would pack in their jobs and take up a coke habit after receiving UBI, they would dismiss the idea out of hand. So, why do they assume the rest of us are a grand away from idleness and vice?

UBI has been trialled around the world, and has produced some promising results. In February 2021, Michael Tubbs, the mayor of Stockton, California, launched the Stockton Economic Empowerment Demonstration, which handed 125 people $500 per month over two years without any rules on how to spend it. Independent researchers from the University of Tennessee and the University of Pennsylvania found that the programme helped participants pay off debt, secure full-time employment and improve emotional health. Only 28 per cent of the programme's participants were working full-time when the programme began. A year later, 40 per cent had full-time jobs. A control group of people who weren't given money was tracked over the same period; only 5 per cent got full-time jobs. Bailey and Cable's concerns were also put to the test. The money was paid to participants on a debit card, allowing researchers to track how they spent it. Only 1 per cent of the cash went on tobacco and alcohol; participants spent the rest on essentials: food, utilities, auto and services.[21] Economists and politicians remain divided over UBI, and more research needs to be done. But this is not a time for complacency; we must be radical.

Reforms to the welfare system will provide people with greater security with their housing. Still, the fact remains that the people most vulnerable to homelessness are not living in the right kind of housing. According to the Centre for Housing Policy, '38 per cent of the whole PRS [private rented sector] comprises low-income households'.[22] This group is more likely to live in overcrowded dwellings in poor condition, and are more likely to be dealing with unscrupulous landlords. Market forces leave them more vulnerable to extortionate rent hikes and no-fault evictions, often issued by landlords who are cashing in their pensions. If we want to end housing insecurity and eliminate endemic homelessness, we must embark on a radical and comprehensive social-housing-building programme. Social housing, council estates and tower blocks have negative reputations. They're seen by many as sinkholes, full of crime and vice. But what is a council house? A home that offers fairer, more affordable rents and free ad hoc repairs, and can be lived in for life. What's so bad about that?

In the last five years, I've lived in four different properties across London. One of those was a temporary placement; in two others, I had to leave due to dishonest landlords. I'm now living in another box in south-east London. I don't have many possessions, and the walls of the box remain pasty. Bare. Decorating seems futile. At the back of my mind, I know I can never settle; the next eviction letter is on the horizon and will soon be in my face, propelling me into another frantic race against time to find my next four walls. And I worry that I'll fail this time, that I'll get the letter during a pinch, and that I'll have to go through all this, again.

There are millions of people in this position in the UK, evidenced by the fact that more than that number overwhelmed the benefits system when the government finally decided to lock the country down in March 2020. Fear of losing one's housing should not be a constant worry in twenty-first century Britain.

I'm conscious of the fact that I've presented a seemingly intractable problem that won't be solved by anything short of a political and social revolution that would require a political movement that simply doesn't exist. Even if it did, it would cost billions in taxpayers' money to pull off such policies. If moral imperatives hold no sway with you; if money is your concern, and you think spending it on the homeless is wasteful, consider this: it costs far more to do nothing. The primary reason for ending homelessness should be preventing the tragic human cost, but let's be frank about this: homeless people are a burden on society. Homelessness places immense financial stress on the police, the criminal justice system, the prison service, the health service and local authorities. Research conducted by Crisis found that 'if 40,000 people were prevented from becoming homeless for one year in England, it would save the public purse £370 million'.[23]

Even if all this convinces you, you might be asking yourself: what can I do to help engineer the enormous changes you've advocated here? Most of us, myself included, are mere passers-by, who look on the misery we see every day with anxiety and hopelessness. I'm not sure I have all the answers, but one thing I am sure about is that homeless people are just that – people. Start with the Golden Rule: treat them as you would want to be treated if you were homeless.

The big homeless charities are unanimously opposed to people handing over cash to rough sleepers. They'd far prefer it if you gave it to them. Their argument for this is perfectly cogent: rough sleepers abuse alcohol and drugs, and giving them more money allows them to buy more booze, more drugs, making their lives worse. But don't you think you would fancy a wee tipple if you were on your arse? I certainly did. So, why shouldn't they? In fact, why not share a can or two with your new homeless mate? Remember, they're just people, after all. If, like me, you're inter-ested in finding long-term solutions to this mounting crisis, we have to organise. Join a campaign – or start one. One that puts pressure on the government to make these changes.

Ending homelessness can be a reality. At the beginning of the pandemic, the government announced the Everyone In scheme, designed to protect rough sleepers from coronavirus. The government claims that 90 per cent of rough sleepers were helped off the streets.[24] That figure has been disputed, but there was a notable change in the number of rough sleepers one saw at the height of the UK's first lockdown. We see a similar phe-nomenon occur during the annual winter cold snap. Suddenly, homelessness rises to the top of the agenda: appeals are made, funds are raised, and people are taken off the streets. Then the emergency passes, the temperature rises, and we rediscover our apathy. What this demonstrates is that homelessness is not intractable. It's a problem that has a clear solution that is well within our means. All we lack is the will to solve it. It seems that we have to ask ourselves some serious questions: How do we want to be remembered in our time? Are we content with being a nation of navel-gazers, who, when faced with real crises, were preoccupied with nationhood and identity, unmoved by the suffering we saw all around us?

If you find yourself thinking that I'm living proof that upward mobility is all about grit and determination, then I invite you to consider: how many books like this have you read? How many people like me have you met? I'm a walking, talking anomaly. Almost everyone I know from the system is damaged somehow. They are off the map, in prison or dead.

I've thought deeply about how I made it through all this relatively unscathed. Somehow, I've always found the will to bounce back from any adversity I've faced. This fills me with guilt, as this virtue is an accident of birth. This mix of genes, environment and circumstance is a lottery that we've all emerged from, and that's fine. But life is not a game to be won or lost; society should reflect that. Yes, there is a line where the state's responsibility ends and personal responsibility begins, but how do you expect people to make the right choices when they're not available? Nothing grows in a desert.

Who knows what kind of life Lucy would have had if social services had truly cared for her and noticed the exploitation going on under their noses? Maybe she wouldn't have suffered the pain of having a child taken from her, and an adulthood plagued by severe mental illness. If the system didn't set care-leavers up to fail, then Sunita wouldn't have had to choose between remaining in a chaotic refuge and a doorway. If one's needs instead of one's means determined access to housing, then vigilantes like Stuart Potts wouldn't have to risk a prison sentence to look after desperate people in his community; vulnerable kids like Louis wouldn't have to pose for photographs in his sleeping bag to convince authorities to act; and sickness wouldn't make compassionate hard workers like Harry lose everything.

Our crippled social infrastructure doesn't only ruin lives, it ends them. If society treated mental illness and addiction like a health issue instead of an iniquity, then maybe I wouldn't have had to watch Joules Humm weep when he showed me the building where his son took his own life; I could have been spared the anguish of learning that Mick drowned in the same river that we used to play chess next to; and Tony Starr wouldn't have had to learn that his beloved brother had died alone and desperate, far from home.

I've come a long way since my nights on the bridle path. Getting published in the *Guardian* was a pipe dream and I can't describe the thrill of opening my favourite paper, the paper that taught me to read, that shaped my ethics and interests, and seeing my byline. I'm in a better place, but I still carry deep psychological scars from my time in the system. The anxiety from those scars can dominate my every waking hour; it darkens my dreams, makes me scared of my own shadow. Happy tablets merely blunt its edge. I don't want more people to suffer like me or worse, and they don't have to. Change is within our grasp. All we have to do is reach.

Acknowledgements

This book would be nothing without the contributions of Lucy, Sunita, Stuart Potts, Louis, my brother Odge, Noel, the Starr family and Harry. Thank you for your courage and sincerity. I'd also like to thank Becky Gardiner and Terry Kirby for taking a chance on me and being the best teachers I've ever had; *Guardian* feature writer, my mentor, friend, and the best interviewer in the business, Simon Hattenstone, for his patience, company, advice and bonkers phone calls; *Guardian* head of features Kira Cochrane, for believing in me, being a brilliant editor and an even more brilliant person; the wonderfully talented Homa Khaleeli, Jenny Stevens, Chris Michael, Stephen Moss, Natasha Reith-Banks, Sarah Habershon and everyone on *G2* and *Guardian* Cities. I'm running out of adjectives for brilliant, talented and wonderful, but they all apply to Ella Gordon and Matthew Turner, without whom this book would not have been possible. Finally, a special thanks to a very special boy, Dom . . . No, I take that back. What did you do, really? Sure, you stood between me and a stabbing and stuck with me through thick and thin, but other than that, you've been a bit rubbish.

About the Author

© Joe Yule

Daniel Lavelle is a freelance feature writer from Manchester. He left care at nineteen and experienced homelessness for the first time not long after. He graduated from Manchester Metropolitan University with a BA in History while he was living in a homeless hostel. He writes regularly on topics such as mental health, homelessness and culture for the *Guardian* (for whom he co-authored the series 'The Empty Doorway' with Simon Hattenstone) and has written for *New Statesman* and the *Independent*. He has an MA in Journalism from Goldsmiths and in 2017 he received the Guardian's Hugo Young award for an opinion piece on his experience of homelessness. 'The Empty Doorway' won Feature of the Year at the British Journalism Awards 2019 and was shortlisted for a National Press Award. He lives in London.

Notes

All sources accessed 6 June 2021.

Introduction

1   Fitzpatrick, S., Watts, B., Pawson, H., Bramley, G., Wood, J., Stephens, M. and Blenkinsopp, J. *The Homelessness Monitor: England 2021*. London: Crisis, March 2021.

2   Homeless Link Research Team. *Full Report: Young and Homeless 2018*. Homeless Link, 2018.

3   The Centre for Social Justice. *Finding Their Feet: Equipping care leavers to reach their potential*. Centre for Social Justice, January 2015.

4   Pleace, N. and Bretherton, J. *Crisis Skylight: Final Report of the University of York Evaluation*. London: Crisis, 2017.

5   Heath, L. 'Just one social home delivered for every 175 households on waiting lists.' www.insidehousing.co.uk, 17 December 2021.

6   Cameron, D. 'Full text of David Cameron's speech.' *Guardian*, 8 October 2009.

7   Children's Commissioner. 'Thousands of children growing up in shipping containers, office blocks and B&Bs.' www.childrenscommissioner.gov.uk, 21 August 2019.

8   Local Government Association. 'One in 10 new homes was a former office.' www.local.gov.uk, 18 January 2018.

9   BBC News. 'Harlow office block "ghettos" should be closed, says MP.' www.bbc.co.uk/news, 13 February 2020.

10 Berg, S. 'Building surge hints at comeback of the council house.' www.bbc.co.uk/news, 24 February 2020.

11 Rugg, J., Rhodes, D. *The Evolving Private Rented Sector: Its Contribution and Potential.* Centre For Housing Policy, University of York, 2018.

12 Shelter. 'Two million renters in England made ill by housing worries.' www.england.shelter.org.uk, 15 January 2020.

13 BRE Group. 'New BRE Trust report shows poor quality homes in England cost the NHS £1.4bn per year, and wider society £18.6bn.' www.bre.co.uk, 20 May 2016.

14 Child Poverty Action Group. 'Child Poverty Facts and Figures.' www.cpag.org.uk, 2021.

15 Doward, J. 'UK elderly suffer worst poverty rate in western Europe.' *Observer,* 18 August 2019.

16 Worrall, P. 'Factcheck: Are the Conservatives putting 20,000 police on the streets?' www.channel4.com/news, 13 November 2019.

17 BBC News. 'Crime figures: Violent crime recorded by police rises by 19%.' www.bbc.co.uk/news, 24 January 2019.

18 Action Hunger. *When 'Social Need' and 'Innovation' collide together sometimes something very special emerges.* Action Hunger, 2017. Available at https://www.local.gov.uk/sites/default/files/documents/Action%20Hunger%20-%20Vending%20machines%20for%20the%20homeless.pdf.

19 Berg Olsen, M. '"Misguided" vending machine for homeless people scrapped after three months.' *Metro,* 5 April 2018.

20 Care Quality Commission. *Housing with Care: Guidance on regulated activities for providers of supported living and extra care housing.* Care Quality Commission, October 2015. Available at https://www.cqc.org.uk/sites/default/files/20151023_provider_guidance-housing_with_care.pdf.

21 Russell Cooke. 'Charities and the Freedom of Information Act.' www.russell-cooked.co.uk, 6 February 2020.

22 Hiller, A. 'Number of registered charities reaches highest level in almost a decade.' www.thirdsector.co.uk, 16 January 2018.

Chapter One: Is Charity Broken?

1   Beckett, F. *Clem Attlee*. Richard Cohen Books, 1997. p. 63.
2   *National Minimum Wage Regulations 2015, Part 6*. www. legislation.gov.uk, 2015. Available at https://www.legislation.gov.uk/ukdsi/2015/9780111127964
3   Jordan, B. *Social Work and the Third Way: Tough Love as Social Policy*. Sage, 2000. p. 114.
4   Emmaus. 'Emmaus in the UK.' https://emmaus.org.uk/about-us/history/emmaus-uk-history/
5   Public Administration Committee. *The Big Society: Further Report with the Government Response to the Committee's Seventeenth Report of Session 2010–12 – Public Administration Committee*. 2012. Available at https://publications.parliament.uk/pa/cm201213/cmselect/cmpubadm/98/9805.htm
6   Watt, N. 'Cameron promises power for the "man and woman on the street".' *Guardian*, 19 July 2010.
7   Taylor, D. 'Complaints filed against charity over removal of EU rough sleepers.' *Guardian*, 14 May 2018.
8   Emmaus St Albans. *Annual Report and Financial Statements*. Emmaus, 2016. Available at https://emmaus.org.uk/hertfordshire/wp-content/uploads/sites/29/2019/07/EMMAUS-ST-ALBANS-2016-ACCOUNTS.pdf
9   Clarke, A., Markkanen, S., Whitehead, C. *Emmaus: Valuing Success: An Economic Evaluation of Emmaus Village Carlton*. Cambridge Centre for Housing and Planning Research, 2008.
10 BBC News. 'Jacob Rees-Mogg: Food banks "rather uplifting".' www. bbc.co.uk/news, 14 September 2017.
11 'Street (Respondent) v. Mountford (A.P) (Appellant) Judgement'. UK House of Lords, 2 May 1985. Available at https://www.bailii.org/uk/cases/UKHL/1985/4.html
12 YMCA. 'Accommodation.' https://www.ymca.org.uk/about/what-we-do/accommodation
13 Hattenstone, S., Lavelle, D. 'The homeless death of Jake Humm: "it was my deepest, darkest fear".' *Guardian*, 24 September 2019.

14 Day, R. 'Police find body in river in the search for missing Michael
    Leadbetter.' *Manchester Evening News*, 16 March 2017.

Chapter Two: Trauma

1   Greater Manchester County Record Office. 'Greater
    Manchester Gazetteer.' Available at https://web.archive.org/
    web/20110718144349/http://www.gmcro.co.uk/Guides/Gazeteer/
    gazzs.htm
2   Evolve Housing. *Breaking the cycle of trauma, the connection
    between trauma, mental health and homelessness.* Evolve Housing,
    18 June 2018. pp. 5–6.
3   Aston, P. 'School owner threatens revenge on dole.' *The Birmingham
    Post*, 11 August 1999. Available at https://www.thefreelibrary.com/
    School+owner+threatens+revenge+on+dole.-a060492297
4   Worcester News. 'Teacher who lied is jailed.' *Worcester News*,
    2 May 2002.
5   Garcia Murillo, L., Ramos-Olazagasti, M., Mannuzza, S. and
    Xavier Castelleanos, F. 'Childhood Attention-Deficit/Hyperactivity
    Disorder and Homelessness: A 33-Year Follow-Up Study.' *Journal of
    the American Academy of Child & Adolescent Psychology*, 2016, vol.
    55 (11), pp. 931–6.

Chapter Three: Care, Criminalisation & Displacement

1   Department for Education. *The national protocol on reducing
    unnecessary criminalisation of looked-after children and care leavers.*
    Department for Education, 27 November 2018.
2   Howard League for Penal Reform. 'Ending the criminalisation of
    children in residential care.' www.howardleague.org, 2018.
3   Pidd, H., Wolfe-Robinson, M. 'Care homes accused of being too
    quick to call the police on children.' *Guardian*, 6 November 2019.
4   Her Majesty's Probation Service. 'Care Leavers in prison and
    probation.' www.gov.uk, 12 August 2019.

5   Oakley, M., Miscampbell, G., and Gregorian, R. *Looked-after Children: the silent crisis*. Social Market Foundation, 2018.

6   Green, C. 'Care home kids smoked, took drugs and did card tricks on the streets for cash to buy takeaways.' *Manchester Evening News*, 24 September 2018.

7   BBC News. 'Abuse scandal dates back 50 years.' www.bbc.co.uk/news, 7 March 2007.

8   Scheerhout, J. 'Care home boss delivered me into the clutches of evil Savile, says victim.' *Manchester Evening News*, 7 April 2014.

9   UK Government. 'Leaving foster or local authority care.' https://www.gov.uk/leaving-foster-or-local-authority-care.

10   Children's Commissioner. 'Leaving Care.' https://www.childrenscommissioner.gov.uk/help-at-hand/leaving-care-your-rights/

11   Howard League for Penal Reform. 'Privatising children's social care.' www.howardleague.org, 2019.

12   All-Party Parliamentary Group for Runaway and Missing Children and Adults. *No Place at Home*. APPG, September 2019.

13   Razzall, K. 'Teens in care abandoned to crime gangs.' www.bbc.co.uk/news, 20 May 2019.

14   See note 12 above.

Chapter Four: Independence

1   Sky News. 'A diverse and divided Britain: the people of Oldham's view.' Sky News, 2016. Available at https://www.youtube.com/watch?v=uQCn-6N9hng.

2   Howe, D. *White Tribe*. Directed by Paul Wimshurst. Diverse Productions, Channel 4, January 2000.

3   Howe, D. 'Why I left Oldham with a feeling of dread.' *New Statesman*, 28 June 1999. Accessed 6 June 2021.

4   Tenant Referencing UK. 'Tenants on zero-hours contracts are being refused accommodation.' www.landlord-referencing.co.uk, 16 December 2020.

5   Crane, M., Joly, L. M. A. and Manthrope, J. *Rebuilding Lives:*

Formerly homeless people's experiences of independent living and their longer term outcomes. The Policy Institute at King's College London, 2016.

6   *Housing Act 1988.* Available at https://www.legislation.gov.uk/ukpga/1988/50/section/21.

7   Ministry of Housing, Communities and Local Government. 'Government announces end to unfair evictions.' www.gov.uk, 15 April 2019.

8   Harrison, N. 'Care leavers in higher education: new statistics but a mixed picture.' Department of Education, University of Oxford, 1 September 2020.

9   Centre for Social Justice. *12 by 24.* Centre for Social Justice, 2019.

10   Gill, A. 'Six reasons why leaving care sometimes isn't the step forward it should be.' www.centrepoint.org.uk, 18 July 2017.

11   Office for National Statistics. *Milestones: Journeying into adulthood.* Office for National Statistics, 17 December 2019.

12   Department for Education. 'Extending Personal Adviser support to all care leavers to age 25: Statutory guidance for local authorities.' Department for Education, February 2018.

13   Booth, R., Butler, P. and Campbell, D. 'NHS, social care and most vulnerable "betrayed" by Sunak's budget.' *Guardian,* 3 March 2021.

Chapter Five: Fighting the Housing Crisis

1   Curtis, R. and Elton, B. 'Goodbyeee', episode 6, *Blackadder Goes Forth.* Directed by Richard Boden. BBC, 1989.

2   *Housing Act 1980.* Available at https://www.legislation.gov.uk/ukpga/1980/51.

3   Carlin, G. *Life is Worth Losing.* Directed by Rocco Urbisci. HBO, 2005.

4   Disney, R. and Luo, G. 'The Right to Buy public housing in Britain: A welfare analysis.' *Journal of Housing Economics*, vol. 35, pp. 51–68.

5   BBC. '20 December 1979: Council tenants will have "right to buy".' On This Day 1950–2005, www.bbc.co.uk.

6   *Hansard*. 'Council House Rents'. House of Commons Deb. 16 December 1981. Vol. 15, cc362–402.

7   Wilson, W., Morgan, W. *Rent Levels Affordability and Housing Benefit*. House of Commons Library, 22 June 1998. p. 6.

8   Office for National Statistics. 'Earnings time series of gross weekly from 1938–2016'. [Excel file]. Office for National Statistics, 25 October 2018.

9   See chapter five, note 4 above.

10   See chapter five, note 4 above.

11   BBC News. 'No-fault evictions to be banned in England.' www.bbc.co.uk/news, 15 April 2019.

12   Cox, C. 'The homeless people living on the banks of the Salford canal – and fishing for their food.' *Manchester Evening News*, 25 June 2017.

13   *Legal Aid, Sentencing and Rehabilitation of Offenders Act 2012*. Available at https://www.legislation.gov.uk/ukpga/2012/10/section/144/enacted.

14   'A Bed Every Night.' www.bedeverynight.co.uk.

15   Lobb, A. 'Andy Burnham: I'll end rough sleeping in Greater Manchester by 2020.' *The Big Issue*, 10 May 2017.

16   Pidd, H. 'Andy Burnham elected mayor of Greater Manchester.' *Guardian*, 5 May 2017.

17   Ministry of Housing, Communities and Local Government. *Homelessness Statistics*. www.gov.uk, 13 September 2013 (updated 22 April 2021).

18   Ministry of Housing, Communities and Local Government. *Rough sleeping snapshot in England: Autumn 2020*. www.gov.uk, 25 February 2021.

19   BBC News. 'Covid: New tiers "not up for negotiation" after Manchester row.' www.bbc.co.uk/news, 24 November 2020.

20   Barker, N. 'Burnham launches homelessness prevention strategy with 30,000 social rent homes planned.' www.insidehousing.co.uk, 14 May 2021.

21   Ministry of Housing, Communities and Local Government. *£3.2 million emergency support for rough sleepers during coronavirus outbreak*. www.gov.uk, 17 March 2020.

22 Walker, A and Allison, E. 'Quarter of Manchester homeless people housed in hotels for lockdown have left.' *Guardian*, 27 April 2020.

23 Cambridge, E. 'Squatter "ruined remembrance Sunday service by setting off firework" before being attacked by furious mourners.' *Sun*, 10 November 2019.

24 Halle-Richards, S. 'Traffic cone hurled at squatter who set off fireworks in Remembrance Sunday fracas has been auctioned off – for a very good cause.' *Manchester Evening News*, 27 November 2019.

25 Blakey, A. 'Everything a judge told "appalling" Stuart Potts as he jailed him for launching fireworks at Remembrance Sunday event.' *Manchester Evening News*, 11 November 2019.

26 Christodoulou, H. 'Squatter who launched fireworks into crowd of war vets at Remembrance Sunday service as a "mark of respect" is jailed.' *Sun*, 11 November 2019.

27 Green, C. 2019. 'Council houses in Oldham will now only be rented to those "in need" – meaning nearly 20,000 people on a waiting list will be ditched.' *Manchester Evening News*, 26 February 2019.

28 Conservative and Unionist Party. 'Get Brexit Done: Unleash Britain's Potential.' *The Conservative and Unionist Party Manifesto*. Conservative and Unionist Party, 2019. p. 19.

29 Soady, A. '"Right to buy" discount could be increased for tenants.' www.bbc.co.uk/news, 11 March 2012.

30 Ministry of Housing, Communities and Local Government. *Right to Buy Sales in England, October to December 2020*. Ministry of Housing, Communities and Local Government, 15 April 2021.

31 See chapter five, note 7.

32 Barton, C. and Wilson, W. *What is affordable housing?* House of Commons Library, 19 April 2021.

33 Joseph Rowntree Foundation. *Affordable Rents compared to traditional social rents*. www.jrf.org.uk, 13 July 2018.

34 Ministry of Housing, Communities and Local Government. *Use of receipts from Right to Buy sales: Government response to the consultation*. Ministry of Housing, Communities and Local Government, 19 March 2021.

35 National Housing Federation. *People in Housing Need*. National Housing Federation, 15 September 2020.

36 Housing, Communities and Local Government Committee. 'Protecting the Homeless'. *Protecting the homeless and the private rented sector: MHCLG's response to Covid-19*. 31 March 2021. Available at https://publications.parliament.uk/pa/cm5801/cmselect/cmcomloc/1329/132905.htm.

Chapter Six: Dependency

1 Royal College of Psychiatrists. 'Two-fifths of patients waiting for mental health treatment forced to resort to emergency or crisis services.' www.rcpsych.ac.uk/news, 6 October 2020.

2 Pleace, N. and Bretherton, J. *Crisis Skylight: Final Report of the University of York Evaluation*. Crisis, University of York, 2017. p. 21.

3 Royal College of Psychiatrists. 'Psychiatrists see alarming rise in patients needing urgent and emergency care and forecast a "tsunami" of mental illness.' www.rcpsych.ac.uk/news, 15 May 2020.

4 Royal College of Psychiatrists. 'Addiction services not equipped to treat the 8 million people drinking at high risk during pandemic, warns Royal College.' www.rcpsych.ac.uk/news, 14 September 2020.

5 Crisis. 'Prison leavers.' www.crisis.org.uk/ending-homelessness/law-and-rights/prison-leavers.

6 Addiction Center. 'What is Methadone?' www.addictioncenter.com/opiates/methadone.

7 Matthews-King, A. 'Residential addiction services in England cut by third amid drug overdose and funding crisis, figures show.' *Independent*, 13 July 2019.

8 O'Hara, M. 'Charities are providing drugs and alcohol services in place of the NHS.' *Guardian*, 27 June 2012.

9 See chapter six, note 4.

10 Home Office and Department of Health and Social Care. *£148 million to cut drugs crime*. Home Office and Department of Health and Social Care, 20 January 2021.

11 Dodd, V. 'Ministers spurned drug tsar's guidance of £900m funding to tackle misuse.' *Guardian*, 21 January 2021.

12 James, A., Sinclair, J. 'Addiction services need more investment.' *Guardian*, 22 January 2021.

Chapter Seven: **Dying Homeless**

1 Office for National Statistics. *Deaths of homeless people in England and Wales: 2018.* Office for National Statistics, 1 October 2019.

2 National Records of Scotland. 'The estimated number of deaths of people experiencing homelessness increased to 195 in Scotland in 2018.' National Records of Scotland, 5 February 2020.

3 See chapter seven, note 1.

4 National Records of Scotland. *Homeless Deaths 2017 and 2018.* National Records of Scotland, 5 February 2020.

5 Cox, C. 'As a man collapses yards from Deansgate, grim video shows how a new strain of super-strong drugs is blighting Manchester city centre.' *Manchester Evening News*, 21 December 2017.

6 Karolinska Institutet. 'Spice: A hundred times more potent than cannabis.' www.ki.se/en, 2020.

7 Matrix Diagnostics. 'Synthetic cannabis is escaping current drug tests.' www.matrixdiagnostics.co.uk, 17 February 2020.

8 User Voice. *Spice: The Bird Killer – What Prisoners Think About the Use of Spice and Other Legal Highs in Prison.* User Voice, May 2016.

9 McCoy, T. 'How this chemist unwittingly helped spawn the synthetic drug industry.' *Washington Post*, 9 August 2015.

10 Rettner, R. 'Synthetic Marijuana Linked to Seizures, Psychosis and Death.' *Huffington Post*, 2 July 2017.

11 *Psychoactive Substances Act 2016.* Available at https://www.legislation.gov.uk/ukpga/2016/2/contents/enacted.

12 Perraudin, F. '"It's worse than heroin": how spice is ravaging homeless communities.' *Guardian*, 15 April 2017.

13 *The Dark Side Of Britain: Spice.* UNILAD, 2018. YouTube: www.youtube.com/watch?v=iL-0287WLFA.

14 Osuh, C. 'Two men jailed for life for beating homeless man to death and then setting fire to his tent.' *Manchester Evening News*, 11 August 2016.

15 BBC News. 'Homeless man found opposite Houses of Parliament dies.' www.bbc.co.uk/news, 19 December 2018.

16 Brennan Z. 'Legal – but lethal: How your child can buy drugs online as easily as you order your Waitrose groceries.' *Daily Mail*, 12 June 2013.

17 American Addiction Centers. 'The Effects of Mixing Spice (K2) and Alcohol.' www.alcohol.org, 27 March 2020.

18 See chapter seven, note 2.

19 Armstrong, G. 'Appeal to trace relatives of Glasgow man found dead within Glasgow Green area.' www.glasgowlive.co.uk, 8 July 2019.

20 Loney, G. 'Police still searching for relatives of man found dead at Glasgow Green.' www.glasgowlive.co.uk, 29 July 2019.

21 Shelter Scotland. *Evidence of Gatekeeping in Glasgow City Council.* Shelter Scotland, July 2018.

22 Brooks, L. 'Glasgow council facing court action over lack of housing for homeless people.' *Guardian*, 2 October 2019.

23 Stewart, C. 'Shelter Scotland drops legal action against Glasgow City Council over homelessness.' *Glasgow Evening Times*, 14 January 2020.

24 Johnsen, S. and Teixera, L. *Staircases, Elevators and Cycles of Change: 'Housing First' and Other Housing Models for Homeless People with Complex Support Needs.* London: Crisis, 6 March 2010.

25 Scottish Government. '1,187 drug-deaths in 2018: up 27% in a year.' www.gov.scot/news, 16 July 2019.

26 Iacobucci, G. 'Drug deaths: Scottish minister vows to tackle "public health emergency".' *British Medical Journal*, 2 December 2019.

27 BBC News. 'Scotland's drug deaths rise to new record.' www.bbc.co.uk/news, 15 December 2020.

28 BBC News. 'Eight found dead at Glasgow hotel for homeless since April.' www.bbc.co.uk/news, 30 September 2020.

29 Boffey, D. 'Dane launches street magazine to help drug users fund their habit.' *Guardian*, 8 September 2013.

30 Bachlakova, P. 'Sådan hjalp sexarbejdere med at få gjort Sexelancen *populær*.' www.vice.com, 3 May 2017.

31 Dolan, K., Kimber, J., Fry, C., Fitzgerald, J., McDonald, D. and Trautmann, F. 'Drug consumption facilities in Europe and the establishment of supervised injecting centres in Australia.' *Drug and Alcohol Review*, vol. 19, issue 2, 2000. pp. 337–46.

32 BBC News. 'Consumption rooms for legal drug-taking around the world.' www.bbc.co.uk/news, 18 April 2013.

33 BBC News. 'Self-injection rooms plan for Glasgow drug addicts given green light.' www.bbc.co.uk/news, 31 October 2016.

34 Herald Scotland Online. 'Westminster "standing in the way of saving lives" on Glasgow safe drug consumption room.' *The Herald*, 5 November 2019.

35 McGivern, M. 'Drugs activist Peter Krykant won't be charged over overdose prevention van.' *Daily Record*, 20 January 2021.

36 Housing First Europe Hub. 'The History of Housing First.' https://housingfirsteurope.eu/guide/what-is-housing-first/history-housing-first/.

37 Homeless Link Policy and Research Team. *'Housing First' or 'Housing Led'? The current picture of Housing First in England.* Homeless Link, June 2015.

38 McCarthy, N. 'The American Cities with the Highest Homeless Populations in 2019.' *Forbes*, 14 January 2020.

39 Kaplan, M. 'Mark David Chapman and the assassination of John Lennon.' *New York Post*, 8 December 2020.

40 McEvers, K. 'Utah Reduced Chronic Homelessness By 91 Percent; Here's How.' www.npr.org, 10 December 2015.

41 Trewern, M. 'The city with no homeless on its streets.' www.bbc.co.uk/news, 31 January 2019.

Chapter Eight: **Precarity**

1 Ministry of Housing, Communities and Local Government. *Assured Tenancy Forms.* Ministry of Housing, Communities and Local Government, 15 November 2012 (updated 1 June 2021).

2   Lavelle, D. 'Only 39 rogue landlords and agents hit with banning orders.' *Guardian*, 5 April 2021.

3   Booth, R. and Rawlinson, K. '950,000 apply for universal credit in two weeks of UK lockdown.' *Guardian*, 1 April 2020.

4   Cameron, D. 'David Cameron's EU speech: full text.' www.bbc.co.uk/news, 28 November 2018.

5   Office for National Statistics. *Employment in the UK: January 2020.* Office for National Statistics, 21 January 2020.

6   Tolhurst, A. 'Record figures reveal almost one million workers on zero-hour contracts.' www.politicshome.com/news, 18 February 2020.

7   Citizens Advice. 'Check if your dismissal is unfair.' www.citizensadvice.org.uk/work/leaving-a-job/dismissal/check-if-your-dismissal-is-fair/.

8   Gov.UK. 'Universal Credit.' www.gov.uk/universal-credit/what-youll-get.

9   Sandhu, S. 'One in 10 Universal Credit claimants paid late, with some waiting up to 11 weeks for first full payment.' *iNews*, 10 July 2020.

10 Owen, J. 'I was sanctioned for going to a funeral.' www.bbc.co.uk/news, 30 January 2018.

11 Bloom, D. 'Universal Credit: Two thirds of councils warn benefit has increased homelessness.' *Daily Mirror*, 4 April 2019.

12 Jayanetti, C. 'Benefits freeze will leave tenants across Britain facing rent arrears of £1,000.' *Guardian*, 13 March 2021.

13 Department for Work and Pensions. *Housing Benefit Claimant Factsheet: Removal of Spare Room Subsidy.* Available at https://assets.publishing.service.gov.uk/government/uploads/system/uploads/attachment_data/file/271013/housing-benefit-factsheet-1-removal-spare-room-subsidy.pdf.

14 Butler, P. 'Welfare changes drive rising poverty and food bank use, study finds.' *Guardian*, 5 November 2019.

15 Citizens Advice. 'Getting a council home.' www.citizensadvice.org.uk/housing/social-housing/applying-for-social-housing/getting-a-council-home/.

16 Marsh, S. and Walker, A. 'Tens of thousands made homeless despite UK ban on evictions during pandemic.' *Guardian*, 8 November 2020.

17 Craw, D. W. 'These are the places you're most at risk of a no-fault eviction.' www.generationrent.org, 19 November 2019.

Conclusion: Ending Homelessness

1 Lammy, D. 'There is something rotten in Westminster when MP's walk past dying homeless people on the way into work. 24,000 people homeless on our streets this Christmas and our Government playing reckless with a No Deal Brexit. Plague on their Houses.' [Tweet] Twitter, 19 December 2018.

2 *Hansard*. 'Homelessness.' House of Lords Deb. 20 December 2018. Vol. 794, cc1923–6.

3 Office for National Statistics. *Deaths of homeless people in England and Wales: 2019 registrations*. Office for National Statistics, 14 December 2020.

4 Museum of Homelessness. 'Homeless deaths spiked by a more than a third in 2020.' www.museumofhomelessness.org, 2020.

5 Hambidge, S. 'Farms can help disadvantaged young people.' www.bournemouth.ac.uk/news, 16 July 2018.

6 Jay, A., Evans, M., Frank, I. and Sharping, D. *Interim report: A Summary. Independent Inquiry into Child Sexual Abuse.* Independent Inquiry Child Sexual Abuse, 2018.

7 See chapter three, note 2.

8 Manchester Metropolitan University. 'Research: exploring the workforce wellbeing of children's home workers.' www.mmu.ac.uk/research, 2020.

9 Poole, S. 'If austerity is (almost) over, what was it anyway?' *Guardian*, 1 November 2018.

10 Alston, P. *Visit to the United Kingdom of Great Britain and Northern Ireland: Report of the Special Rapporteur on extreme poverty and human rights.* United Nations General Assembly, 2019.

11 Office for the United Nations High Commissioner for Human

Rights. *Fact Sheet No. 21: The Right to Adequate Housing.* www. ohchr.org, 2014.

12   Shelter. 'When universal credit can be paid direct to a landlord.' https://england.shelter.org.uk/housing_advice/benefits/when_ universal_credit_can_be_paid_direct_to_a_landlord.

13   Thorp, L. 'Weighing six stone and barely able to move – this man was denied vital benefits and told to go and look for work.' *Liverpool Echo,* 3 February 2019.

14   Thorp, L. 'The money Stephen Smith was wrongly denied by the government for so long will now pay for his funeral.' *Liverpool Echo,* 2 April 2019.

15   Bulman, M. 'More than 17,000 sick and disabled people have died while waiting for welfare benefits, figures show.' *Independent,* 14 January 2019.

16   *Hansard.* 'Debate on the Address.' House of Commons. 12 November 1936. Vol. 317, cc1081–155.

17   van Parjis, P. *Arguing for Basic Income: Ethical Foundations for a Radical Reform.* Verso Books, 1992.

18   Yang. A. 'The Freedom Dividend.' https://2020.yang2020.com/ policies/the-freedom-dividend/.

19   BBC News. 'Shaun Bailey: Tory mayoral candidate says universal income would be used for drugs.' www.bbc.co.uk/news, 3 March 2021.

20   Cable, V. 'Universal basic income is only a sticking plaster to get us through coronavirus – it won't treat the economic crisis to come.' *Independent,* 31 March 2021.

21   West, S., Baker, A., Samra, A. and Coltrera, E. *Preliminary Analysis: SEED's First Year.* Stockton Economic Empowerment Demonstration, 2020.

22   See Introduction, note 11.

23   Crisis. 'Cost of Homelessness.' www.crisis.org.uk/ending-homelessness/homelessness-knowledge-hub/cost-of-homelessness/.

24   See chapter 5, note 36.